Mrs. E. H. Carbutt

Five Months' Fine Weather in Canada, western U.S., and Mexico

Mrs. E. H. Carbutt

Five Months' Fine Weather in Canada, western U.S., and Mexico

ISBN/EAN: 9783337188788

Printed in Europe, USA, Canada, Australia, Japan

Cover: Foto ©ninafisch / pixelio.de

More available books at **www.hansebooks.com**

FIVE MONTHS' FINE WEATHER

IN CANADA, WESTERN U.S., AND MEXICO

BY

Mrs. E. H. CARBUTT

LONDON
SAMPSON LOW, MARSTON, SEARLE, & RIVINGTON
Limited
St. Dunstan's House
Fetter Lane, Fleet Street, E.C.
1889
[*All rights reserved*]

FIVE MONTHS' FINE WEATHER

IN

CANADA, WESTERN, U.S. AND MEXICO.

ON Saturday morning, 11th August, 1888, after a wonderfully quick passage, we found ourselves so close to New York, that we were almost certain to land in the evening, and, with the exception of a solitary croaker, who had prophesied misfortunes of all kinds ever since we left Queenstown, all the passengers packed their trunks, put on their best clothes, and prepared joyfully for land. However, the croaker was right this time. As we were sitting on deck after lunch, suddenly there was a horrible noise, and we were covered with soot and steam. The spindle to the high-pressure cylinder valve had broken inside the crossheads !

One's first idea was naturally that the poor fellows in the engine-room must be terribly scalded and knocked about, but happily no one was injured. That fear relieved, we could feel the bitter disappointment of the delay. Not only must we spend another dreary night in the stuffy cabins, but no doubt we should lose the race we were running with the new much vaunted *City of New York*, and anyhow, we had lost the glory of making the fastest passage on record.

A beautiful French steamer of the Transatlantique line passed and jeeringly offered to tow us in. Next day we saw with great satisfaction that she had not arrived in time to land her passengers in the evening, and when we learnt that the *City of New York* had done very badly, we felt almost consoled; but it was a very dull afternoon. A canary flew out from New York to welcome us, and a big fish swam about close to the ship for a long time, some said it was a shark, and some said it was a sturgeon.

The engines were got to work again after four hours' delay, and the run after dark was very interesting as we passed the immense hotels and tea-gardens in Coney Island and other favourite resorts, flaring with gas and electric lights. An American charged us strictly not to omit visiting West Brighton in the morning, when we should see "hundreds of thousands of men, women, children, cats, dogs, and other living creatures all bathing together." The Elephant Hotel was just distinguishable by its curious shape.

We stopped outside Sandy Hook for the night, and next morning at six o'clock we were all up, dressed, and breakfasting, eager to see the new world.

The harbour of New York is exceedingly pretty; the *Umbria* seemed to be going all the way to the hotel, we passed so far up the river. The statue of "Liberty," by Bertholdi, is very effective, the position is so fine, facing down the harbour as if welcoming the new comers. I suppose the design was not taken from the frontispiece of *Truth*, but it looks very like it—the lines are too straight, and the pedestal too large and heavy. The saying current at the time of its presentation to America by the French nation came to one's mind: "All the liberty France ever had she gave to America."

Immediately after breakfast, the Custom's officer came on board, and took up his position in the dining-saloon. Everybody had to pass before him and sign a declaration he had nothing liable to duty. I noted that one gentleman declared two bottles of whisky and 150 cigars, and was allowed to take them in free. The whole business of disembarking was very wearisome, not the less so because of the heavy rain that fell all the morning. However, we were agreeably surprised with the Custom's House. We had been told over and over again that the officers were rude and rough, and did their best to annoy the traveller, often upsetting all his goods on to the ground, and leaving him to re-pack as best he might; while ladies spoke of heavy charges on old clothes, on the pretext that they were new. It used to be the rule to bribe the officials, but new men had been lately appointed on purpose to stop it, and should any one offer a bribe to one of these, the consequences would be serious. We had made up our mind not to bribe, as a few hours' delay at the docks would be better than a few weeks in New York, should we hit upon the wrong man.

When, after weary waiting, our turn came, we found a very gentlemanly, quiet-mannered person, who did not look in the least bribable. He examined everything most minutely, opening with special interest any parcel, such as a bit of needlework or a few gloves wrapped in paper, even looking into a tiny parcel containing net for veils, which could have hardly covered any contraband goods ; but whatever he touched he replaced, and at the end, he kindly helped us to lock up and strap our trunks. Of course the journey before us did not require new clothes or finery of any kind.

There is one point I was never able to clear up, as everybody told a different tale, viz. : do diamonds pay duty when unquestionably private property ? I was particularly asked what I had, but I had absolutely none, not even a ring. Some ladies put on their jewellery under their cloaks, and I noticed a gentleman with a magnificent solitaire in his rough tie, the only diamond out of place that caught my eye in America, where I was told everybody wore them all day long. A few years ago a gentleman I knew took over one brooch, and had to pay 170 dollars duty, although it was for a present ; but lately an American dealer is said to have passed a quantity free, simply by taking the precaution of having a monogram stamped on each case, which was taken to show private ownership.

I saw a Custom's officer unfasten and examine a few sticks and umbrellas tied together, perhaps six in all, and another furious at having to spend the morning finding out the exact sum a lady had to pay on two fans she had brought from Paris to give to her daughters.

At last we were free, and got into a landau, which is probably the oldest article in America, so dilapidated was it ; windows shattered, doors broken, lamps gone, and lining in tatters. The New York roads were worthy of it, such holes, such bumping, and thumping, and shaking. We arrived at the Windsor Hotel about 10.30 a.m.

It must be to this landing on Sunday that is owing the wonderful luck that attended us through our journey. We had almost perpetual fine weather, and where storms did occur, they always seemed to be arranged for our advantage, as the heavy rain at Montreal, which filled the Lachine Rapids and the Montmorenci Falls, near Quebec, and the snowstorm which delayed the Denver and Rio Grande train just long enough to enable us to enjoy the whole of the grand scenery in full daylight.

After Edward had gone round presenting some letters of introduction, and making arrangements for our onward progress, he returned to the hotel for me, and we spent the short time we had in New York in seeing as much as we could. We went first to the top of the tower of the Produce Market, fourteen stories high. Of course there is an elevator. The view is glorious—all New York, the harbour, the statue of Liberty, the Brooklyn Bridge, the two rivers, everything is visible from this tower, and New York looks far better from there than from the level.

The streets are dirty and badly paved, the shops have no smart appearance, the elevated railway is unsightly, and the whole place covered with telegraph and telephone wires, just like great cobwebs, except for the rough poles at every corner leaning all ways, so that one feels disappointed with New York, except as seen from the tower. Of course I only speak of the first impression. There are some very fine buildings in the commercial part of the city, and some handsome churches, but the whole effect is shabby—the elevated railroad is a hideous disfigurement ; it is built down the middle of the street, mostly on trestles or columns, so that cinders from the engine, or anything dropping from the trains may fall on to the heads of the passengers below.

New York " licks creation " in hotels. The Windsor Hotel far surpasses any I know in Europe, for the comfort and elegance of the apartments, the luxury of the table and, what is very rare in America, the quick service. The universal weak point is the washing apparatus. Of course it is not always possible to secure a room with a bath, and then the arrangement of the tiny basin with the two taps over it is maddening. One keeps knocking one's head against the taps, and any incautious movement of the sponge catches the chain which holds the plug, and all the water disappears. The theory of hot water conveyed to every room is delightful, but in practice one generally has to let both taps run for half an hour before one discovers which is the hot water tap.

We found acceptable accommodation all over the States and Canada with hardly any exceptions, that is, good according to the American style, clean, comfortable bedrooms, and meals better than one could expect in towns only a few years old. The service always bad, and the hotel people always disobliging. The meals are at stated hours, and while it is impossible to get breakfast at the early hour promised, it is equally impossible to get dinner a moment after the fixed time. The cook goes home, and the manager himself cannot keep him. I often wondered what an invalid would do in an American hotel. What we most disliked was the waste of time at meals. When we had examined the lengthy *menu*, and chosen our food, we had to wait half an hour until it was cooked. Then everything came on together, and was piled around us. My soup, fish, meat, potato, everything on its tiny dish, in a circle round the one plate that was meant to serve for the whole dinner, and Edward's portion in tiny dishes round his plate. Of course things got cold.

The great want in American hotels which is much felt by Europeans is the omniscient porter of continental Europe, or the friendly landlord of English inns. The guide-books are very poor things, the waiters are generally strangers, so there is no means of obtaining information. The American landlord is rarely seen; we saw him occasionally, and found him a curious creature. He is delighted to discuss the weather or politics with you, but if you ask a question as to how best to visit the neighbourhood or the price of carriages or anything connected with his business, his dignity is up in arms at once. He considers himself a gentleman, and you want to treat him as if he were a hireling. As for the clerks at the hotel offices, they are proverbial for impertinence even in America.

The following is a specimen of their manners. Our linen had returned from the laundress, and an important piece was missing, so Edward went to the office and asked the clerk to make inquiry. "You must have counted wrong," said the clerk; "nobody wants your things." This was in one of the best and oldest established hotels in the States.

Tuesday, August 14*th.*—We went on board the Hudson River steamer at 9 a.m. for Albany. We would gladly have rested and seen a little more of New York, but everybody said we must reach the Yellowstone Park not later than the beginning of September, and we had much to do before then.

On going on board, we deposited our hand-baggage in a parcel office in the steamer. Hand-baggage is a very important article on America, for you are never sure when you will see your trunks again. The first lesson the traveller learns is that he is the last person whose convenience is to be considered. If the station-master or the carrier does not feel inclined to worry about the luggage that evening, though it may cause you to lose your train next day, there is nothing to be done. So it is wise always to have a few things in a "grip," which is the American for hand-bag, and as there are no porters at the stations, you have to carry it yourself, so you must not have it heavy. The steamer was very large and luxurious, with comfortable seats, and we had a lovely day on the river, which is very wide and beautiful in its way, but not the least like the Rhine, as New Yorkers fondly imagine. The size of the river is impressive, the handsome residences near the city look very attractive, further on the Palisades are both curious and beautiful, then come the pretty towns nestling at the foot of the cliffs, and the Catskill mountains in the background.

An excellent lunch made us still more contented. It was our first experience of negro waiters, who are better than any others when well trained. They move about as quietly and as gracefully as cats. Some of the large establishments must choose them for their looks, as I never saw a good-looking negro anywhere else. One or two of the waiters on the steamer were splendid men with no trace of negro features except their skins, which were black as coal, and seemed to have been beautifully polished. They really look as if they blacked themselves like boots instead of washing, the gloss on them was so bright. White and black men are never seen working together as waiters, either all are negros or all white. At the conclusion of our meal, we tipped our waiter, who evidently did not expect anything, and some Americans at the same table reproved us for so doing, but everywhere else we found the waiters as anxious for tips as any German, and the bell-boys especially tiresome. The bell-boy is a functionary whose duty it is to answer the bells and transmit the orders to the waiter, chambermaid, or whatever servant's service you require.

It may prove useful to some if I give the result of our experience. It is no good tipping any one unless the traveller means to make some stay in an hotel;

Then he should tip the head waiter to give him the same seat at every meal. After that, he must square the waiter in charge of his table. Table d'hôte is always served at tables accommodating from four to ten people. In that way he will secure attention, and earlier comers will be kept waiting until he is served.

We arrived at Albany at 6.10 p.m., and took the train at once to Saratoga, where we arrived at 8 o'clock, and walked across the street from the station to the monster United States Hotel just opposite. It is built round a large garden, and contains 916 rooms. We expected to see great magnificence of dress and extravagance generally, and were disappointed to see a very common, dull-looking set of people. The principal beaux of the place seemed to be the hotel clerks. As we left very early next morning, we saw nothing more of the place except the pretty main street with its big trees. Our small bedroom, with bath, on the fourth storey, tea, and breakfast, cost ten dollars.

Wednesday, August 15th, was a hard day. We left Saratoga at 8.20 a.m., and arrived at Caldwell, on Lake George, about 9. We did not leave Caldwell until past 10 o'clock, instead of 9.40, and were, in consequence, late all day. We spent four hours zigzagging from side to side of Lake George, landing one passenger here, and taking off another there, sometimes crossing the lake only to deliver a case of mineral waters. Saratoga was a dreary-looking pleasure-resort, but Lake George is charming. The English element in the American character has discovered this healthy outdoor fashion of holiday making. The lake is full of little islands, and on them and on the side of the lake, people camp out in tents, regardless of mosquitoes, do for themselves with the help of canned foods of all kinds, and spend the summer days boating, playing tennis, fishing, flirting, and generally enjoying themselves. At some points there were small, rough hotels, and at every landing there was a merry crowd greeting the coming and speeding the parting guests, and shouting jokes as long as the steamer was within hail.

Unfortunately, the scenery, though pretty, is monotonous, and we were very glad when we got to the end and took the train to Fort Ticonderaga, where we joined the steamer for Plattsburgh. Lake Champlain is more beautiful, as well as much larger than Lake George. The shores are sometimes flat and cultivated, sometimes rocky and hilly, but always there are the beautiful Adirondack mountains in the distance. The weather was changeable and threatening, which improved the scenery by the lovely variations of colour and cloud effects.

Both steamers were very comfortable. We had no time for supper at Plattsburgh, where we took the train again and arrived at Montreal about 11 p.m., after a shaky run, very tired and thirsty. The customs' examination at the Canadian frontier was nothing.

The Windsor Hotel at Montreal is large and handsome, with good rooms, but wretched food and service. It faces on to the square and the new Roman Catholic cathedral built on the model of St. Peter's at Rome.

It rained incessantly the two days we were in Montreal, with occasional thunderstorms, so that, but for the great kindness of our fellow-traveller on the *Umbria*, Sir Donald Smith, we should have seen nothing of the place; but he sent his brougham, notwithstanding the deluge, to take us round the town and the favourite Montreal recreation-grounds, the cemeteries, which are certainly unusually large and elegant. The drive is called "Around the Mountain," and most of it was through the Protestant cemetery. The driver regretted we did not allow him to take us through the Roman Catholic cemetery, which, he said, was much larger, but we had seen as many tombstones as we cared for. At last we reached the view which, even in the rain, was very fine—all Montreal, with the big Victoria Bridge, and as far away over the plains as the mist and clouds would permit.

Sir Donald also asked us to dine with him at no less than 1157, Dorchester Street, where he has built a beautiful house, fitted up with American woods which ought to be better known here, the colours are so pleasing. Sir Donald showed us his magnificent picture-gallery, where he has a fine Turner, a Millais, a Boughton, two large M'Whirters, and many very valuable old masters. But his great pride is his matchless collection of ancient Japanese porcelain and curios, of which we only saw a few, as they were not yet arranged. The collection was formed by an Englishman who lived many years in Japan. He died recently, and his wife would only sell the collection as a whole, and, though many had the will, only Sir Donald had the power to buy such a prize; and still people have been heard to say that wealth does not add to one's happiness!

Next day we drove in pouring rain, still enjoying Sir Donald's brougham, to Lachine, but while we waited for the steamer, the rain cleared off, and we had a splendid run down the rapids, which are curious, but not so exciting as we expected from the picture on the advertisement, which represents a Red Indian pilot in full war-paint steering through rocks which barely afford room for the steamer to go through them, while billows mountains high threaten to overwhelm her. Now there was no Indian pilot, no billows to speak of, and apparently no particular danger to any one who knew the road.

On reaching Montreal, we were transferred to the comfortable s.s. *Quebec*, and started at once for that city. The scenery looked very lovely in the gorgeous sunset, and in the bright starlight night. We met a Montreal acquaintance on board, who said, as every one says, that the French element in Eastern Canada grows stronger daily. The employers of labour have much difficulty with the French workpeople, who are Roman Catholics, and keep too many religious holidays. We noticed that everybody in the streets seemed to be speaking French, and several men we spoke to could not understand English.

Saturday, August 18*th*.—Up at 5.30 to see the fine approach to Quebec, which is called Kébec by the natives. It was a splendid day, with baking sunshine and a refreshing breeze. The town is on a steep cliff, with steps for streets. We ascended in an elevator, and after rushing first to Dufferin Terrace, which overhangs the St. Lawrence river, for the view, we went to the St. Louis Hotel for breakfast, and then took a carriage and drove the round of the sights of Quebec. The roads are equal to those of New York and Montreal, that is, they are disgraceful. First we went to the Citadel, where we found Lord Stanley taking his morning walk on the terrace, which is said to have the finest view in America. I should say from our experience it is the only one of its kind—so peaceful and civilized. It is very lovely; but it is a great thing to say that it is the most lovely in the land of the Yosemite and Niagara.

Lord Stanley was amused at my disappointment on finding Canada so French. He thinks that the French element is overpowering the English in the eastern provinces, but that it is because the English go west, where there are better opportunities for men of energy. He thinks the trade of the country is not diminishing, but is changing. From the Citadel we drove to the Plains of Abraham, passing the beautiful new Parliament buildings and many splendid Roman Catholic churches by the way. There is nothing to see at the Plains of Abraham, except a cricket-ground, a jail, and a wretched monument to Wolfe, so we hurried away over some queer roads and down break-neck hills, through the town, and along a good country road to the falls of Montmorency, which are ninety feet higher than Niagara. There is a steep staircase, or rather, series of ladders, down the cliffs opposite the falls. I struggled down to the first landing-place, whence I could see the rainbows on the spray. Edward went to the bottom to look up at the falls. There is nothing in Europe to equal them. There was abundance of water, owing to the recent heavy rains, but occasionally there is hardly any. Some ladies told me they had seen them almost dry. It was lucky I spoke to these ladies, for they told us to be sure to visit the Natural Steps. The drivers always try to avoid the extra journey, and assure the unwary that there is nothing worth seeing. Our driver was very loath to take us, but we insisted on going there, and were well rewarded, though there was a long, rough walk and a steep scramble through a wood to get to the Steps, which reminded us of the Strid at Bolton, but magnified and glorified. The stream flows through a rocky gorge, and its bed really is a succession of long steps. It is a brown stream, and appears to be full of gold dust, which turned out on examination to be sawdust from timber cutting up-stream. Such is the effect of sunshine. After rambling about for some time, we went back to the Point Levis Station, on the south side of the St. Lawrence, and took train back to Montreal, where we supped at the hotel, and then went back to the station, expecting to get at once into our sleeping-berths, which had been engaged beforehand, in the Montreal Pulman car. We found that some one else had got them. Of course he had not bribed the conductor—all conductors are immaculate—but we had to tramp about the station for more than an hour until the train came in with the Boston car, where happily we got two lower berths, and made our first night's journey in a Pulman sleeping-car—not much sleep, so we were not sorry to be turned out at Kingston Junction at 5.30 a.m., but we were horrified to find that there was no boat ready to take us to the Thousand Islands, and no breakfast to be had. We had a short train journey to Kingston itself, where we roamed about in a famishing condition until the official who sells the steamer tickets took pity on us, and gave us some of the coffee he keeps for the workmen, for he is a temperance worker, and wisely gave the men coffee to keep them off beer. A man had carried our rugs, &c., to the boat, and as Edward was asking the ticket-seller what he ought to give him for it, a voice in the background called out, "Give him what you'd give him in Yorkshire; you come from Leeds or thereabouts, I know." We turned, and saw a stout party, who said he came from Bradford, but unfortunately he took another boat, and so we saw him no more. It was not an interesting journey until we reached the islands in about an hour and a half. After that, it was very pretty, but monotonous. The islands are of all sizes, from tiny rocks to quite important islands with several large houses and parks, still far too small for sport of any kind; and as the river is rather dangerous for boating, with occasional rapids, it must be very monotonous living on an island. We arrived at Alexandria Bay about noon, and took up our quarters at the Thousand Islands House, a very good hotel, where there were some very fine men among the black servants. One, I think, was the handsomest man I ever saw; he was very tall and splendidly proportioned, had perfectly regular features, and was as black as night. I should have liked to bring that man home for a footman, but probably English servants would not like to have a negro among them. No American ever sits down to meat with a coloured man. At the railway dining-rooms there is a separate table for the black men, and if there are any Chinese, there is another table for them. The conductors generally sit among the passengers, who would be thought absurdly arrogant if they objected. I should often have preferred our coloured brethren, for the railway conductor, though sometimes extremely kind and pleasant, is often insolent. I took the address of the head waiter at the Thousand Islands House, meaning to visit his shop in New York. He was a wonderful manager. I never saw such perfection of waiting as at this hotel. He gave directions by signs, and the rapidity and graceful movements of these waiters were charming. They carried heavily-laden trays on one hand high above their heads. I watched with great interest, expecting to see collisions between going and coming waiters, but everything went as smoothly as if by clockwork. I never saw a black woman-servant, except once, in the whole of our journey. After dinner, Edward took a boat, and went to present his letter of introduction to Mr. Pulman, who lives close by, in a house costing 50,000 dollars, which he has built on an island he bought for 40 dollars twenty-five years ago, before fashion had discovered the Thousand

Islands. He kindly showed Edward over his house, and gave him a letter to his firm at Pulman Town, where his works are.

Monday, August 20th.—We were called at six, and started by the 8 o'clock steamer for Gananoque. We found afterwards that there were two other boats later in the morning, but all the hotel people assured us the 8 o'clock was the only boat. We had to wait five hours at Gananoque, with nothing to do but eat a bad dinner and watch some magnificent butterflies, and crickets, that looked like butterflies when flying. I heard afterwards these were katydids. They make a loud noise when flying. At last the steamer called for us and took us back to Kingston by the other side of the river. At one stopping-place, where there was an enormous hotel, we saw a little boat containing two people, completely overturned by the wind suddenly catching the sail. Of course there was a rush of other boats to the rescue, but they were barely in time. I should not like to stay here, it seems as if such accidents must be frequent. There is a strong main current and numbers of cross currents and windy corners, and everybody does without professional help. We took the boat train to Kingston-junction, and the 3.32 train to Toronto, where we arrived at 10.45 p.m., and found a comfortable room at the Queen's Hotel. Next day we walked and trammed round Toronto, which is a very handsome, prosperous town. We sought diligently for the magnificent parliament buildings, whose photograph was in every shop window, and only discovered late in

in Canada, Western U.S., and Mexico.   19

the day that they were not yet built. We took the 5 o'clock train, arriving at Niagara about 8.15, and took the bus to Clifton House Hotel, on the Canadian side, a long way from the station, and directly opposite the falls. I shut my eyes all the time we were driving, not to catch any glimpse of them on the way, as I wanted to see the full glory at once. I do not know why Niagara should be more to me than any other fine sight, but so it was. I do not think a glimpse of Paradise would fill me with greater awe and enthusiasm, and still it kept recurring to me how many people had said the first sight of Niagara disappointed them. I have heard many say so. When at last I saw it shining in the brilliant moonlight, the whole extent visible from our bedroom balcony, I felt that nothing mortal could equal the glory of it, the loveliness and the power, and the fulness of content it seems to put into one's heart. Here at last is something without weakness or failing, perfectly beautiful, resistlessly strong, the roar of the waters musical and satisfying. It was delicious to wake in the night and hear the roar.

In the morning we took a carriage and drove first to the rapids, admiring the Cantilever Bridge on the way. The immediate vicinity of the falls, both on the American and the Canadian side is public property, but below the bridge everything is enclosed, and has to be paid for.

A rather dangerous-looking elevator takes one down to the rapids, where there is a long promenade close to the water. This is the place where poor Captain Webb was last seen alive. The pace is tremendous, and the big waves, or rather upheavals of water, stand far above the general level. It is a marvellous sight!

From the rapids we drove over the Suspension Bridge to the whirlpool. We ought to have seen this from the Canadian side, but our driver had different interests from ours, so he took us to the American side, where there is no elevator, and we had a dreadful pull down and up the 180 steps. The whirlpool, from that side, is decidedly disappointing. Then we drove to the top of the American Falls, where everything has been done to assist visitors. Railings have been put close to the edge, so that one can lean quite over the falls, and looks through the lovely green water and watch it take its great leap.

Our great adventure was passing through the Cave of the Winds. First we had to take off all our own clothes and put on special flannel suits and macintosh hoods, long jackets and trousers, and rough boots and stockings, both alike, so that we were comical-looking objects. Then we went down a long winding staircase in a tower to the foot of the falls. From here a guide led us and two gentlemen along wooden platforms and up and down little stairs, scrambling over rocks, drenched by spray and mixed up with rainbows, making desperate efforts all the while to look at the immense falls which were thundering in our ears. At last we got round to the other side of the first part of the falls, of course comparatively a small part, but bigger than all the Swiss wasserfalls put together.

Then comes the tug of war! the guide disappears behind the water, and you dash in after him and find yourself scrambling along the side of the rock, no path, no rope, nothing but a little ledge up and down anyhow. It is impossible to see, or hear, or even breathe, for the spray and wind and noise of the cataract which thunders past close to your head, and you cannot stop to admire for fear your breath will not hold out. I was quite happy, but then I had the assistance of the guide. Poor Edward was dreadfully upset. About half-way through, there is a drop of about three feet or more, and when he saw me go down this, he thought I had gone for good. He could not get his breath for some time after we came out.

We heard afterwards that this really is a very dangerous adventure, and many lives have been lost. A lady fell last year, and was never seen again. It was supposed she was jammed amongst the rocks at the foot of the falls, but these accidents are not put into the newspapers to frighten people and spoil trade. It is certainly quite unfit for any one with the slightest weakness of the heart, lungs, or nerves, but for strong people it is a queer experience well worth the trouble, and reminded me of the delightful sensation out hunting when one faces a fence one is not quite sure one will get over.

From the cave we drove to the Three Sisters Islands to see the rapids above the falls, and then through Prospect Park, and over the other Suspension Bridge back to the hotel.

After early dinner, we walked along the Canadian side to Prospect Point, where Table Rock formerly stood, and where was the old Cave of the Winds, associated with Professor Tyndal's name. Here there was no cataract to pass under, and come out the other side, but a kind of path under the main fall, and each person went as far as his powers allowed, Professor Tyndal going further than any one else. Now only a short piece of the beginning of the path remains. We went down to it by the elevator, and walked most of the way, when to our amazement we saw some gentlemen in complete macintosh suits solemnly do the five or six yards good path with a little spray falling over them, evidently thinking they were accomplishing the same feat as Professor Tyndal.

Of course we paid our respects to Mrs. Webb, and bought a large photograph from her.

I wish to say that there is not a single objectionable advertisement near Niagara, as one so often sees described in books. They swarm in fitting places, but we did not see one that marred the scenery, either at Niagara or anywhere else in America. Another note is that the Clifton House Hotel and the Queen's Hotel, in Toronto, are almost the only hotels in America where salt-spoons are found.

Thursday, August 23*rd.*—We walked to Prospect Park, on the American side, and went down by the elevator to the steamer, which goes close to the American Falls, and as near as it can get to the Horse-Shoe Fall.

Not only does this give one a better idea of the height of the falls, but it enables one to see the curious break in the middle of the Horse-Shoe Fall. Part of the rock has fallen since our visit, enlarging this break. The steamer approaches the Horse-Shoe Fall twice, and when it reaches a certain point, the water takes hold of it and swings it round. We landed on the Canadian side, and while walking along the cliff, met a fellow-passenger on the *Umbria*, who expressed himself much disappointed with Niagara.

All through our journey we kept meeting "Umbrians."

After dining early, we took the train to Chicago. It had to come from New York, and was two hours late, so we did not start until 4.45. We had a row with the hotel porter and the United States customs' officer, who was so angry because he was not tipped, that he deliberately smashed my box. After turning over everything, he found the photograph of Niagara, which he declared was dutiable, being "a picture," but he had no time to inquire how much we must pay, so the baggage could not be put in the Chicago van, but must be examined at Port Huron about 1 a.m. After we got to our carriage, the hotel porter followed us, and offered to get the trunks put in the through van if we would give him a quarter. We declined to do business with him, so we had to pass them at Port Huron, which was no misfortune, as we saw the train put on to the enormous ferry-boat to cross the river. We had nothing to pay on the photograph after all.

We got tea that evening very comfortably on a Pulman dining-car.

Tea is generally pretty good, except that one sometimes gets preserved milk, but dinner is not to be commended. Perhaps one would be less critical were it not for the expectations raised by the advertisements. Whose mouth would not water at the prospect of a meal "combining all the delicacies of the Atlantic and the Pacific, with the game and fruit of the countries passed through." This is the modest description given by the Northern Pacific Railroad of its Pulman dining-car fare.

One does not sleep well in a Pulman car. There is a peculiar smell, and it is very like being in one's coffin. No wonder there is a smell about the bedding, for it is never aired. As soon as the passenger rises, the porter comes to do up the bed and turn it back into seats. He takes away the linen, but the blankets and mattresses are shut up inside the berth at once until next night. In the daytime the cars are delightful. We took the drawing-room on this journey. This is a little snuggery cut off the rest of the car, with its own washing apparatus. It is very comfortable, but only having windows on one side, it is not so convenient for seeing the country, so we did not take it again.

As usual, we were hours late, and only arrived in Chicago at 12.40 p.m. The country passed through was very uninteresting and poor-looking, much of it still uncultivated. Chicago is a wonderful place, with magnificent buildings of a massive style of architecture, as if they were expected to stand a siege. Pulman's offices are one of the finest, but many far surpass anything of the kind here, for they are only private commercial buildings, and still they are built regardless of expense with blocks of granite often ten feet square at least. The public buildings are very fine too, but the roads are the same as usual, only dirtier, and the place is smothered in smoke. The whole town is built on a swamp, and has been raised eleven feet above the original surface, so there is naturally great difficulty with the drainage. We admired Chicago very much; it is not only fine, but it is characteristic of its inhabitants, and copies no European city.

The Palmer House Hotel is very dirty and uncomfortable. Charges very high. I had my breakfast brought to my room one morning, and the extra charge for the service of bringing it was one dollar! The Richelieu Hotel is said to be excellent.

We spent our first afternoon in a general survey, and took the cable car to Lincoln Park, the new promenade along the shore of Lake Michigan. The road there goes through a tunnel under the river lighted by electricity. The tramcars here are run like trains, several together, at a great speed, and everybody must get out of their way. I saw a policeman seize the horse in a private carriage, and force it out of the way of an approaching car, as if the whole place belonged to the tram company. The American policeman has no nonsense about him; he would and does make short work of any troublesome people. He carries not the sword in vain.

On our return to the hotel we found an immense crowd awaiting the arrival of Mr. Thurman, the Democratic candidate for the office of Vice-President. Another crowd came with him and filled the enormous hall of the hotel—there must have been over 1000 inside the hotel. Judge Thurman is a sweet-looking gentleman, but seemed far too old for public life, at least for electioneering. He was very tired, and refused to speak a word for a long time, but the crowd would not be appeased, so at last he came forward and said in a low voice that he " guessed he saw Democrats before him, and if Democrats, they were reasonable people, and when he told them he had travelled three hundred miles, and made nine little speeches, they would not expect a speech to-night, as he heard a few people were coming to hear him speak to-morrow, and he wanted to save his voice and strength till then." A lady spiritualist was waiting to present him with an address and a picture representing a prophetic vision she had had concerning him. It was very indistinct, but seemed full of angels, and an enthusiastic politician rushed about all the time thrusting into everybody's hand cards with a picture of the Democratic leaders, and the inscription, Vote for Cleveland and Thurman, and buy your carpets at the City of Paris Store, 138, State Street.

Next day Judge Thurman had an outdoor meeting of about thirty thousand, but we could not attend, for Edward went off to see Mr. Armour's stock-killing establishment, five miles out by train. He did not see the oxen led from one pen to another by the trained decoy ox, but saw the old fellow standing there having accomplished his work of treachery. He is a great pet of all the men. Edward saw both oxen and pigs killed and cut up. The cleverest thing is the contrivance for fetching the hair off the pigs by revolving discs with sharp flat springs. He saw the sausage-making, the potting and sealing of the canned beef, and the refrigerating chambers and cars, which are kept at a temperature of 36 degrees. The cars are double, the inner one being protected by the air space between it and the outer car, and only the ends are filled up with ice. Edward was astonished to see how dirty the surroundings were. The places where the work is actually done were very clean, but outside that, all was careless and slovenly. Armour employs 5000 to 6000 men, and kills one and a quarter million hogs a year, besides 500,000 cattle, and 100,000 sheep.

On his return, Edward called at Mr. Armour's office. The clerk glanced at the clock, and said: "Mr. Armour is away at lunch, he will be here in a minute and a quarter," and he was. He spends his life in that office; early in the morning and up to any time of night that there is any business to do. It is hardly worth while being a millionaire in Chicago. The clerks arrive at 8 a.m., have three-quarters of an hour for dinner, and remain always until six, and later if required, and until three on Saturdays. Mr. Armour is very kind to his people, and works harder than they do. He told Edward that now he had found employment for all former waste products. He made glue, oil, grease, &c.; the most valuable bit of an ox, his leg bone, is sold for knife-handles. He seized Edward's coat. "Why," said he, "these buttons are made of dried blood." He has a secret process of making for 40 cents (1s. 8d.) a pound the isinglass used for clarifying beer, formerly brought from Russia at three dollars (12s. 6d.) a pound. Everything not otherwise utilized is made into "fertilizers," *i.e.* manure.

After dinner, which is early here, Mr. Armour sent one of his clerks with his carriage to take us to see his grain elevator. We had a horrible drive to it through clouds of black dust and a multitude of evil smells. The grain elevator is situated on the side of the river, as much grain is brought to it by boat and transferred to the railway cars. There is storage-room for 2,250,000 bushels (of sixty pounds). The building is 155 feet high, and 550 long by 112 wide, and contains four tracks, on each of which twelve cars can stand while the grain is poured into them from above. The engine which works the twenty-eight elevators is of 1500 horse-power, and each elevator carries 7000 bushels an hour. First, we saw the grain shovelled out of the cars by large scoops, two men with scoops in each car. It looks like ploughing; these men hold down the scoops, and a rope fastened to an engine outside pulls them along. They empty an immense waggon in seven minutes. Then we saw the "Jacob's ladder" bands with buckets, which run over pulleys at 570 feet a minute to convey the grain to the top to be weighed and poured into the ships or cars ready to take it away, or if for storage, into enormous bins 75 feet deep, and 12 feet square. What pleased me most were the splendid views of Chicago from the top windows of the immense pile. Though it was past 6 o'clock on Saturday evening, the men were still working, and the foreman came to ask our conductor if he should begin to empty another lot of waggons that evening. After leaving the elevator, our young friend drove us round the town, first down Dearborn Avenue, the property of Mr. Palmer, the hotel owner. It was a swamp when he bought it, but he made a sea wall to the lake with a fine promenade, and reclaimed the land, built himself a splendid mansion, gorgeously decorated, and then sold off the other land at prices which paid for everything. We saw numbers of fine houses, and our guide kept saying, "You see that large house? the owner built that out of one speculation," or "that man found a mine out west, and built that house out of it," &c. Money seems to be made here quickly, but not easily.

Business-hours are dreadful. There can be no social life or interest in music, literature, politics, or science, when men are at their offices twelve hours a day. The shops were open, and masons and road-menders, &c., at work that Saturday evening, and afterwards we noticed that not only do Americans work all Saturday, but often on Sunday.

Sunday, 26th August, was desperately hot. We had a dinner worth recording.

Mock Turtle Soup
Fried Soft-shell Crabs.
Brandy Peaches.   Stuffed Mangoes.
Boiled Capon, Cream Sauce.
Corn on Cob.   Tomatoes.
Sweetbreads with Mushrooms.
Frog Legs à la Maître d'hôtel.
Punch Siberian.
Pies.   Cakes.   Ices.   Coffee.

The crabs were nasty—the soft shells give one the impression they are out of season. Frog legs good.

Dinner over, we turned out to see what we could. After vainly endeavouring to extract any information from the hall porter, we got into a cable car for South Park, four miles out, and went as far as the car would take us, which was some way past the park. It looked very gay and pretty, with plenty of visitors ; then, after coming back a little way, we changed to another car that went to Jackson's Park by the lake side, which is also very pretty and nicely kept, but both badly want good trees. It was a great rush and scramble to get seats in the homeward cars. We jumped on as the car was coming up to the park, and coming pretty fast, too, and kept our hold until some one got out, and then we managed to get room to perch for the return journey.

The cars carry as many as can find foot-hold. In the country where the road is clear, they go at great speed, up to fourteen miles an hour.

Next day I spent alone, roaming round the town and looking at the shops, which are poor and dear. Some moderately good peaches were marked 35 cents each, which did not seem to be cheaper than the English. In New York, too, they were dear. Perhaps the abundant and cheap peaches are found in the Eastern States. We paid only 5 cents each for large ones in San Francisco in October, but they had no flavour. American peaches are hard, and are cut into slices and eaten with cream for breakfast. I visited the school of art, where they have Mr. Boughton's "The Last Minstrel." In the meanwhile Edward had gone to Pulman Town, about three-quarters of an hour by tram. This is entirely the property of the Pulman Palace Car Company, who have laid it out nicely, with trees and open spaces, and is occupied by their 4000 workmen.

The only place where drink is sold is the bar of the hotel. On the whole Edward was rather disappointed. There was nothing new in the iron-working machinery. The wood-carving machinery was interesting, and the works for making the brown paper wheels, which are said to be a great success. They are made of layers of brown paper pasted together and compressed by hydraulic pressure, becoming so hard, that they can be turned up like wood to fit the steel tyre. The Pulman's cars are very handsomely upholstered in plush, and expensively decorated. Inlaid woods had gone out of fashion, and the new cars were being decorated with natural woods polished to show the grain. The company kindly sent Edward by special engine to the South

Chicago iron and steel works, where he saw four blast furnaces in operation smelting Lake Superior iron ore, which is very rich, containing 60 per cent. metallic iron. Each furnace produces 1300 tons a week. The steel works were stopped for want of work. Business is always slack at the presidential election, and of course this, which turns on the Free Trade question, is more disturbing than usual.

Protection does not always keep the wolf from the door. I was astonished to find from a local paper that there is great poverty even in this prosperous city. The articles in this paper were written by a lady who has taken employment in a number of trade establishments, just staying long enough in each to see how it is carried on, and she gives her experience. It is a pitiful tale, quite equal to "The Bitter Cry of Outcast London." Here the misery of low wages is increased by the excessive cost of living. It seems extraordinary that there should be actual starvation here in the centre of the great corn-lands, and especially now, when the harvest is above the average. A gentleman told us he had been visiting in the country, and to show him how fine the corn is, his friend drove him in a two-horse waggon into a field, and standing up in the waggon, they could not look over the top of the corn. Corn, in America, I should mention, always means maize.

Edward's final excursion was to see the new tunnel under the lake to bring water to the city. There is one already, but the new one is to run four miles out, to make certain of getting pure water. A crib is to be sunk, with a large wrought-iron cylinder, two miles out, to facilitate working. In the afternoon we moved on two and a half hours by train to Milwaukee, a very pretty, bright-looking, brand-new town on the edge of Lake Michigan, almost exclusively inhabited by Germans. It was curious to hear every one talking German and shouting, "Ach ja!" "Je wohl!" A large party were at the station to greet some returning friends, which they did with great enthusiasm. It is said the Germans keep very much to themselves in America, and, if strong enough, try to Germanize the public institutions, having in some places actually caused the public day-schools to teach in German. This makes the genuine Americans very angry.

The Plankington Hotel is poorly conducted and cheaply gaudy. We were disappointed, as Mr. Armour had spoken of it as very fine, being the property of his friend, the great Milwaukee millionaire, Plankington. There is a kind of tradition that a millionaire should always build a hotel. We started for Minneapolis next day at 11.15 a.m. There was no Pulman car on the day train, so we had a very fatiguing journey. It is not usual to have Pulman cars on what are called local trains. The ordinary cars are not uncomfortable, but they are very noisy. As soon as the train starts a man comes selling newspapers; he goes through all the cars, banging the doors after him, then he comes back and brings round a cargo of books, mostly pirated editions of "Robert Elsmere" and Rider Haggard's books. Then he goes round with apples and pears, then ba-

D.

nanas, then dried figs. At each visit he requires your attention, and sometimes one gets cross at the perpetual interruptions.

There are always babies in ordinary or Pulman cars. Children do not have a good time in America. When a few weeks old their travels begin. They swarm in hotels, little dots of two or three years old taking meals at the table-d'hôte at seven and eight o'clock in the evening, and those of riper years, such as six, roam all over the hotels alone, playing with the elevator boys and the waiters. They look very delicate. On this occasion there were several babies in the car, and they all screamed. There was not much to see on the way; we seemed to go over endless swamps, past many lakes, and very poor-looking soil, mostly not cultivated or even used as grazing-land.

Nothing astonished me so much in America as the immense tracts of totally unoccupied land even so far east as this. Later on we met a gentleman who had a cattle ranche in Texas. He told us his cattle were driven up every year for sale to Miles City, Dakota, a town on this line of railway, the whole way on free land, feeding on the grass they pass over. He thought this would be the last year they could do it, as the land was being quickly taken up. At half-past three we reached Kilbourn, which is a pretty little place; and at half-past four, Camp Douglas, where there are some remarkable rocks standing out of the plain and curious round, flat-topped hills. A little before five o'clock we came to a tunnel, which is such a curiosity in this flat region that a city has been named after it—Tunnel City. Just as we entered the tunnel an unlucky passenger opened the car door, admitting a blast of sulphur that almost poisoned us. A lady with a terrible cough was half killed. The single-line tunnels are very suffocating, being so narrow. We had tea at La Crosse, and after that ran along the bank of the Mississippi all the rest of the way. It was really lovely; the sunset glow on the broad river and the pretty banks, and the big steamers and rafts, were all delightful, but the mosquitoes, which swarmed into the cars, were not delightful. We must have taken them to the hotel, for they worried us all night. I slept with a veil on. We arrived at Minneapolis at 11.55 p.m., and got a cab for a dollar to the West Hotel. We had great difficulty in getting our luggage, as the station-master said it was too late for any one to bother about luggage.

West House is a first-rate hotel, very handsomely built by the millionaire West, and splendidly furnished in excellent taste. We were thankful to get to a comfortable room, with a bath, for we were grimy and dirty beyond description. Very bad coal is burnt on the railways here, very smoky, and with an unpleasant smell.

Thursday, August 30*th.*—Our first care was to go to the Northern Pacific agent, to make inquiries about the Yellowstone Park. We had had so much advice on the subject that we were quite at sea. It ended in our buying the forty-dollar round-trip tickets, which are certainly the most satisfactory arrangement. All trouble is taken off one's hands, and time and opportunity given to see everything worth seeing. A lady and gentleman in the office told us they had just returned from the Park, and had had wet, cold weather. They advised us to take plenty of wraps and waterproofs, which we did, and found them dreadfully in the way, as we did not have a drop of rain.

Minneapolis is a charming town, with some very fine buildings. The cause of its prosperity is the water-power supplied by the once beautiful Falls of St. Anthony, which are now utilized for everything—the water carried off in little channels to mills and works without number. Edward presented his letters of introduction, and then we visited the celebrated Pilsbury and Company Mills. The Company present visitors with a card, on which is printed :—

"STARTLING FACTS.

"Fact No. 1.—Mill A is the eighth wonder of the world.

"Fact No. 2.—Mill A grinds 9,500,000 bushels of wheat yearly.

"Fact No. 3.—Mill A has a capacity of 7000 barrels daily.

"Fact No. 4.—Mill A makes more flour than any other two mills on the globe.

"Fact No. 5.—The mills of C. A. Pilsbury and Co. could feed two cities as large as New York."

It is supposed to be the largest flour-mill in existence, and has every new appliance. The flour goes through four hundred operations before it is ready for use. We were shown all over the immense place, which is beautifully clean, but very hot. Every precaution has to be taken against fire. We got a splendid view of the town from the top. Then we went to some lumber works, which were very interesting. We saw the tree floating in the river, then drawn up a tram-line by chains, and put on to a wonderful machine that cut off the rough outside uneven layer, and passed it on to other machines, which made it into planks, planed them, cut them into lengths, and piled them in several heaps, according to length, in the yard. Then we went back to "the most magnificent hotel in the world" (see advertisement), looking in at the Exhibition on our way. It was very poor. Next morning we had a delightful excursion to Minnehaha Falls on the motor car; we had only seven minutes to run across the road and through a little wood to the Falls, and back to the car. They deserved a much longer visit, for it was a pretty spot, and the Falls are well named, they are such sparkling, laughing waters. We should be very proud of them in England, but in America people are accustomed to bigger things.

At 4.35 p.m. we started by the Northern Pacific Railroad for Livingstone Junction, for the Yellowstone Park. The country was very uninteresting at first, and, not having got accustomed to the sleeping-berths, the night was very disagreeable. I tried really going to bed, as most people do, but never repeated the experiment. I was always the earliest riser, as I thus secured the lavatory before the other ladies were up.

Saturday we spent mostly on the platform at the back of our car—a capital place for seeing the country, as the Pulman is always at the end of the train, unless there is a private car on. Of course it is very dusty, but that is of no consequence. We met an Englishman on his way to join his brother at his ranche in Wyoming, who had been over here several times before. He told us that a few years ago he and his brother were detained at Livingstone a few days, just as the boom in land was going on, as it was thought Livingstone would become a great centre. They bought land at the beginning of the week, and so rapid was the rise in price that they sold it at the end of the week at a profit sufficient to cover the expense of their whole trip. Livingstone did not succeed as expected, so land has gone down again. This seems to be the history of most western towns. It is quite a common question to ask about a place, if it has had a boom; it seems to be a kind of distemper to be got over in youth. Our friend also explained to us how the places get such wonderful names. A trapper he knew married and settled at a place on the line. His name was Gustav, and his wife's name Minnie, so he named the settlement after themselves, Mingusville. It is situated between Bismarck and Gladstone. At first the country was very uninteresting; then we got to the prairies, which were not covered with grass, but with sage-brush, a pale, silvery, olive-coloured plant with a delicious smell. I have some now sewn in muslin. An infusion of it is sometimes used in the place of quinine. At half-past one we reached the Bad Lands, which are wonderful. Everything is burnt, and turned curious colours, bright red and yellow, &c. The rocks are the oddest shapes, and there are mounds of all sizes and fossil trees. There was hardly any vegetation, and what there was looked uncanny—such metallic greens and blues. It is said that in places there are coal-seams exposed to the air and burning perpetually. We were a long time passing through this desolate district, which made us reflect what a terrible journey it must have been for the early settlers, who had only bullock-waggons. After that the country again became monotonous and uninteresting, except for the wild sunflowers, which made a blaze of colour along the roadside. The train reached Livingstone in the night, and went on West, leaving our car on a siding. The station had been burnt down the night before our arrival, and the remains were still smouldering. We had to pick our way through them to the hotel for breakfast next morning.

We left by train at 8.15 for Cinnabar, through a very wild and pretty valley, passing the Devil's Slide on the way—a curious wall of stone in one block, fourteen feet across, running straight up the hill, with another wall parallel to it, not so strongly marked, and all the clay between washed away. At Cinnabar we took seats on the coach roof, and had a lovely drive up the valley of the Garrison River, a very steep pull, to the Mammoth Hot Springs Hotel, where we arrived very tired, hungry, and dirty. It was very hot, so I declined further exertion that day, having plenty of letters to write; but Edward started for the Hot Springs after dinner, and went past them to the Devil's Fireplace, a narrow hole extending far into the ground, and said to be very hot. A ladder is placed for the benefit of those who care to enter, but few fancy the descent. There he met two young fellows, who persuaded him to go on with them to a hot lake set apart for men to bathe, and had a delightful bath. The hotel here is very good and comfortable. It has a good view of the terraces of the hot springs and Liberty Cap, a large rock supposed to resemble in shape the cap on the dollar. I had a bath in the evening, and was alarmed by a terrible grasshopper kind of creature that had come direct from the springs through the pipes. Still, the lady at Santa Barbara whose ablutions were disturbed by a large tarantula, fared worse than I did.

Monday, September 3rd.—We started at eight o'clock in a charming little carriage and pair called a Surrey. A nice young fellow from Helena we had talked to the day before introduced us to our driver, a merry, chatty old gentleman, who showed us everything on the road, and drove very carefully. The road is generally very good, but occasionally there is a stream to drive through or a rocky bit, and sometimes the road goes dangerously near the rotten ground round the springs. Miss Bates describes both the Yellowstone and the Yosemite as dangerous and very fatiguing expeditions, but both have been wonderfully improved since she visited them. We met neither difficulty nor danger at either. The fourth occupant of our carriage was a gentleman from New York, who travelled with us from Minneapolis, and was very quiet and pleasant. There must have been over thirty carriages of all kinds. Some large 'busses, others holding six or eight people, and a few like ours. It is prudent to settle on the day of arrival how one wishes to go round the Park, for there is no changing on the way, and disagreeable fellow-travellers would spoil all pleasure. The long procession kept together through the steep defile of the Golden Gate, so called because the rocks are covered with bright golden yellow moss. The gate itself is a pillar of rock on the precipice side of the road, which really is like a gate-post. After reaching level ground we scattered to avoid dust. The first point of interest is the Obsidian Cliffs, entirely composed of this volcanic glass which is quite black. There were a few boiling springs, but wonderland is not reached until lunch-time at Norris Geyser Hotel. After the meal we all walked on ahead of our carriages to the First Geyser Basin. There would be about sixty of us—no guides—the steam and smell and noise direct one where to go. Anything more uncanny, horrible and extraordinary than this dreadful place does not exist! Boiling springs sending up columns of steam, some clear, some black, some sulphur, close together. Some throbbing like great machines, and the water sinking out of sight, and then rushing up again with a terrible noise. One little geyser playing every two minutes, others at longer and irregular intervals. The most appalling is called the Hurricane. The water is shot out of the rock sideways with tremendous force and noise, not continuously or apparently regularly, but as if some great struggle was going on inside. The ground is uncomfortably hot, and sounds quite hollow. It is white like lime, with bright-coloured spots, where there is iron or sulphur. There are dozens of springs, some only bubbling, some throwing spray or drops a foot high —all boiling. If there is a Mouth of Hell on earth, it is certainly here. Going on, we came to a mud geyser, which immediately started its performance for us. It always bubbles, and it seems to get excited, and in three places in the pool the mud dashes itself higher and higher and more and more violently up to about four or five feet high, raising the level of the whole basin, which is about fifteen feet diameter, about a foot. After some minutes it gradually quietens and subsides. A sad thing happened here last year. Some visitors had a pet dog with them, and somebody having thrown a stone into the boiling mud, the poor little thing thought it was meant for him, and jumped in. He sank out of sight instantly. We went on to the Steam Valve and another large basin, but neither did more than bubble, so we went into the wood, where we found a magnificent geyser that had killed the trees round it, and covered them with incrustation. To our delight it began to work, and was soon throwing up water to the height of fifty or sixty feet; quite a great stream was made by the overflow. It performed twice. The Minute Geyser refused to do anything for us. I put my finger into a hot spring at leisure, but I took it out in haste. It was scalding. All over the park at every turn, amongst the trees, at the top of the hills, at the side of icy cold rivers, everywhere are boiling springs—mostly mineral water, but unfortunately so full of alkali that they cannot be used for medical purposes. In about an hour the carriages picked us up, and we drove on.

The Beryl spring is a lovely light blue semicircular pool standing about three feet above the road like an ornamental marble basin. The spring builds this basin itself by depositing the lime contained in the water. We passed Beaver Lake, so called because beavers abound there, and have built a dam zigzag across the lake. Their houses look like piles of sticks. It is forbidden to kill anything in the park, so it is hoped by-and-by there will be plenty of the wild animals there which are being rapidly exterminated outside. We only saw beavers, a snake, wild ducks, little birds, a few butterflies, and large dragon-flies, and traces of elk. Some of the other party saw a bear, which are pretty common, and are said to come down to the hotels at night to eat the refuse thrown out for the pigs.

We passed some very pretty lakes and rivulets, all full of curious colours, and near the hotel we forded the rapid Fire Hole River. It was the third time we had forded a river in our forty miles' drive to Lower Geyser Basin. We were seven and a quarter hours on the way, arriving shortly after five o'clock. A very decent hotel, like a Swiss chalet with tiny rooms, quite clean. We visited the Gibbon Falls on our way, and had a difficult scramble down the steep hill-side without much reward, as there was hardly any water. We met numbers of camping parties. Sheep-farmers and people of that kind in the neighbouring country bring all their families and numbers of servants, in waggons and on horseback, and live in tents on canned food. Unfortunately they cover the park with rubbish—it is littered with cans, which of course last for years. As a whole the park is ugly; there must be nine dead trees to one green one.

Tuesday, September 4th.—Drove off at seven o'clock, and followed the Fire Hole River for some time. First we saw the Paint Pots. Like everything else, this has been over-described. It is very curious to see the mud bubbling up, but it is not brilliantly coloured. It is very fine, and generally white, tinted in places with pink and blue. There is a tiny little spring close by that clucks like a hen. The noises of some of the boiling springs make one's flesh creep. As one bends over them, and looks down into the bottomless depths, groans and wailings seem to rise from them as if prisoners in torment. The next great sight was the Excelsior Geyser, which kept us waiting two hours, not only in a blazing sun, but in clouds of steam from the Prismatic Lake and the Turquoise Lake, both lovely and of marvellous colouring, but disagreeable to be near, because of the sulphur-smelling steam, which damps one's clothes and one's spirits. The Excelsior Geyser itself is in a lake with rocky sides about fifty feet high when it is quiescent. When at work the whole surface of the lake rises considerably. At last the performance began, and we all stood on the brink and watched the water begin to bubble in different places, then the centre became more and more agitated and the Geyser rose, first quite small, then higher and larger, until we had to fly from the torrent of water and stones that were thrown hundreds of feet high and yards over the edge. One gentleman was badly hit by a stone. It was an absurd sight to see us all flying, after having chosen our positions so carefully to get the best possible view. This piece of the park which contains the Excelsior Geyser, the lakes, and several boiling springs, is a desolate region, all brimstone and alkali, and so horrible to look at that it is called "Hell's Half Acre." A soldier of the garrison was loitering by the Prismatic Lake when we first arrived, and he puzzled us by telling us it was the "Spasmodic" Lake. We did not know what it might do. A little further on we found the Grotto, Giant, and other geysers, all silent except for steam, and then the Devil's Punch Bowl, a curious hill which the spring has built around itself. The ground is so rotten for some distance that we could not drive near it, and even had to pick our way carefully on foot. This rotten ground is the only danger of the park. Since our visit a carriage was overturned by the ground giving way under two wheels, and was rescued with difficulty. Happily the visitors had got out to look at something. It is said that people have been badly burnt, and even killed by falling through the rotten edges of the springs and geysers, which are never protected, but these casualties are not put in the papers.

The most beautiful object in the park is the Castle Geyser. The formation is really like an old castle. Almost every geyser builds up some kind of house for itself with the deposit from the waters, and this is called the formation. Often the shapes are very remarkable, as the Grotto, which has almost roofed itself in. The Castle performs very irregularly. It was very lively all the time we were within sight, rising to about forty feet, but it did not go off properly until after we had left. Those who stayed all night at the Upper Geyser Basin Hotel saw it rise to the height of 150 feet, and said it was glorious.

We arrived at the Upper Geyser Basin Hotel after fourteen miles' drive, and had lunch, after which I went with others to visit the neighbourhood, which is the headquarters of the geysers, but Edward was so unwell, he preferred to sit on the veranda and watch Old Faithful, which is close by, and goes off every sixty-five minutes, and is as fine as any. It is a very serious drawback to the Yellowstone Park that the air, or steam, or something, seeks out everybody's weak point and attacks it. Edward felt his rheumatism, as did many others, those with weakness of the heart were quite ill, weak throats and chests suffered. There were very few of us free from pain. About a dozen of us got a soldier who happened to be loitering near, to act as guide. There is a garrison in the park, to prevent visitors shooting wild animals, or defacing the scenery, or carrying off specimens, or annoying the geysers by throwing in stones or soap to make them work. It is extraordinary that soap cut into thin pieces and thrown into a geyser will cause it to perform. I met people who had done it; but, unfortunately, after we had left the park, otherwise

I might have got a new testimonial to the efficacy of "Pears." We saw the Lion play, and afterwards the Lioness and the Cubs, a large geyser with four little ones round it. We admired the formation of the Sponge, so like a sponge that one is astonished to find it hard to the touch; the Beach, just like a bit of seashore, and many others much alike, some silent, some extinct, one born only three months ago, and one a year old. The Bee-hive, and several others well known by name, have not gone off for years. Our guide told us he had been on the spot over a year, and had watched the geysers carefully. He said none except Old Faithful worked at regular intervals, as they were said to do formerly, but his opinion was that they never had done so. Some would remain quiet for months and then break out again and perform daily or several times a day. We saw the Minute Man Geyser, not large, but a very pretty one, which really did go off every minute, and a quite new geyser which has this peculiarity :—all the water thrown up falls back into the basin, and recedes into the depths again, none escapes. The Beauty Spring is a large pool, very transparent, and full of lovely colours. The beauty of the large springs consists in the colouring. They are supposed to be bottomless. The centre is dark blue, and has a weird, unfathomable look, the sides are formation deposited by the spring, and shine light blue, green and white through the clear water, bubbles rise continually like messages from below, and, bending over, one hears strange noises. Altogether, the horrible desolation, the dead trees, the glaring white ground, the steam, the sulphur smells, the choking white dust, the uncanny noises, and the geysers going off all around in the most startling fashion, make a scene to be remembered with interest, but never with a wish to revisit it. All is marvellous, but desperately ugly and disagreeable. It corresponds in America to the chamber of horrors at Madame Tussaud's.

We drove back to Lower Geyser Basin that night by a shorter route, and had the luck to come upon the Grotto Geyser in full play. After dinner, my diary was a source of great uneasiness to an American lady. She felt sure I was saying disagreeable things about Americans, which was certainly not the case, as my only entry about them was my amusement at the perpetual question, as I stood admiring something, "Now, have you anything like this in Europe?" (invariably pronounced "Your 'ope.") In the Yellowstone Park, I could conscientiously answer that we had not. Jonathan is rather touchy. I was speaking of a very pretty girl we had met riding through the park. I remarked, she reminded me of an English girl, because she was so sunburnt. A stranger from the other end of the table called out he "begged to inform me there were pretty girls in America." I explained I thought the American girls took better care of their complexions, and so peace was restored. There were no other Britishers in the park except a young Englishman, settled in Helena, and a Welsh parson, also settled in America, and who was actually tramping through the park without any money in his pocket and living on the charity of the drivers, or any one who might hear of his case. I believe he slept in the stables. We met very few English travellers during the whole of our journey. Our room this time was in the dependance, close by a hot spring. It was funny to trot downstairs and fill one's pitcher, like Rebecca, every time we wanted a little hot water. We had to be careful in the dark, as there was no railing round the basin.

Wednesday, September 5th.—By returning to the Lower Geyser Hotel, instead of sleeping at the Upper Geyser Hotel, as many did, we saved ten miles in this day's journey, only leaving thirty-two miles to the Cañon. We started soon after seven o'clock, and, except that the road was extremely bad, there was nothing remarkable before lunch. We had then reached a dreary spot, miles from any habitation, and found there two tents and a delightful Irishman, who lives here with one assistant through the season to provide lunch. He gave us an excellent meal of hard-boiled eggs, pie, potted turkey, ham, tongue, tea, coffee, &c., and was so chatty and merry we enjoyed our stay there very much. He intimated that he had been one of Mr. Forster's victims, but I think it was his joke, he did not look outrageous. Soon after leaving here we reached Mary's Lake, the highest part of the park. It is merely a collection of rain-water with two outlets. Then we had to take a great round, owing to the rotten ground, to get to the Sulphur Mountains, hills entirely composed of sulphur, and at the foot a large yellow spring bubbling violently. It was very curious and ugly. At one point we were within seven miles of the Yellowstone Lake; occasionally people go there from the Cañon, and have some fishing, which is poor, as the lake is overstocked and the trout are unhealthy and unfit for food.

We arrived at the Grand Cañon Hotel about three o'clock, meeting on the way the landlady, head waiter and two maid-servants riding for pleasure on the ponies which should have taken visitors up the Cañon. We luckily preferred walking, as it is only three and a half miles to Inspiration Point, the end of the path. It was the very best time of the day to see the Cañon as the afternoon sun shone straight down it, bringing out the beautiful colours in the cliffs, red, yellow, brown, and occasionally blue, with a lovely green river dashing down the middle, sometimes over rocks with white, angry waves, and occasional pools of darker green. The path which runs along the top of the cliff is quite easy, but there are points jutting out into the Cañon from which the finest views can be obtained, which are rather dizzy climbs. Look-Out Point is easy and the view from that magnificent. The Cañon is glorious, very deep, and with rocks curiously shaped into pinnacles, turrets, even animals, and wonderfully coloured. The Falls are grand, but the Cañon is even more lovely than the Falls, and it is utterly unlike anything in the Old World.

We looked down into two eagles' nests. An eaglet in one was raging and scolding a strange bird that was taking a mean advantage of the old birds' absence to steal the baby's food. In the wood that skirts the Cañon we saw numbers of chipmunks, or ground squirrels, so tame and so inquisitive that they come within a yard of one's feet, and gaze most intelligently at the stranger. Inspiration Point is extremely fine. We were three and a quarter hours in the Cañon that afternoon. Next morning we got up early and went to Look-Out Point to see the morning sun shine down the Cañon from the other end, but we preferred the evening sun. We also went down a steep path to the platform on the edge of the Lower Falls, whence one looks straight down over the Fall, which is 350 feet high and has an immense volume of water. The Upper Falls are smaller, but also very pretty. The hotel is a rough wooden building, very cold, badly managed, and uncomfortable. Food uneatable. Some people go back from here over Mount Washburn on horseback, a very fatiguing ride. Opinions were divided as to whether the views did or did not repay one for the trouble. It is also a considerable addition to the expense. Our journey was entirely covered by the forty-dollar tickets—hotel accommodation, carriages, and all. We thought it very cheap.

At ten o'clock we started for the last day's drive in the Park by a new road direct to Norris Geyser Hotel, passing the beautiful Virginia Falls. The river does not fall, but runs over a steep bank of rock sloping very rapidly from a great height, at a point where the hills draw close and make a narrow gorge with curious rocks. We found a large party at Norris Springs

Hotel, the Press Association of Dakota, eighty of them, with their wives and sisters; a very lively set. One of them addressed himself to us, and finished by presenting us with "his card," which turned out to be a tract. Our driver turned up his nose with disgust. "Why," said he, "he's a sky pilot." A queer old fellow, our driver, X. Beadler! He is lame from a gunshot wound in the thigh, received years ago in the rough old times when he was a miner and used to act as guard to the bullion waggons. The road robbers were so bad then that fights were constantly occurring. It is his boast that he never gave up his gold, he always "shot first," and had thus killed many men. At last a vigilance committee was organized to put down the robbers and he was made captain. After many days hunting for the suspicious characters, they arrested over one hundred men, gave them a fair trial, and hung twenty-two. This settled matters so far as the public was concerned but Beadler had many fights afterwards with the friends of the men hung. The State is going to give him five thousand dollars. Last year the proposal to do so was lost by one vote; but this year, it is said, he is certain to get it. He was a delightful driver, and should be secured at once by any English visitor. Some of the old robber race still remain, for only last year the Northern Pacific train was stopped and looted by four men, who failed to break into the strong bullion safe but "held up" the passengers. "Holding up" signifies the American brigands' custom of making the victims hold up both arms to show that they have no weapons, while their pockets are picked. They are placed in a line and one robber covers them with his revolver while the others secure the plunder.

From Norris we drove back to the Mammoth Hot Springs the way we came, stopping to obtain some specimens at the Obsidian Cliffs. We arrived about a quarter to five, before the rest of the party, and so secured a good room, and then went off to the hot springs as I wanted to see them before changing my dusty garments. We climbed from one basin to another, admiring the extraordinary formations and the colours, from pure white to dark chocolate, green, pink, and yellow. One place looked just like a shop-window with silks puffed out for exhibition, of every shade, from cream to dark brown. In the basins are lovely fringes and tracery of formation, sometimes like seaweed—in another place like large fans. I picked a bit of formation out of the hot basin, and, to my surprise found a living tiny worm on it. The water was too hot to keep one's hand in a moment. We could hardly tear ourselves away, and only gave ourselves time to rush back for dinner. Next day we rested, read and wrote letters, and said farewell to our fellow-travellers, who all left in the morning. It was this morning that we were amused to see an American child about five years old come into the coffee-room, seat herself at a table, summon the waiter, and order her breakfast, which she had all alone.

Very few new arrivals came, as the season is nearly over. Last year there were four inches of snow on the 1st of September.

Saturday, September 8th.—We started, in the company of the Dakota editors, for Livingstone, where we lost our friends, who had special carriages into which they kindly invited us, but we were only going to Helena. We were kept waiting so long at Cinnabar, apparently to please the conductor, that we had no time, as promised, for tea at Livingstone. Punctuality is not the soul of business on American railways. We were not to arrive at Helena until 1.45 a.m., so settled ourselves to sleep, but about midnight a poor little mite of three years old, who had been dragged all through the park and was utterly worn out, suddenly found expression for her misery in a series of shrieks and wild sobbing. After vainly endeavouring to soothe her with apples and iced water, the father carried her off to the smoking-room. Fancy an English child consuming apples and iced water at midnight! But I think the oddest meal I ever saw living being partake of, was the evening repast of a boy of ten or so on the Hudson River steamer. He ate a Vanilla cream ice with bread-and-butter! We passed through a tunnel lined only a small part of the way with wood. It goes through some coal seams, and it was very pretty to see the coal sparkle as our lights passed it. The Cosmopolitan Hotel at Helena is rather rough. We had a good room, pervaded by a strong chemical smell from a shop on the ground floor. On the whole we were comfortable, but the food was bad.

Helena is a wonderfully pretty place, not in itself, but from its position. The glow of the sun on the red plains, the sand clouds, and the blue mountains in the background, reminded us of Mr. Goodall's Eastern Pictures. There is a Chinese quarter, principally gambling-houses, which is the great Chinese vice. They live principally by market-gardening.

We got a beautiful view of the town, which is on the slopes of some hills, with the plain in front of it and the distant mountains, from the Reservoir Hill, where, too, we met a Scotchwoman, happily married and settled, but rather home-sick. Still, she liked Helena better than San Francisco, she said, where she had formerly lived, and where she had seen several murders in the streets. I never heard a good word spoken for San Francisco by any one who had lived there, even Californians dislike it, and go east as soon as they have made money.

Monday, September 12*th*.—We started in a "Surrey" and pair for Marysville and the Drumlummon Mine, three and a quarter hours' drive up hill, through very pretty scenery. Both the Northern Pacific and the Montana Central have a line to Marysville, and run each one train a day each way, though there is nothing but the mine at Marysville, another mine starting somewhere a few miles further up the hills, and some wretched cottages on the way. Mr. Bayliss, the English manager of the mine, and his pretty wife received us very kindly. It is great satisfaction to have such a specimen of English beauty in Helena, which is rather noted for pretty women. It was also very pleasant to hear once more the English language, as she is spoke at home. The Americans in the West are very difficult to understand, all the vowels are pronounced " aw," and the consonants are rather slurred over.

The celebrated Drumlummon Mine is in the side of a hill. After putting on rubber boots and mackintoshes we walked to the entrance, where we were seated on a car and pulled along some way on a level to where there were many men working, far away inside the hill; there were cuttings both above and below. We descended two hundred feet and saw more rock-drilling. Part of the mine was closed, to put in a large engine for hoisting up the quartz, and to sink the shaft deeper, to one thousand feet. After lunch, such a treat after table-d'hôte meals, we went through the mills to see the quartz crushed. It first goes into a machine like the Marsden stone-breaker, from which it falls into stamps, where it is pounded small, and then is washed through wires and over large plates covered with quicksilver which picks up most of the gold and silver and every three hours is removed and the precious metals separated from it by heat and made into bars on the premises.

The impoverished ore is then washed over "concentrators," machines with endless sheets of india-rubber running in an opposite direction to the flow of water. The heavier particles of ore cling to the india-rubber, while the sand is carried away by the water. This gives a mixture of metals, which is sent to California to be smelted. All the machinery was American. The English cannot make mining machines to compete with Americans, owing to their want of experience. The Drumlummon Mine is principally a gold mine—60 per cent. gold to 40 per cent. silver.

After a cup of tea with Mrs. Bayliss, we started at four o'clock, and arrived in Helena at 6.40. Our driver was very chatty; he told us thirty years ago he was so far gone in consumption that the doctors said he could not live a month. He came off at once to Helena, to try the mountain air as his last chance, and he had become quite strong, though he still had a nasty cough, and had married and lived as if in ordinary health, except that he could not do indoor work. He was quite well even in their desperate winter weather, with thirty and forty degrees of frost. Helena, he told us, was a friendly, sociable, little place, nobody at all proud, not even the sixteen millionaires who are the boast of the town. Everything is very dear, and wages very high. A bricklayer gets seven dollars a day; Mr. Bayliss has to pay his black cook forty dollars a month, and he told us the man who pulled us on the tram-car got about 250$l.$ a year in our money. Lately a newly-arrived clergyman thought it was only right to get up a fund for the relief of the poor and the congregation took up the idea heartily, collected 1600 dollars, formed a Committee, and then could not meet with any one who would receive the money. The hero of Helena is Mr. Kruse who discovered the Drumlummon Mine. This is his history as told to me, and it is the history of hundreds of men, except for his extraordinary good luck. He starts off with a pony, a sack of flour, a piece of bacon and a pick, and for months he prospects for gold. Nobody will trust him with half a dollar, for he is a low drunken fellow. One day he sticks his pick in the ground and props himself on it, to eat his bacon, gets up to go away and notices that his pick has knocked up some gold quartz. He sticks up a mark to show that he has been there, goes off, registers his claim, and sells a quarter of his find for 2,000,000 dollars, builds a fine house and marries the prettiest girl in Helena, and the whole country round attends his wedding feast.

Tuesday, September 11*th.*—Left Helena at 9.15 a.m. We passed through the Rockies by the Mullen Tunnel. After this we constantly saw Chinese working on the line as plate-layers, &c. It seems that the North Pacific Railway are having disturbances about employing Chinese cheap labour, and the white men are calling on the state authorities to forbid it. In Pierce County the farmers are in need of Chinese labour to take the place of the Indians, who generally come in swarms at the hop-picking season, but from some unknown cause have not come this year. White labourers could not be procured in sufficient number, but the State will not allow the Chinese to come, and the magnificent hop crop will be lost.

The railroad goes through an Indian reservation, the Flatheads, and from the train we saw many fishing or standing by their wigwams. Once when the train had stopped, an Indian galloped past, first on the line and then up the steep rocky bank, without slackening pace, like a cat. He seemed to have a very loose seat, but they are said to be perfect horsemen. As the scenery was very fine we sat on the platform at the back of the carriage all day. The run along the Clark's Fork of the Columbia River is exceedingly beautiful, much finer than any river I know. Very high cliffs, often covered with golden moss and many sharp curves, the broad beautiful river sometimes widening into lakes and sometimes crushed into narrow gorges. At Heron we had to change carriages to get into the Tacoma sleeping-car. There was a great crowd and a rush but we circumvented the Yankees and secured two lower berths.

Wednesday, September 12*th.*—Was not a happy day. A baby screamed for eleven hours without ceasing. Then we had no dinner, for at Ellensburgh a large Republican convention arrived, carrying brooms with which they meant to, and afterwards did, " make a clean sweep," and they devoured everything on the dining-car. We were alarmed when first we saw them and we made at once for the cook and asked him if there would be enough. He first inquired were they Republicans or Democrats, for, he said, the Republicans eat most, but the Democrats drink most. We got nothing until supper-time except a handful of broken biscuits, crackers they call them. It would have been quite easy for the cook to procure more food from the large stations we passed but that is not the way in America.

They are a patient people, and put up with the worst train service ever heard of, something like the Scotch service on August 10th and 11th.

Trains are almost invariably behind time, hours being wasted at roadside stations without apparent cause, or trains sometimes creeping on over level ground at the rate of six or eight miles an hour. The pace from Pasco Junction to Yakima was not equal to that of an ordinary tram-car and unfortunately there was no scenery. We passed some nice bits later in the day when crossing the Rockies. We saw the beginning and the end of the old Switchback Railway that goes over the top of the mountain, used before the tunnel was constructed, now only used if the tunnel is blocked, as it is very steep and dangerous. As soon as we reached the western slopes the country became beautifully green, with hop-grounds and forests of fine trees. Here we first saw the forest fires, which spoil the scenery very much, not only by destroying and blackening the timber, but by the smoke, which has the effect of a fog. Many are lighted by sparks from the engines or by fires left burning by squatters and spread by the wind, but many are started by natural causes, it is said by the dry boughs rubbing against each other. We arrived at last at Tacoma, where there is an excellent hotel.

The town of Tacoma is very prettily situated on Puget Sound, with the lovely snow-topped Mount Tacoma standing solitary in the background. This district is misty, and often people stay a week at Tacoma without discovering the mountain, but we luckily had the pleasure of his company most of the time we were there. It is a baby town, not yet on any map, but has already some good shops and pleasant dwellings. The small wooden houses are running up like mushrooms. The new comer orders a house as he would a coat, and it is ready by the end of the week.

The steamer from Tacoma to Vancouver started at 3 p.m., and stopped all night at Seattle, another baby town, which is the most prosperous of all, as coal and iron have been found in the vicinity. The English Moss Bay Iron Company is starting large works there, and the Seattle, Lake Shore and Eastern Railway will soon be finished, and will connect the town with the North Pacific Railroad. There is a large hotel, the Occidental, where we got an excellent dinner, after roaming through the streets and admiring the prosperous, busy, go-ahead little place.[1] We slept in our cabin, because the boat started about 4.30 a.m., and amused ourselves for an hour by throwing things into the water to see the phosphorus. Next day we had a very disagreeable, foggy journey, and arrived two hours late at Vancouver, so that we could get no dinner, only tea and cold food, although Vancouver Hotel is one of the best in America. It was only by chance that we got our luggage, as I happened to be sitting on my box when the man came to take it on shore, and I asked if it were going to be examined by the Customs' officers on board. He told me all baggage was to be taken into custody until Monday. I explained that we had nothing with us except our boxes, no grips, so the officer very kindly examined ours at once. Next day, Sunday, was foggy and disagreeable, but we were satisfied to rest, as we had secured a cosy sitting-room. There we met an English clergyman who had just returned from the Alaska Expedition and was much

[1] The whole town was burnt down a few months after our visit.

delighted with it. His accounts of the scenery were most tempting, but it proved too late for us to go, as it is very cold up there.

Vancouver, the terminus of the Canadian Pacific Railroad, is the rival of Tacoma, the terminus on Puget Sound of the North Pacific Railroad. Tacoma has the advantage of a second great route, the Shasta, to San Francisco, and has a richer district at the back of it, besides being equal to Vancouver as a port. Certainly Tacoma seemed more prosperous, as houses there could not be run up fast enough, while in Vancouver there were numbers to let. Formerly this little village was called Fort Moody, a better name than Vancouver, which is a source of trouble and mistakes, owing to its being the name of the important island close by. We were told that Lady Burdett Coutts had presented a peal of bells to Vancouver. I forget which she meant them for, but the wrong place had got them, and meant keeping them. There were shoals of Chinese and many shops of their curios. We were making a few purchases, when we were astonished at hearing our name, and there was actually a former constituent settled in Vancouver, and prosperous.

We went to see the s.s. *Batávia*, just arrived from China with emigrants for the States. They were packed like herrings and were a horrid-looking lot.

People give them a bad name up here, but afterwards I heard them well spoken of. I fancy they are very badly treated. Sometimes, we were told, the Chinese get obstreperous on the voyage. Then they are battened down and the steam hose turned on. They pay fifty dollars each for their wretched accommodation. I tried hard to buy a joss direct from an emigrant. Of course there are plenty in the shops, but I thought if I could get a true joss direct from a believer, it would bring me luck, and I wanted one of the funny ones which fold up into lockets, and are hung round the neck, but nobody would part with one.

We had a splendid drive in the park, which is simply a piece of primeval forest, with good roads cut through it. The trees are enormous, and moss grows on the lower branches like wool on sheep. There were very few living things; a few rooks and chipunmaks, some gigantic slugs and a frog were all we saw, but bears and deer are plentiful inland. At one point we had to walk through a narrow path amongst the big ferns which cover the ground, to see the biggest tree of all, which is more than thirty feet round the trunk and immensely tall. The shell beach is another of the great features of the park. It is a large piece of ground near the water, which is formed yards deep of nothing but shells. Immense trees, most of them seventy feet high, and some probably more, are growing on this great shell bed. It is used to mend the roads like gravel, numbers of carts were taking it away for that purpose.

The drive round the park is ten miles long, with lovely views on to English Bay, the Narrows, and Burrard's Inlet. The mountains on the other side of the water, opposite Vancouver, with the white Mission village on the shore, are very pretty. As we approached the town we saw a boatful of Indians bring some deer they had shot to sell for a dollar a piece. I regret to say that a few hours afterwards we saw them helplessly drunk. It is strictly forbidden under heavy penalties to sell spirits to the Indians, but they get them somehow.

Tuesday, September 8th.—We started for Banff, 648 miles east, at 12.45 p.m. When past Wharnock we got a magnificent view of Mount Baker, a lofty, snow-covered mountain, standing alone, like Mount Tacoma. It is sixty miles off, on U.S. territory. The scenery was pretty from the first, but the grand part began at Yale, and from there to Banff, so far as we could see, there was not a mile where the scenery was not extraordinarily beautiful. The line crosses four ranges of mountains, the Cascade, the Gold, the Selkirks, and the Rockies. It is always night, unfortunately, when the Gold range is crossed. All the way, except at a few large stations, there is hardly a trace of human habitation except the people working on the line and here and there a small timber place and, very rarely, a squatter's miserable hut and bit of clearing, and a few Indians. It must have been a very difficult road to make, and is a great triumph of engineering. We, on the last carriage, often saw the engines and front carriages on the curves in front of us—once we saw the two engines and seven carriages ahead of us. The Fraser Cañon begins at Yale, the scenery of which is described as "ferocious." It is very wild and grand, but I think the Thompson Cañon, which we passed after bed-time, is still more terrible. Perhaps the moonlight increased the effect. We had a good supper at the little hotel at North Bend. Next morning I was up at five o'clock, and got a glimpse of the reddest sunrise I ever saw. The heavens seemed to be on fire. Unfortunately, just then the train was running due east. Breakfast was on a dining-car and was very good. There cannot be anything finer in the world than the run this day, with such diversity of scenery, all wild. Lovely lakes, glorious snow mountains, grand rocks, wild streams dashing in perpetual rapids and many whirlpools to join immense rivers, and forests wherever trees can find foothold. The gorge of the Illecilliwaat is very narrow, and about ten minutes past Albert Cañon station the train stops to allow passengers to go into a balcony and look down three hundred feet to the river. Then comes the steepest rise, where a big eight-wheeled coupled engine pushes the train, and we had great excitement over the breaking of the iron pin fastening the bar and coupling it to our carriage. A young engineer had been explaining to us all that this arrangement was most dangerous, and when the broken pin went whizzing past his head, he was wild with delight at the confirmation of his opinion. After passing through miles of snow-sheds and much zigzagging, on account of the steep ascent, we reached Glacier, where we dined, and where we would willingly have spent a week, so beautiful is it, surrounded by snow mountains with glaciers in every direction. The highest peak is named after our kind friend "Sir Donald" (Smith); it is a rocky tooth far away in the sky. The road rises some way after Glacier and then

F

descends rapidly. We came soon to one of the most beautiful views I ever saw. The mountain-side is very steep, as are all the surrounding mountains, and covered with pine-trees, and we looked down from the train, almost a bird's-eye view, into a magnificent valley full of bright green pines and firs and yellow cotton-wood trees and the Beaver river meandering quietly through it. The whole valley was filled with a slight haze of smoke from forest fires, of which there were plenty of small ones near the line, but later on we came to the enormous fire which caused the smoke. It seemed to cover many acres of forest. After dark we passed many fires, but none so large as this. The rain that fell while we were at Vancouver had extinguished many of them. They brought that perpetually recurring ten shillings for chips at home to my mind. After passing through the narrow gorge bridged in one place by a fallen tree, down which the Beaver river runs to join the Columbia, we ran a long way on the level, having the Selkirks on one side and the Rockies on the other, and then we ascended the Rockies to Field, where we supped. After that, all was dark until we reached Banff at 11.30 p.m.

Banff is 4500 feet above sea-level, and there is a good hotel, for which all supplies have to be brought from Winnipeg. There were only twenty-five guests on account of the lateness of the season, as snow may come any day. In July and August there are sometimes 120 visitors in the hotel, besides numbers living in tents and wooden huts, and no doubt, when this delicious place is better known, it will become the

Switzerland of America. The first afternoon and the morning of the second day were rainy, but not bad enough to prevent our visiting the pretty bits close to the hotel, i.e. the Falls of the Bow river and the Pontoon bridge. The mountains which surround the valley were glorious with fresh snow. Some are very lofty, some are bare rocks, some wooded a long way up, and the autumn tints were very fine, especially the brilliant yellow cotton-wood trees. The Canadian National Park occupies the whole valley, which is in shape something like a star-fish, with the hotel in the centre. It is far more beautiful than the American Yellowstone Park, and is much recommended as a health resort on account of the pure bracing air. It is quite out of the mining district, so there were no specimens about, and no miners with their amusing tales of their successes and disappointments.

One of the most interesting tales was told us by a Scotchman on the Seattle boat. He was a railway man by trade, but whenever he had made a little money he had set off to the gold district to "prospect." Sometimes he had done well, but once he found a very rich vein and sank a shaft and found it grew richer as he got lower, so he spent on it all he had and all he could borrow. The fame of it spread, and many wanted to share his venture and offered good prices for the half or the quarter, but nothing would induce him to part with the smallest fraction. This time he thought he would become a colossal millionaire. Suddenly, to his horror, the vein ceased. It ran straight into the earth in the form of a V and he had just hit the centre of it, so, besides losing all he had saved, he had to work for months to repay what he had borrowed.

Another amusing mine story was of one that promised well but turned out badly, so the owners put up large engines, and arranged somehow to cart and train regularly to a certain point a large quantity of rich ore, which was reported in the newspapers, and then secretly carried back to the mine. Then the owners went to New York and sold the mine to a company for two millions.

Saturday, September 22nd.—We took a carriage for the whole day and drove first to the Devil's Head Lake, nine miles off, getting back to lunch. Happily the day was magnificent and the rain had put out the forest fires, so that the views were quite clear. It was a very pretty drive up a valley due east to the lake, which runs thirteen miles, but unfortunately turns a corner, so one only sees the beginning of it. It is all shades of blue and green, according to depth, light, and shadow, and sparkles like diamonds in the sunshine. The colouring of the trees and rocks, and the peculiar red tinge of the turf make a wonderful picture. The Devil's Head is a rock on a mountain close by. We could not see any likeness to a head at all. On our return, we stopped to look at a shop said to be kept by a man from South Kensington Museum, but I am sure Professor Flower would faint if he saw those atrociously stuffed birds and beasts. There was a live beaver in a box outside, baking in the sun, which seemed very unhappy.

After lunch we drove in the opposite direction to a sulphur spring, high up on the mountain-side, where there is a small hotel with baths. The view from it is very fine down a valley opposite: another ray of the star-fish. Then downhill again to the Grotto, a hot spring in what looks like the cone of an extinct geyser. It is reached through a long underground corridor, the platform being over the stream that carries away the water from the spring, and at the end is a place to bathe from, though how any one can enter such a gloomy pool, only lighted by a hole in the far-away roof, I cannot imagine. From there we went to the station to inquire about the freight train that was to take us back to Field next day, so that we might get the scenery by daylight, and that settled, we went down the valley past the Bow Falls and past a mountain whence an immense mass of rock fell about six weeks ago at 11 p.m., frightening everybody by the terrible noise. This is a very pretty valley, and Mr. Van Horne and other gentlemen connected with the Canadian Pacific Railroad have selected very choice lots down by the river to build. They can only get leases of the land, because it is national property.

Sunday, September 23*rd.*—We started by freight train for Field at 12.30 p.m. The guard was exceedingly kind and gave us the view seats in the tower of his van and pointed things out to us. When we looked for him and his man at Field with a view to tips they were nowhere to be found. It was a marvellous journey; such cliffs and precipices, and such gradients. A second engine of great size and power held us back on the descent, besides a break on every carriage, and the guard admitted that if once the train got its head there would be nothing for it but to jump off. Everywhere on the Canadian Pacific Railway the greatest care is taken, and every possible precaution and safeguard are used, and constant vigilance. I counted fifty roadmen at work between Field and Donald, a distance of fifty miles. The hotel at Field is small and rather earwiggy, but very fair. Unfortunately, there is nothing to do, as there is no walk to take, unless one goes up or down the line, or up the side of the cliff. We were desperately hungry, because the sandwiches we brought from the Banff Hotel were made of such coarse salt bacon we could not eat them, but we had to wait until long past seven o'clock for dinner because the cook was out for a walk. The east-bound train rushed in, supped, and disappeared in the darkness, making one feel very lonely. There was only one other guest—a Mr. De Wolff, who is running a mine in Mt. Stephen, 1200 feet above the railway, in connection with smelting works at Vancouver. His idea is that in course of time many mines will be started in this district, and all the smelting will be done in Vancouver.

Next day we joined the west-bound express at 9.10 a.m., and spent the day on the platform at the end of the train enjoying the glorious scenery. Dined at Glacier, and supped on the dining-car. We were fortunate in getting two comfortable lower berths, but we rose early to see the Thompson Cañon, which we had passed by starlight on our way up. To our disgust the morning proved foggy, so we did not see all of it, but what we did see was very wild. The train crawls along a shelf cut in the steep mountain side, hundreds of feet above the mad, whirling, dashing river. Much of the line between Banff and the flat district near the sea is made on such steep slopes of drift, or clay, or sand, that the greatest, unceasing precaution is necessary to get along safely. Men go over the line just ahead of every train to see that all is right, no slip occurred, and nothing fallen from above, and at times the train only goes about five miles an hour. Luckily this is generally when the scenery is finest. All day it was fine. The Fraser river was our constant companion nearly all the way. First a torrent dashing through narrow gorges amongst lofty mountains, it finally widens into a broad river. In the wild part there were terrible rapids and whirlpools, where the water appeared to be twelve to twenty feet higher at the sides than in the troughs. The Indians manage to get about between the many dangers in their little boats, salmon fishing. The Fraser river is full of salmon, which the Indians catch and dry on little platforms in the sun or with fire under. We saw some of them in a little canoe going through a very dangerous bit of river to a rock in the middle, where they had a salmon net. Canning salmon is a great industry all along the coast, as the rivers are full of them. We once saw a whole train-load go off east. Sometimes an Indian catches a dog-salmon, a fine-looking fish, but unfit for food. If he thinks he will not be found out, he cans it, to the disappointment of some poor creatures far away. We never got any salmon equal to British or Irish salmon—the flavour is inferior. Mount Baker was at its best again, as the day was so fine, and we had a delightful journey back to Vancouver. This Canadian Pacific Railroad trip is worth all the trouble of coming to America. We could spend a month at Banff, there is so much to do and see for which we had not time, and from many of the other stations interesting trips can be made by boat on the Columbia River, or into the neighbouring valleys, besides unlimited opportunities for mountain climbing.

Wednesday, September 26th.—We rested and enjoyed the comforts of the hotel and visited a timber-mill where very large logs are cut. The largest we saw cut was forty-two inches by twenty-five inches, but they have been made there twenty-four inches square by one hundred and eighteen feet long. These long balks are for the Chinese market. The cutting is done by two circular saws five feet in diameter, one above and a little in advance of the other, working together. They can thus cut logs up to four feet six inches in diameter. Most of the machinery was old-fashioned. The finest thing there was an Indian workman, a magnificent fellow, tall, strong, and graceful as a panther. His face was very peculiar, a long hooked nose and straight wide mouth, with a strong line each side. He would make a perfect Mephistopheles, and would not need to go on tiptoes when he wanted to be impressive. He was wonderfully solemn generally, but in the pauses of the work he turned to make quite Mephistophelian gestures to his friends, and then his face became all grin. I watched him a long time. He was the finest Indian I ever saw. Generally they are short and ugly, the women very coarse.

Thursday, September 27th.—The park we visited the previous week was formally opened by the mayor. Forty carriages of all kinds went in procession, all decked out with flags, of which, I regret to say, there were as many American as British. We left Vancouver by the 2.30 boat for Victoria. As we waited for the Canadian Pacific Railway express to come in, we saw a train-load of sand very rapidly emptied on to the pier by a sand plough. The wooden piles of the pier are constantly destroyed under water by a worm called the torrido, which makes a hole, at first no larger than a darning-needle, but as the worm grows, so the hole enlarges to the size of a man's finger—many remedies were tried to destroy the worm, but nothing succeeded except creosote, which is too expensive, so now the piles are being surrounded by sand. We had a delightful passage to Victoria. To our astonishment Mt. Baker reappeared when we had got some way from land, and we passed through a school of whales spouting and leaping occasionally out of the water. Puget Sound is full of large islands, very like the Thousand Islands, but on a grander scale. When evening came on, after a fine sunset glow, the stars shone out in thousands. It is curious that often there is very little colour at sunset in the west, but a splendid glow in the east.

We arrived at Victoria at nine o'clock. The electric lights were visible long before we arrived, and by them we were able to notice what a roundabout entrance there is to the harbour. We walked to the Driard Hotel, of which we had heard much, but were disappointed, as the cooking is very inferior. The rooms were good. Victoria is a pretty place, with a nice park and a Chinese quarter, where we managed to do a little shopping by signs. We also bought at an English shop some Indian carvings in black stone. It is a kind of slate and is only found on the Hydahs Indian reservation. In Vancouver Island we saw very funny-looking Indians.

The great excursion is to Esquimaux, the British naval station and headquarters of the Pacific fleet. It is quite at the mercy of any enemy who might take a fancy to it. There were plenty of old-fashioned muzzle-loading guns and even two six-inch breech-loading guns, but none of them were mounted and the carriages were safely put away in the stores. There is a large graving-dock and a small machine-shop for repairs, built by the Canadian Government. We drove back by the Gorge, a pretty bit, where an arm of the sea winds up like a river. A kingfisher was in possession of the place. At night we got on board the s.s. *T. J. Potter* and slept in our cabin, as she sailed at 4 a.m. The Custom officer awoke us at six o'clock, but passed our luggage without examination, so I think he might have let us sleep. At eight o'clock we stopped at Port Townsend, another baby town, very prosperous, placed at the extreme end of the peninsula that separates Puget Sound from the sea, on American territory. The whole peninsula is one dense forest, which has been bought up by a large company in San Francisco, greatly to the annoyance of local folk. It seems no single person or firm may legally take up from the State more than a certain quantity of land, but this company gets people to claim and take up, and then buys from them, and is powerful and clever enough to hold its own. Here we saw a horrid creature, a great octopus, clinging to a pile of the landing-stage. We thought there was another further back under the platform, and there were also some enormous white sea anemones or fungi, some feet below the water, so that we could not see them clearly. Port Townsend expects to be eventually the great port of this district; it is nearest the ocean, and all boats going to Vancouver and Tacoma must pass it, but at present it has no railway nearer than Tacoma.

At Seattle we changed from the *Potter*, which remained there until 3.30, to the *Hasselo*, a ricketty old boat with a large stern paddle-wheel, which started at once. We wanted to catch the night-train for Portland and had to pick up some of our goods at the Tacoma Hotel, but when we arrived we were told the train was four hours late, so we decided to stay all night at the hotel. Next day we learnt a train had been sent off at the usual time with the local traffic. That is always the way in America, it is impossible to obtain information. We should have been glad to take the night-train, because the run to Portland is very ugly and flat. The railway company is reclaiming a piece of shore at Tacoma by putting out a pier, and filling in the space between pier and shore by washing down the hill-side into it with a powerful stream of water through a hose-pipe. This interested us, because it was the system employed formerly in hydraulic gold-mining, now forbidden, on account of the damage caused by the débris, which covered the lower country and ruined the agriculture.

After a weary journey, nothing interesting, not even the ferry across the Columbia River, with slight rain all day and much mist, we arrived at Portland at 2.30 p.m. We had been told over and over again that it was very late in the season for fine weather in this district, that if rain once set in it would probably go on for months, so, as it had set in and looked as if it meant continuing, and as, moreover, we learnt that the Northern Pacific train had been delayed two days on account of a burnt bridge, and we should have our train to ourselves, we decided to go on at once and miss the Columbia River. Portland looked very doleful as we drove to the hotel for letters, quite in vain, and the cabman made us pay an extravagant fare. Portland seems to be a declining city, killed by its new rivals on Puget Sound. Perhaps sunshine would have altered its appearance, but it looked quite mouldy and forgotten, the streets empty and forlorn.

We had a very comfortable journey to San Francisco in the almost empty car. Teas and breakfasts on car, and dinner at Sissons. There was an interesting negro in charge of the car, who wanted, as so many do, to come to England, where they think they will escape the contempt shown for their race by Americans. This man was born in the Bahamas, and had been in charge of some lower department in a place of business or warehouse in New York. One young fellow after another had come under him, learnt from him, and been passed over his head. At last he went to the "Boss," and asked him if he were not to be advanced. "Impossible," said the master, "except porter, there is nothing else open to you because of your colour." So he left, but found it the same everywhere. I did not know what to say to him, there are so few negroes in England that they are looked upon as curiosities, and there are plenty of our own people to do the work. He gave a terrible account of their condition in California. He said they could expect no justice against a white man; no Court would decide in favour of a coloured man whatever the case might be. A white conductor went further than this. He said all justice was sold. A rich man might do anything he liked, from murder downwards, with impunity. This opinion we heard again and again from Californians, and indeed pretty well all over the States. As far as I could judge from their own accounts, Mr. Bryce's book is simply a pretty picture of what things ought to be; but in fact there is but one judge and one law, the almighty dollar. My black friend meant to go back to the Bahamas when he had saved a little money. There, he said, a man was a man whatever his colour, and respected according to his conduct; everything was open to all, and coloured men might be soldiers or policemen, or anything they were fit for. We often found men in America who looked forward to returning to Australia as a happier country than the United States. It is a great trouble to genuine Americans that recent comers do not amalgamate with them and become one people. The Irish are of course the worst, for they are not only most interested in Irish affairs, but they use their political power as American citizens to forward their plans and intrigues in the old country; but the Germans also remain Germans, and congregate together and keep up home associations and their attachment to the Fatherland, and the English, too, are said to keep themselves together, and never forget the land of their birth.

The journey from Portland to San Francisco occupied a night, a day and a night. There is very pretty scenery. Mount Shasta, a glorious snow-covered giant, was visible all the morning, but, unfortunately, was clouded over when we were at Sissons, which lies just at its foot. There is a long and difficult rise to Sissons, 3555 feet above sea-level. Often we could see the line doubling on its track four and five times. A young fellow got out at a station on the hill-side, and went straight up to a station some way above, arriving as soon as the train, but quite exhausted. The descent is more gradual and is through a great grazing country, partitioned into immense estates, and covered with fine horses and cattle. Then the train gets into the Sacramento Valley, which might have been made for its accommodation, and follows it until dark, passing some curious rocks looking as if giants had commenced to build there, something, I suppose, like the pillars of Staffa, and a delicious cascade, that falls over banks of moss under drooping trees—a fairy spot. It was at Red Bluff, on this line, that I met the first beggar I had seen in America.

Tuesday, October 2nd.—We reached San Francisco at nine o'clock, an hour late, on a foggy morning, and were disgusted with the difficulties of the arrival. We had to get out of the train at Oakland Pier, and wait until all the luggage was transferred, before getting into the immense ferry-boat, which took us across in half an hour to San Francisco. Here we landed on a tumble-down, dirty platform, and went through shabby wooden buildings amongst a crowd of screaming, hustling hotel-touters, who knocked us down and trampled upon us and tore us to pieces. Of course we had checked all our baggage (25 cents each), and, avoiding the hotel 'bus (25 cents each), took the cable car (5 cents each) to the door of the Palace Hotel. This is, on the whole, a good hotel, though the service in the restaurant is very bad, and I should think the drainage doubtful. Perhaps we should have done better if we had taken our meals in the table-d'hôte room. Here we tasted terrapin. It was like minced mutton with an innumerable quantity of small bones. Squab, we found, is only American for pigeon, and Californian champagne is very bad for the price, but so were all the Californian wines, Zinfandeln, &c., we got at the hotel; but it is said some of them, when got from the wine-merchants, are really quite good. The principal thing to do in San Francisco is to loaf about China-town, visit the Joss-house, a dark room up a very steep staircase over a chemist's, with some huge idols and some finely carved and coloured shrines with candles burning before them, Roman Catholic fashion; and make desperate attempts to see the views from different points. Our experience was that, however fine the morning, as soon as we came within a quarter of an hour of any point we were making for, a great sea-fog rolled in and swallowed up everything. We managed to see the sea-lions, an inferior kind of seal without fur, which dwell in multitudes on a rock opposite the dirty Cliff House Restaurant, and we heard them bark. They make a great noise. From there, too, we first caught a glimpse of the Pacific Ocean, not much, on account of the fog. We had miles of cable car, and "dummy engine" train, on this round. The country is all sand dunes, and this road goes past great tracts of cemeteries. The Freemasons have their own, the Odd Fellows theirs, anything to distinguish one man from his brother worm. Friendly societies are more thought of here than with us. Men wear little brooches to show that they belong to certain societies—even the President of the American Institution of Mechanical Engineers wore a little brooch to make people aware of the fact. The variety of these badges is endless, some gentlemen wearing several at once. We visited the United States Mint where we saw nothing new, but we learnt something new about our old neighbours in Swansea. The official guide, in his speech to a large party of visitors, after describing how as much as possible was got out of the ores here, continued, "The refuse metal is then sent on to Swansea, where labour is at 5 cents a day!"

Colonel Taylor took us to the Fire Station to see the twelve o'clock drill. At the electric signal the horses rush to their places in front of the car, the men come sliding down poles instead of down the staircase, and all is ready in two and a half seconds. I was disappointed with the business. The firemen did not even take their places on the car, nothing was done at all except harness the horses. The harness is hung over the car and when the horses take their places it drops on to them, leaving nothing to be done except to buckle the belly strap and clinch the collar clasp. Then, too, it was not a fire engine at all, it was only a salvage car. These things are all over-described. Edward being much interested in the cable cars, we visited several of the stations to see the engines at work and how the whole thing was done. There is nothing pleasanter to travel by, or quicker, or safer when they have a fair chance; but I must say when we were in a car that dashed like lightning down an incline much too steep for horse cars and saw other cable cars tearing along towards us at right angles along cross streets, so that the slightest mistake on the part of either driver would dash the two cars into each other, I felt less charmed with them. The longest cable is 36,000 feet, the steepest incline 1 in $5\frac{1}{2}$, the price 5 cents everywhere. This 5 cent piece is the

G

lowest coin in circulation in California; coppers can only be used to buy postage stamps.

Colonel Grey, formerly chief engineer to the Northern Pacific Railway, took Edward to see the Union Iron Works, a large shipbuilding yard with a hydraulic graving-dock. They were building two fast cruisers for the U.S. Government to go nineteen and a half knots an hour, and carry two 8-inch and six 6-inch guns. No armour plating except a protected deck over the machinery.

It was during our stay in San Francisco that Mr. Cleveland finally decided on the exclusion of the Chinese, to the great delight of everybody except the Chinese themselves, on whom it fell so unexpectedly that two thousand were said to be even then on their way to San Francisco, many of them having resided there before, but all were to be refused admittance.

Travellers are told that Chinatown is full of bad characters, and that it is not safe to go there after dark without police escort, but this seems to be only a means of extorting money. Nothing does ever happen to the inquisitive tourist. Most of those who employ the Chinese speak well of them. On the railways it is found necessary to put them in gangs under Chinese heads, as they quarrel with white overlookers, but they work steadily and never strike. That is probably their great fault in the eyes of the American workman. They make good private servants, too. Colonel Grey told us he had had a Chinese butler in his service thirteen years, with complete charge of the wine and the silver. Twice the man had been summoned home by his mother; the first time, because she thought it time for him to take a wife, and the second time, because she thought it only right he should come to visit his wife and see his child—each time he was away six months. It seems grandmother first and then mother rule in Chinese families. Another less pleasing anecdote told us as true, was of a Chinese servant who, after fourteen years' satisfactory service in one family, went into a violent passion over nothing particular, pulled out his knife, and killed three people.

"Johnny," as he is called, looks very good-tempered and cheerful. Still I sympathize with the Americans in wanting to get rid of them. So far there has been free trade in labour and nothing else, and the land is being filled with strange races. We were told that the horrible low Poles, Russians, &c., who swarm into London and our manufacturing towns, fill all the works in the big Eastern States manufacturing centres, and take very low wages, so that the natives are forced to go West. Still, I cannot think how California will get on without the Chinese, for now they do all the work, make the railroads and keep them in order, do the washing and the cooking, and most of the field-labour.

With the assistance of a gentleman in business in San Francisco, Edward made a calculation as to the relative comfort and prosperity of the labouring classes in England and California, taking into consideration on one hand the high wages paid, and on the other the extravagant prices of the necessaries of life. The result was, that while a single man can live as well and save more money in California than he can in England, a married man with a family will be rather worse off. Rents are so high that many working men live in boarding-houses. Clerks, railway conductors, and people of that class rarely have houses of their own, because American women dislike housework. The woman, who in England would put her pride in her comfortable home, and would herself work to keep it clean and tidy, and prepare her husband's meals with loving hands, is in America a fine lady with fashionable hat and stylish costume, and would not for a moment think of putting her hand to brush or kettle, it would seem to her a degradation, so they live at hotels or in boarding-houses with great expense and little comfort.

The election excitement was very great all the time of our visit, and occasionally small processions in curious fancy uniforms with bands of music would look in at the hotel and give us a tune. Nobody seemed to pay any attention to these processions as they passed along the streets, there was no tail of cheering politicians. There is quite a different feeling about these things in America to what there is in England. The procession is not a popular demonstration—it is an advertisement.

We never got to see the whole of the Golden Gate Park. We reached the band stand one Sunday afternoon, and found hundreds of carriages and a number of pedestrians listening to the music. Close by is a pleasing monument to the composer of the "Star-spangled Banner," the American National Air. The fog came pouring up from the ocean before we had been there ten minutes, so we fled. The same afternoon we took a car up a steep street and then got into a bit of waste ground on the top of a hill, from where we had a magnificent view of the Bay and the Golden Gate. The sun was setting gloriously, but still streams of fog were pouring across the Park, happily missing the town for once. We walked back down California Street and Nob Hill, sometimes called Snob Hill, and saw the large houses of the millionaires, each with two entrances, one for use and the other as an excuse for an immense flight of steps. Our excursion to the Presidio, the military reservation, was as unlucky as that to the Golden Gate Park. We got some pretty views on the way, and admired the trim officers' quarters, but as soon as we started to walk to the particular view we had come for, the fog calmly rolled over the hill, and covered it up. The shops in San Francisco were very good, finer than any others we saw, but most to be admired was the extraordinary number of cake shops. People go to them for meals, just taking tea, coffee or chocolate, and cake. We tried them once or twice for afternoon tea; but that is not their object, they are for poor people to make a solid meal. In one shop the man told us they cut up fifty cakes a day.

We left San Francisco in the evening, and arrived at Raymond, the end of the railway towards the Yosemite Valley, at 7 a.m., Tuesday, the 9th October, after a miserably cold night in the Pulman car. We had a wretched breakfast at the tiny hotel there, but, after that, all was well with us. We had secured the box seats on the coach for the whole journey, there and back. The drive to the White Soda Springs was pretty, winding through a forest. Here we got an excellent lunch, well cooked and pleasantly served by the landlord and his family. To my astonishment, I saw in the visitors' book that one of our party complained that he could not get enough to eat! No doubt I have been as unjust in some of my criticisms. After leaving the White Soda Springs the scenery became very grand as we rose higher and higher on the mountain side. Occasionally there were glimpses of distant hills away towards the sea, but the valley and the opposite hills were sufficient of themselves to make the drive delightful. The finest distant view was from the top of a steep hill, at a place feelingly named by some pedestrian "Perspiration Point." The immense trees, oaks, cedars, and pines of different kinds, with the golden green moss on their trunks, and the bushes of all colours, with the variations of light and shadow on the ground as the sun shone through the trees, and the cloudless blue sky, were a good preparation for the grander beauties of the valley. We had a very pleasant, good-looking driver, Tommy Gordon, very careful at the dangerous corners. The roads are rough, so that we were pretty well shaken and tired. Poor hotel at Wawona.

Wednesday, October 10*th.*—We got up at five o'clock, according to orders, but could get no breakfast until 6.40. We started about seven. Our new driver, Uriah Toby, was a big, handsome, solemn fellow, a very fine whip. We dashed down the steep hills and round the sharp corners at a splendid pace. I do not suppose we went any slower because of my delight in his prowess. His skill was wonderful. I spent the day with one eye on his driving, and one on the scenery. He must come of a Yorkshire stock. Certainly he was the best specimen of the wild Westerners we met with during our journey. At first the road was much the same as on the previous day, except that the trees were finer, and the pine that bears enormous cones, up to sixteen and eighteen inches long, grows in this forest. Quail abounded larger than ours, also ground and grey squirrels, blue jays, and woodpeckers busy knocking holes in the trees and storing up acorns, sometimes killing the trees by the extent to which they honeycomb them. Fresh deer-tracks were on the road, and we were told rattlesnake were common. Indeed, Tommy Gordon's hat was decorated with the rattle of one he had killed on the roadside with his whip. After driving thirteen miles, and admiring the extensive view from Look-Out Point across the Merced Valley, and over row after row of hills towards the coast, we changed horses, then had two more miles up-hill, and then four miles' rapid descent to Inspiration Point, whence the first view of the Yosemite Valley is obtained, a view never to be forgotten. The beautiful photographs and enthusiastic descriptions can give but a very poor idea of its wonderful grandeur. The next point is called Artists' Point, because it is better for sketching. After a delightful rush down the hillside, and a long drive on the level, we reached the Stoneman House Hotel, quite good, at the end of the valley. We were much tired and shaken, for the road is rough, being torn up by the constant traffic during the dry season. Toby missed every stone and hole he could in a wonderful way, and he brought the coach down the hills and round the corners with admirable skill. Most of the way the road skirts precipices, like a Swiss road. The weather had been very hot ever since we left Raymond, and continued so until we reached Raymond again. So unfortunately, the celebrated waterfalls, the Virgin's Tears and the Yosemite Falls, were absolutely dry, and the Bridal Veil had very little water. This is passed on the right soon after reaching the valley; then the glorious rock of El Capitan, a straight wall three thousand three hundred feet high, perhaps the most beautiful object in the valley, is passed on the left; the Cathedral Rock, the Cathedral Spires, the Sentinel Rock and Dome on the right, and the Three Brothers on the left. The Royal Arches, Washington Column, North Dome, Half Dome, and Glacier Point are well seen from the hotel. Unfortunately, the dust was so deep, walking was out of the question. We made a desperate attempt to reach Mirror Lake on foot, but had to give it up. The journey from Raymond to Clarkes, or Wawona, is forty miles, with four teams of four horses; from Clarkes to the Stoneman Hotel is twenty-six miles, with two teams of four horses. The drivers have only Monday off. Six days in the week they drive these great distances, every yard of the road being such as to require the utmost care. It is wonderful there are not more accidents. The Government of the United States made a present of the Yosemite Valley to the Californian Government, who hold it as a place of recreation for the people for ever. They make the roads, which are fairly broad, and good as the nature of the country allows. There were some curious bits of work. In several places the road was hemmed in too closely by immense trees, so, instead of cutting one down, the exact distance required had been measured on the trunk, and a slice taken off high enough to allow the wheels to pass. In other places, big dead trees having fallen across the road, the obstacle had been sawn across at both sides of the road, and only the middle piece removed. The Government have built the Stoneman Hotel, which is much larger than any of the old ones.

Thursday, October 11*th.*—A blazing day. We started at nine o'clock on a buckboard to see what we could. First to the Mirror Lake, now almost dried up and muddy, but pretty from its situation. In the side of the great walls of rock near the lake is a profile, said by the Indians to be one of their ancient heroes, with a name many syllables long, looking for his lost bride, Tis-saack, to return and bring joy and happiness to his wigwam. It is difficult to feel sentimental about Indian love affairs. No doubt Tis-saack ran away because she was tired of carrying his tent and baggage after him on foot while he rode on ahead. She would also have to do all the hard work, pitching the tent, cooking, getting in firewood, &c., while the devoted husband smoked, fished, or hunted. Let us hope she found an easier situation.

From the lake we went down the valley, past El Capitan, and up the hill (on the opposite side of the valley to Inspiration Point), on the Milton Road, getting some lovely views down the Merced Cañon, where there used to be a road to Madera, now deserted, because three roads into the valley did not pay. From the Milton road we saw the road we came by, and the zigzag from Inspiration Point into the valley. On the Milton side the road is suddenly blocked by a magnificent rock, standing out alone on the hill-side, and has to make many doubles to get high enough to pass it. So rich in beauty is the valley that this rock has not been thought worthy of a name, though it would make the fortune of a Scotch valley. It was the same with some curious rock pillars. The road was very steep and rough, so that on reaching the top we were glad to rest in the shade of some gigantic pine-trees and eat our lunch. As the yellow flowers in my hat had faded to dirty white and looked very shabby, it suddenly occurred to me to take them out, and trim my hat with the beautiful golden moss, which I did with complete success, and gained many compliments from fellow-travellers. I brought that moss home, and it is golden now. On our return to the valley we followed the river, and, leaving the carriage, struggled through the brushwood to get to the pools to see the lovely reflection of El Capitan. About a third of the way up this bare rock a solitary pine-tree has managed to plant itself and grow about one hundred feet. It is very difficult to distinguish it amongst the many lines on the rock, of cracks and inequalities. Our driver had arranged for us to arrive at the Bridal Veil at the proper moment to see the rainbow. To-day it was 3.40. The sun must be at a particular point of its descent to catch the fall, and then it turns it into one immense rainbow. As we saw it, even with so little water, it was very beautiful. We reached the hotel about 4.30, after a delightful day, to find it literally empty—not a creature there, except one Chinaman in the kitchen. At last Edward induced him to make us some tea, but as he said he had nothing to do with the cream, Edward had to go into the cellar and take what he wanted himself.

This night we were the only guests in the hotel, the Boston family who came with us having gone to Glacier Point. The Boston gentleman is a wholesale boot and shoe manufacturer, and employs a large number of Irish, who give him a great deal of trouble with strikes and disputes. His daughter told me how frightened they often were, for the men would wait outside her father's office and would form two lines for him to walk through while they swore at and threatened him. Even men who had been with him twenty years, and received much help and kindness from him, would join the rest. Another traveller was a German gentleman, representative of a soft woollen goods firm, who was making an extended tour, combining business and pleasure. He had been in every West Indian island, all through South America and Mexico, and was now going through the States. These German superior commercial travellers are everywhere, seeking whom they may devour. We had that day an opportunity of testing the American boast of the high wages they pay. On our drive we met a cart with five horses, bringing freight for the Stage Company, so we inquired what pay the driver got. He said he owned cart and horses; he came fifty miles, and was paid three cents per pound; he carried 3500 pounds up and down these dreadful roads, so would receive 105 dollars. Out of this he had to pay twelve dollars for tolls, one dollar for the keep of each horse per day, and his own food, two meals at fifty cents each, altogether forty-two dollars for the journey, so that he would only have sixty-three dollars in hand to cover his own wages, and five days' work and wear and tear of his five horses and cart. Poor pay in a country where the lowest coin is five cents!

Friday, October 12th.—Another blazing day. We started at eight o'clock for a long day's work. We drove to the stables, close to the old hotels, and then mounted ponies for the ascent to Glacier Point. It is a wonderful trail, quite safe and easy, but rather giddy, as at several turns the pony's head is over one precipice and his tail over another, and often, by stretching out an arm, we could have dropped pebbles straight down, hundreds of feet, into the valley. The beauty of it surpasses, I think, anything in Switzerland. For some time we crept up under the Sentinel Point, which towered far above us, but by-and-by we reached his level, and from Glacier Point looked down upon him. Half-way to the point there is a turn in the zigzag, from which the traveller can see both ways, up and down the valley.

It is a dizzy pleasure, as there is a sheer descent of one thousand five hundred feet on each side, but there is no danger. We stopped to visit a flat rock, remarkable both for the view from it and for the curious Agassiz Column close by. This column is composed of three immense stones, one on the top of the other. Most of the rocks seemed to be divided into upper and lower parts, sometimes of different kinds of stone. It was very interesting to note how different the rocks looked from different elevations. For instance, from the valley, the Washington Column looks very fine, but as one rises it fades into insignificance, and seems to melt into the general outline, but the Half Dome looks magnificent from every point. The Cap of Liberty looked but a small affair from Glacier Point, but when one is close to it, it is very fine. This wonderful trail was made by a man called Macauly, from Antrim, who now keeps the little inn at Glacier Point with the assistance of his wife, a pleasant, motherly German, and his two fine boys, who, however, are to go to school next year, and the mother is to go down, too, to make a home for them and keep them out of mischief. Mr. Macauly is a most interesting man. He told us that he had been a sailor, first on the Cunard line, but had joined the Confederate service because the pay was so high. He planned the trail all by himself, although he knew nothing of engineering, just planning it out from place to place by his eye. Every one told him he would never succeed, but he persevered, though often despairing. Seven nationalities, he said, were concerned in making that road—himself (Irish), one Englishman, one Scotchman, a Chinese, two Indians, one American, and a Mexican lad, who worked best of any. It was made in five months, and for seven years he took toll, and then sold it to the State for 2500 dollars. His little inn is beautifully clean, and our lunch there excellent. We should have liked to spend a week there, and make excursions into the forest, though that might not have been safe, for there are bears. His boys saw one a few days before our visit not far from the house. The view from the verandah is marvellous—across the valley to the Nevada and Vernal Falls, the Cap of Liberty, the Half Dome, Cloud's Rest, and, far away in the distance, Mount Lyall, where Mr. Macauly said there was a "living glacier." Glacier Point is so called only because from it a glimpse can be had of this glacier far away. A short distance from the inn is a rock jutting out about twenty feet beyond anything else over the valley, just a bar of rock, as if one had put a plank out over the straight, unbroken drop of three thousand five hundred feet. To my horror I found my husband standing on this stone enjoying the view. He had to come off at once, it was too dreadful, but there were nooks and crannies in the rocks where one could wedge one's self and peer over. At one point the rock is flat, and Macauly has put a strong railing. From here we looked straight down on to the hotel, and shouted, as is usual, until some one down below answered our greeting.

After two hours' rest we mounted our ponies and started for the Nevada and Vernal Falls. By-and-by the track was so steep and rough we preferred trusting our own feet, so got off and walked some way, then up and on again, no longer on a handsome road like Mr. Macauly's, but on just a natural path, very queer at times, round the mountain side down to the valley, where we crossed the bridge over the Illilouette River, passing the lovely Illilouette Falls, then up a tremendous pull to the top of the Nevada Falls, where we got off the ponies, and walked on to the very rock the water falls over. The guide advised our walking down the tiny cañon to the foot of the falls, as the path was so steep and rough. Part of the road before reaching the Nevada Falls is very impressive. On one side, for about thirty yards, there is a steep slope, then it ends. From the track one simply sees that there must be a terrible precipice at that point, and that if one's pony slipped and rolled down the bank, there would be nothing to stop it. From below one sees that it is the edge of an extraordinary amphitheatre of rock, almost perpendicular. Snow's Hotel, at the foot of the Nevada Falls, was closed, so we missed our tea. We scrambled close to the foot of the Nevada Falls, and over the rocks to the very edge of the Vernal Falls, that is, as near as nerves permitted; mine kept me further off than Edward ventured, but still I got to where I could look straight down where the water plunges about four hundred feet without a break. There is a natural barricade of rocks close to the falls. The water washes one's feet within a yard of its plunge. There is no practicable path to the foot of the Vernal Falls. A long way off we climbed over rocks into the bed of the river to get a glimpse of them from below. On leaving the top of the falls we had to ascend a long way to get round a difficult point, then a steep descent, which gradually became easy, until we reached the valley, and indulged in a "lope" (canter) on the flat to the hotel. Our guide was pleasant and obliging; he was the brother of the manager of the stables. It was a glorious day. Those who have time should take two days, spending the night at Glacier Point; indeed, those who have time should spend the summer here.

Saturday, October 13th.—Up at 4.30. Started at 6.10 back to Wawona. We were very sorry to leave the valley so soon, for, though we had seen almost everything, still we should have liked to see everything again, and spend more time at the best points. Not only is the valley wonderfully beautiful, but it is different from any other. The mountains surrounding it are huge piles of bare granite, with precipitous sides and curious shapes, while the valley itself is full of fine trees, with a peaceful, clear river winding through it, reflecting the wonderful rocks above. Then, too, we could gladly have spent hours climbing round the Nevada and Vernal Falls, and many other charming bits. We hurried back to Wawona, because the afternoon is devoted to visiting the big trees of Mariposa. It was very sad to say farewell to the valley at Inspiration Point. There one sees the whole glorious scene at once; a few turns of the wheels and it is gone for ever, not the tiniest glimpse to be had anywhere.

After lunch at Wawona, Toby got a little trap,

as there was only one other visitor, a German gentleman, to take us to the Mariposa Big Trees. It was a very beautiful forest drive. We went past magnificent pines and cedars, but they were nothing compared to the *Sequoia gigantea*, the highest of which reaches two hundred and seventy-two feet. It is odd that there is no English name for them. We left the carriage and stood at the foot of the Grizzly Giant, and felt like ants creeping round him. Our heads did not reach beyond his roots. Another tree has a doorway cut through the middle, twelve feet by twelve feet, for the coach to drive through, and still the tree lives. The biggest trees are named, many after Presidents of the United States. "Andy Johnson" has fallen, and people walk through the hollow trunk without stooping. The German bought two little trees to take home, and somebody said the Earl of Devon had one on his estate in England that had grown sixty feet in twenty-five years. Toby told us the Mariposa trees were four thousand years old, and I read in an American guide-book that they "were present at the birth of our Lord." I did not see any reason given for their subsequently leaving Nazareth to settle here. We bought a little pin-cushion of the bark, which is said to be as good as emery paper for needles.

Sunday, October 14*th.*—Started at eight o'clock for Raymond—a charming drive. Tommy Gordon, the driver, was musically inclined to-day, and favoured us with many songs, one very sentimental, about "marble halls, where my love sits and drinks his wine and thinks of me;" but that soon wearied him, and he went off to

H

a very long comic song about "Jim Jones." I could only catch one verse of it :—

> Then he went to Jersey City,
>   And lived altogether on clams and cheese,
>   He put all his money in his mother-in-law's pocket,
>   And took out a patent for raising fleas.

After dining at Raymond, we got on board the Pulman sleeper, and were taken to Berenda, where we had to wait until 4 a.m. for the Southern Pacific train, which landed us at San Francisco at noon. After looking for letters and finding none, and securing berths on the s.s. *Santa Rosa* for San Diego on the 19th, we went off at once to Monterey to the delightful Hotel del Monte. It was a weary journey of nearly four hours without Pulman car, but the scenery was very pretty, such orchards and vineyards, pretty towns and villages, trees and flowers, and beautiful hills on each side in the distance. We arrived very tired, and indulged in tea in our own room, which we much enjoyed. We were sorry to leave our Boston fellow-travellers, whom we rejoined at Wawona, at 'Frisco. The gentleman was originally a miner, and his wife wore a brooch containing the first nugget he had found. He was going to Sacramento to see an old comrade, still living in the cabin they once shared. Mr. C—— was a very quiet man, but he told us some interesting tales of Californian life when he was amongst the gold-diggers. It must have been a fearful time—no law, no protection for life or property. One man might shoot another, and nobody would interfere—

it was nobody's business; only when matters got too serious they would organize a vigilance committee, arrest the murderers, and hang them. A plank out of an upper-storey window, or the projecting branch of a tree, sufficed as gallows. One of his experiences shows how reckless men can become. A ruffian strolled into town one day, maddened with drink, and telling every one he met that, having already killed eleven men, he meant that day to kill a twelfth, "so that he might have a jury to sit on him in hell;" he did not care who it was, but he meant to kill somebody. First he went up to a man he knew, who was sitting with his dog between his knees, and shot the dog dead with his revolver, but this man had presence of mind to keep quiet, for if he had spoken, or moved to get his pistol, the wretch would have shot him at once. After vainly endeavouring to pick a quarrel with anybody who knew him, he went to a drinking-saloon, where he found a stranger, just come into the town. Now Bret Harte would have made a prettier ending to this tale, but Mr. C—— was not a man to romance, and so it became still more ugly. All the men of the town, seeing his state, and knowing him, slipped quietly away without a word of warning to the stranger. The murderer went to him and stood him a drink, and, as the poor fellow raised the glass to his lips, sprang upon him, knocked him down, stamped on him, and fired five times into him. After this, he thought it wise to retire into the country. Then the others came back, and put the corpse on a cart and drove it round the town to work up the feelings of the community, and a band was organized to go after the murderer and bring him back. After a long search they found him, and fired at him, but he got away, though wounded, and they followed on. At last they found his horse, covered with blood, and then they found him, badly hurt, tied him securely, brought him back, and the townspeople met them outside the town, drove the waggon containing the wounded, fettered wretch under a tree, strung him up to one of the boughs, and drove the waggon away, and so he was hung. There is a want of the heroic about this story!

Tuesday, October 16th.—Rather misty, but the air pleasant. It seems the almost constant mist from the sea is considered one of the charms of Monterey by the visitors from the blazing inland States. We were glad to have a quiet day, roaming on the beach and in the pretty grounds of the hotel, which cover one hundred and ninety acres, and contain a maze like Hampton Court, tennis and croquet courts, swings, &c. There is a large sea-bathing establishment on the beach. The hotel is very comfortable, the great feature being the winding ascending passages instead of staircases. Our bedroom, with bathroom attached, and very good simple board, was only seven dollars a day for both of us. Next day was brighter, so we took the seventeen miles' drive in a little carriage and pair, six dollars. They appeared to be very short miles. This drive, which is remarkably pretty, is almost entirely over the Hotel Company's property. It goes past the old barracks and the Chinese fishing-village to the seaside, which it follows a long way, until it reaches the famous cypress grove, which is said to share with the cedars of Lebanon and some grove in Japan the distinction of being the oldest trees alive. Now, as Toby said the Mariposa trees were four thousand years old, how old must these be? They certainly have the appearance of great age; many are dead, many dying, and the Spanish moss disfigures them badly, and must exhaust them. It grows on every branch. Still, they are very picturesque. We saw plenty of sea-lions, and numbers of coot, wild geese, and very odd-looking birds with long thin bills, flying close past our heads in long, single-file processions. First our driver said they were albatross, and then he said they were pelican. We scrambled over the rocks to look into the pools on the beach at the large mussels and the crabs, and there we found the most magnificent sea-anemones, fully a foot across when open, and of the most brilliant light green. The abellona is plentiful here, but lives in deep water. Every child in England owns an abellona shell I should say, though it does not know the name. We found a little Chinese fishing-village where they were sold, and we bought one, so fresh that part of the fish was still sticking to the shell. Johnny eats them, but no one else does, though they ought to be as good as scallops. It is said if the fish dies a natural death the brilliant colours in the shell fade. We lunched at the Pebble Beach on provisions we had taken with us, our coachman sharing the meal, and telling us of the long drives he had taken English people several times. It was very tempting to hear of the scenery on the road between Monterey, *via* the Yosemite Valley, and Virginia City, but of course the season was too late for us to do it. Further on is a beach of white sand, which was being carted away for glass manufacture. After leaving the lovely coast, we drove through woods alive with quail, and, finally, got on to the high road, which was very rough and dusty. We looked at the Roman Catholic Church, built in 1794 of bricks plastered over and coloured yellow, the court-yard paved with whales' bones, formerly very common here, but now becoming scarce, as the whales have been killed off. I fancy our drive ought to have included the old Mission, of which we saw a photograph afterwards at Taber's shop in San Francisco. The driver told us this church, close to the hotel grounds, was the old Mission, and we then knew no better. At the beginning of the wood there is a colony of tiny wooden houses, not half the size of the smallest Arcachon villas, and frames for tents, which are covered in the season with gay-coloured calico, and let, like the tiny houses, to visitors who take their meals at a second-class hotel in the middle of the colony, all belonging to the Del Monte Company, so that, when the great hotel has its full complement of eight hundred guests, and the second-class hotel, which is also large, is full, and all the villas and tents are taken, the shareholders must make money.

Thursday, October 18*th*.—Rose early, and took the 6.20 train to Menlo Park, where we got a trap to drive to Senator Stanford's horse-breeding establishment at Palo Alto, where he has over 1000 horses. We passed the University he is building, and the grand tomb he is erecting for himself, his wife, and only son, who died a short time ago, and we drove past the house, with a smart garden, and, coming close up to it, like a park meadow in England, a large vineyard. The horse-breeding establishment is in two divisions; one for runners, which looked like a nice lot of hunters, the other for the great American speciality in horse-flesh—trotters. Senator Stanford is supposed to have the finest, and wins all the races. Occasionally he sells some at enormous prices, but the groom who showed us round remarked with delightful frankness, " He never sells any he thinks he can get any good out of." Of course, his standard is very high.

The stables were of the most primitive description, just wooden sheds, whitewashed, and guiltless of fittings, except a few pegs on which the clothing was hung and a few medicine bottles stuck in a corner; none of the trimness and neatness that make English stables so pleasant. The horse's food is brought in a bucket at meal-times; this struck me as being a very good arrangement. Some of the horses were beauties, but very different from anything over here. Electioneer, the original stud horse, now sixteen years old, would be far too heavy for a brougham, but he was a great prize-winner in his day. In some cases a little blood has been introduced and the colts are very handsome. There is a mile race-course for exercising the trotters, who are put into the most comical, tiny, two-wheel traps. The driver has a seat about the size of a postage-stamp, and puts his legs along the shafts. He looks as if he were hanging on to the horse's tail. Unfortunately we never saw a trotting match, but the pace even of these horses exercising was remarkably fast, and the action very fine.

We drove back to the station past a number of buckeye trees. As I had often heard and read of buckeyes, after which the State of Ohio is nicknamed, I got some to bring home. They seem to be a kind of horse-chestnut. On reaching San Francisco we went off to Taber for photographs of what we had seen, and then to the curiosity-shop opposite the hotel, where we got a bowl of Indian wicker-work which holds water, and an old tobacco pouch of the same. These things are becoming scarce, because the Indians can make more by working as ordinary labourers. The dealer told us with pride that he was born and brought up in Wigmore Street, Cavendish Square!

Friday, October 19*th.*—At 9 a.m. we went on board the steam-ship *Santa Rosa*. As Edward had been given a pass, and introduced to Captain Ingall by the managing partner, we were allowed to take our trunk into our cabin, which was roomy and comfortable, and were invited to dine at the captain's end of the table. The *Santa Rosa* is very well managed and prettily decorated. Unfortunately, the fog concealed the coast, and the day would have been dreary had we not made the acquaintance of a cheery, blue-eyed little Englishwoman, Mrs. Hermon, who came with her brother, Mr. Roberts, to California on account of her health ten years ago. San Francisco not suiting her, they settled at San Diego, where she is always well. Mr. Roberts had the post of chief clerk on the railway, and having to go about a great deal on their work, became thoroughly acquainted with the country and started as land agent, doing very well for a time, but the worry and hard work of it, together with his regular occupation, proved too much for his health, and he died about six months before we met her, leaving her hands full, as there was no one else to take up the business, her husband, an architect and a more recent arrival in the country, not knowing anything about it. She has also the fruit ranche they had just started. I asked her many questions about South California and the prospects of Englishmen coming out there. She told me she and her brother had had a good deal to do with young fellows sent out from England. Some were quite unfit for the life, and they had sent them back; others they had started, advised, and looked after. Sometimes, she said, a young fellow would be sent out with 500*l.* in his pocket—too small a sum to be of any service—and then, if otherwise a likely lad, they would persuade him to return the money to his father and work for hire until he had saved something and gained experience of the climate, soil, and methods of cultivation, which are totally different from ours. She said it was best for a lad to bring 1000*l.* with him and buy an uncleared lot. While he is clearing and preparing the land, which he must do with his own hands as labour is too dear to be worth employing, he is gathering knowledge quite as well as if he were apprenticed to some farmer, who would put him to do just the same work. If he buys a cleared lot, he is sure to pay much more than it is worth, and will begin without the necessary knowledge, which can only be gained on the spot. The lad should put up a decent little house to live in, as too rough and coarse a life has a demoralizing effect. She thinks that whenever possible a sister should be sent out with a lad, on equal terms as to profits, because she makes a home for him, and there is so much a woman can do on a ranche; for instance, preserving fruit when it is too cheap to sell. It seems to me a rough life for a girl, but she said there were many nice people settled there now, who had started reading and other societies. When the land is cleared and the olive and orange trees planted which will not bear for some years, vegetables and small fruit should be planted between them. These pay very well as there is a large demand for them; indeed, nothing can be sent away, because the local demand is so great. When the ranche is in working order, Mrs. Hermon considered it ought to pay five hundred pounds a year clear profit, besides keeping the owner, but over and over again she laid stress on the necessity for the farmer to do the work himself, not merely superintend, but labour with his hands. Not only do the Chinese get very high wages, but, as we heard from different sources afterwards, it is dangerous to employ them on account of the jealousy of the white men. In one case a farmer had had fifty acres of raisin grapes ruined by tramps and roughs because he employed Chinese labour. It is very important in California to keep well with the roughs, as there is no redress, and the law is delightfully uncertain.

Mrs. Hermon had seen great evil done by deceitful prospectuses. People come from England, Germany, Italy, &c., lured by their promises, and often staking their whole substance on the venture. In one case a circular was sent offering wonderfully fertile land at three dollars an acre; and when the poor wretches had broken up their homes and come over, the secretary of the company told them they certainly had had land at that price, but now they had nothing under seventy-five dollars an acre. Another company described their land as well supplied with water, whereas there was not a drop to be had until the settler made a deep well. The idea given by the advertisements was of a land where oranges and vines, and all manner of rich vegetation covered the ground, and all the farmer would have to do would be to prune and trim and gather the produce. This is not a true picture of South California. It is a desolate region, except where great labour and costly artificial irrigation have brought out the qualities of the soil. Labour can do nothing there without capital, and it is a question if such a life—mere manual labour at market-gardening—is well repaid by the very small measure of success that seems possible. Whenever we heard of people making money, it was not by ranching but by land speculations.

We had an amusing instance of the accuracy of a prospectus. A fellow-traveller tried to induce Edward to take shares in some company that owned "twelve miles of orange groves." It was so printed on the prospectus, but on inquiry they dwindled to eight miles staked out for orange groves—not quite the same thing.

Santa Barbara was passed at 5 a.m. All day we had alternate fog and sunshine, with only occasional glimpses of the coast, as we were now further out. But this day we saw what we had never counted on meeting so far north—flying-fish in numbers, shining in the sun like herrings, and flying about as if disturbed by the ship. They really did fly, not jump; they turned first one way, then the other. One flew half round the ship. It gave us great pleasure, but it made us feel a desperately long way from home to see these outlandish creatures as common as minnows.

Just before coming to San Pedro we passed a large iron ship stranded on the rocks. It was an English ship, laden with coals, then worth eighteen to twenty dollars a ton, owing to the strike in New South Wales. The captain refused to take a pilot on board, because he had been the journey before and thought he knew his way, though this part is very difficult to navigate, not only on account of rocks, but of the dense masses of seaweed, which choke the screw and render the ship unmanageable. Of course he came to grief, and lost all his own fortune, which he had put in the venture, as well as the ship. San Pedro has no harbour: it is an open roadstead, and passengers go off and come aboard by a tender. This is the landing-place for Los Angeles.

San Diego has a very fine harbour, almost land-locked, but with an entrance twenty-seven feet deep. We narrowly escaped running down a tug; even the captain lost his presence of mind to such an extent that he gave orders in plain English instead of nautical terms, telling the man at the wheel to steer "the other way." From this I judged the danger must have been great. It was evening, and very chilly when we arrived, so that the long journey to the Coronado Beach Hotel, always tiresome, was very unpleasant in the open hotel bus. The hotel is built round an inner court or garden 250 by 150 feet, and is supposed to accommodate 2000 guests in 630 bedrooms. This sounds like a puzzle, but I take it from a printed card. It has seventeen and a half acres of carpet, and the total cost of it was one million dollars. It was almost empty when we were there and very uncomfortable, the charges high. A curious feature in this district is the Bridal Chamber, rooms finer and smarter than the others, specially reserved for newly-married couples. There are bridal chambers on the s.s. *Santa Rosa* and others of the line, and at all the hotels. At the Coronado Beach Hotel, to quote their own words, "The two bridal chambers in suites are exquisite in their appointments of white and gold. It would be a species of literary sacrilege to try and enumerate their charms. In every particular they are the very acme of perfection." By the way, this gives a good idea of the usual style of American advertisements. Generally, people like to hide the fact that they are newly married; but here it is otherwise. Captain Ingalls told us of one happy couple who had engaged the bridal cabin, and came on board in all their bridal finery, but immediately after leaving the harbour the Pacific Ocean proved too much for the bridegroom, and he fell flat on his face in the saloon, and remained there groaning and lamenting until they reached Santa Barbara.

We rested on Sunday, admiring the lovely bay and the brilliant colouring of sea, sky, the distant hills, and indeed everything, in the delicious sunshine. It is supposed that formerly a river ran out here, but somehow it disappeared, and the curious bay is the old mouth of the river, kept open by the sea, but gradually filling up. It is the only harbour in the States south of San Francisco, which is the finest in the world. North of San Francisco there is again no harbour south of Puget Sound. It is said that large vessels can go about seven miles up the San Diego bay, where they are absolutely protected from the ocean by the long narrow tongue of land which stretches from the southern extremity of the bay, due north to the entrance, which is at the north end.

It is this narrow strip of land which widens at the northern end and the so-called North Island, which is practically one with it, that the Coronado Beach Company bought and cut up into building plots. The wonderful hotel was the decoy to bring speculators and settlers, and in that capacity it is a great success, much of the land being already sold and many good houses, as well as a multitude of small ones, already built. Even the chambermaid in the hotel had invested her savings in a villa. The hotel itself is unprofitable, and there were rumours it was bankrupt. There had been an idea that Southern California would rival Florida as a winter resort, and so immense hotels have been built everywhere, but even yellow fever cannot drive people from Florida, and there are very few attractions in California. There are no roads for driving or preparations of any kind for tourists. People are said to drive on the beach in the season, but whenever we went on it, it was too soft even for walking. There are some moderately good shops, in one a tempting display of curiosities, but as they were mostly Mexican silver work and such things, we did not buy much. Still we found a few things we wanted. The sunsets over the ocean are very fine. There are some rocky islands outside the bay which stand out beautifully against the sky.

Monday, October 22nd.—We spent the day with the Hermons, meeting them on the road to Sweetwater Dam in the morning. The drawback of Coronado Beach is the ferry. A car ride to the ferry, then waiting for the boat, crossing, and then another car ride to the main streets of the town, are a bad beginning and finish to a day's excursion, as it means half an hour at each end of the day. We had to walk about a quarter of a mile to catch another car, which took us all the way to Sweetwater Dam and left us there, to see what we could, while it went some way further and returned to pick us up. We only had about half an hour, but it was enough to see the Dam which is a very important work, an immense wall built across the Sweetwater Valley to collect the great body of water that comes down the river in spring, and retain it for irrigation all through the year. The company who made the Dam own the land it is meant to irrigate, which they sell off in five-acre lots for building, and large pipes convey the water along the main roads, and any one may attach pipes for his own property and use as much water as he wishes for house, garden, stables, &c., for a rent of two and a half dollars per acre. The soil is wonderfully fertile when irrigated, and very little of the five-acre plots was wasted in flowers; they are all planted with orange and olive trees. Mrs. Hermon had a ten-acre plot, a special favour, as the wish of the company is to make this the great residential district, so they discourage market-gardening. It is called Chula Vista, and commands lovely views both towards sea and land. Every house built there must cost at least two thousand dollars. Mrs. Hermon showed us how she had planted her ten acres with orange and olive trees, and, for present profit, one thousand strawberry plants, which would yield fruit in December, although only planted in October. The planting being now finished, she meant to discharge the Chinese labourer, who had received forty dollars a month. An American, aged twenty, who did outside work and drove the carriage, received thirty dollars a month, with board and lodging. Mrs. Hermon spoke well of the Chinese, and said they are good, steady workers, but slow. The American can do more and better work in the time if he will, but Johnny has this great superiority, that he requires no watching. He will work all the time as if his master's eye were on him. There was some very fine fruit for dessert—a bunch of grapes weighing three and a half pounds, and splendid apples and pears, but the greatest treasure they had found for me was a live tarantula. They had put it in a bottle, and wanted me to bring it home, but really it was too loathsome.

These spider monsters are found, like the centipedes and scorpions, in turning over new ground; they are all venomous and, it is said, a tarantula bite kills, but Mrs. Hermon's man said he had never heard of any one being injured by either tarantula or centipede, though they are fairly common.

Mrs. Hermon's was quite a large house, and I am sure no English servant would have gone there as maid of all work, but her girl, certainly rather rough-looking, cooked the lunch very nicely and brought it in and changed plates, &c. We noticed everywhere that though wages are high in the States, the work is very hard, and servants are not looked upon as members of the household but as machines. A servant undertakes to do certain work and if she is ill, she is just turned out to make room for a machine in better working order. Of course the servants show just as little regard for their employers. Mrs. Hermon is trying English treatment. After lunch Mrs. Hermon drove us to see several fruit ranches where oranges, guavas, lemons, limes, pomegranates, the third crop of figs, and many other fruits were growing in wonderful profusion. The persimmon, a Japanese fruit, is the most beautiful tree, the fruit is a brilliant red. The Forbidden Fruit looks very handsome, but does not ripen so far north. Of course vines are luxuriant, but they do not pay to grow now, though the grapes are fine muscat and quite large.

We visited an old lady, Mrs. Kimball, who gave us grapes off vines that had not been irrigated since they were first planted, six years ago. Kimball is the great name at San Diego. Many years ago the three brothers Kimball bought an immense tract of land, ten leagues, from a Mexican to whom it had been granted by the Mexican Government before the Americans stole half their country. They paid 30,000 dollars for it, of course quite wild and bare. For years they struggled on, often having to borrow money to pay the taxes, which are levied there on all land, whether cultivated or not. At last they persuaded the California Southern Railroad to come to San Diego, by giving them 40,000 acres and every second block. A block in America is now taken as a term of measurement an eighth of a mile long.

Now the Kimballs are millionaires, but remain very simple people. This Mrs. Millionaire was hoeing her vineyard in a little cotton dress with the sleeves rolled up, but no doubt Miss Millionaire shines in silk and diamonds, and has her eye on the British peerage. It is to be hoped she will not fall a prey to some adventurer like the individual who called himself Sir George Bridges, Bart., and got engaged lately to the prettiest heiress in San Francisco. Luckily he was discovered, before it was too late, to be an American forger who had played the same trick in several towns and been married more than once.

Another ranche we visited was the property of a charming old lady of eighty-four, who came there some years back for her son's health. He died, and now she lives there without kith or kin, or even an old friend near her, and still she seems quite happy.

A visit to Mr. Kimball's olive-mill closed the day. Olive oil making is the rising industry in California, and pays very well, but it requires capital, as the trees have to be planted and do not bear for some years, and the mill and machinery take money. There is no quantity of olives now raised to supply a large mill, but everybody is planting them. Mr. Elwood Cooper has a large olive ranche and mills near Santa Barbara, and the year before last he sold all he made at twenty-five dollars a barrel to go east, and last year at fifteen dollars a barrel. The mill we visited was not even a one horse, it was a one man affair. The process is simple. The olives are crushed stones and all, under a vertical stone roller, then they are put in a tub with holes over a vat, and are very slowly pressed to force out the oil, which is strained, filtered, and bottled, and sold at a dollar a pint. The mast is then put back under the roller, water added, and the same process repeated for second quality oil. The olive-tree growing in California was originally introduced by the Spanish priests, and is called the mission olive.

Mrs. Hermon left us at the car station, and on arriving at the hotel we found that, although she had driven us about all the afternoon, we had spent a dollar and a half in car fares. There is a car line to the Mexican frontier, but as there is nothing to see except the boundary-stone, we did not make the excursion, but devoted ourselves to the immediate neighbourhood. San Diego expects to eventually occupy an area four miles by eighteen miles, without Chula Vista, and National City, and the whole of this is already divided into town lots, twenty-five feet by one hundred and twenty feet, at prices varying from eighty-five to five hundred dollars a lot. This information was given us by the estate agent, living like a hermit at the top of University Heights. We had come up by car, and seeing fellow-creatures, he had emerged from his office to take advantage of such an unusual occurrence. As we laughed at the idea, he waved his hand proudly to draw our attention to the four houses in view, one of them his own office. "All these," said he, "were built since last May." They were miles apart. The long tram-lines are built, like the large hotels, not for profit in themselves, but to induce people to buy lots and build.

Another car journey took us all along the narrow strip called Coronado Beach, and round the south end of the Bay to the town, in about an hour, with, of course, several changes of car. The sandy waste was marked off into building-plots all the way, some streets already graded, and a few trees planted. In some places the beach is only about thirty yards wide and just above sea-level. It looks as if the waves would go right over it in rough weather. Quite at the south end of the bay there is marshy land, which affords some shooting.

Thursday, October 25th.—We left San Diego at 9 a.m. by the California Southern Railroad, and had a pretty run to East Riverside through the Temecula Cañon, passing every now and then towns, with graded streets, and trees planted, and everything but houses. They look very comical, but the pity of it is, that it stops ordinary cultivation. If one building-plot is sold, the rest cannot be reconverted into agricultural land. After changing cars, a run of twenty minutes took us to Riverside, the show place of California. As we were trying to arrange about a carriage to take us round, a gentleman joined us whom we had met before, and who owned a good deal of property in this district, and insisted on acting as showman and standing treat with the carriage. It was a great advantage to have him with us, as he told us all about the great Riverside Irrigation and Land Owning Company, and took care that we saw all the best parts. We drove over wide roads decorated with aloe and palm trees, past gentlemen's houses, each with its orange ranche, to the Magnolia Avenue. The magnolias were planted, but died with one consent, and I do not think they would have been more beautiful than the pepper-trees and gum-trees. There is also a cyprus avenue, handsome but gloomy.

We were struck with the great neatness and care required by the orange-trees—not a weed was to be seen. The soil must be kept broken, so that the sun and air can reach the roots, and they must be irrigated three times a year. The orange becomes profitable when six years old, improves until it is sixteen, and continues in its prime for many years, being a very long-lived vegetable. At sixteen and after it is said to bring in a profit of 80*l.* sterling per acre. We saw some olive plantations and quantities of grapes drying in the sun on trays for raisins; it is the sun that turns the white muscat to purple. Seventy-thousand boxes of raisins were exported from Riverside last year. We saw the sorting and packing establishments in the town, but did not admire them. It was all handwork, and the fruit was too much fingered. Chinese were packing raisins in boxes, which were also made on the premises. A man told us he nailed together 600 boxes a day, and as he put all the nails he used into his mouth, and there are ten nails in each box, we calculated that he must take daily a good dose of iron, and we suggested an addition of a little quinine. There are two crops of grapes a year, but they are not very profitable.

An Englishman called Gage, formerly a little jeweller, started a store here a short time ago, and, after looking about him, devised a new system of irrigation, and has opened up another large tract of land, and so he is rapidly becoming a millionaire.

Riverside is a teetotal settlement; wine is not allowed even in the big hotel. They were building more schools. The first thing done when a new settlement is really started is to put up a big schoolhouse.

We came on to San Bernardino at 5.30 p.m, arriving at six, and put up at the new Hotel Stewart, which was good though not finished. San Bernardino is a very pretty little place, and appeared prosperous. We spent a morning rambling about and eating the delicious grapes of the vineyards that surround it, and in the afternoon started for Los Angeles, just the same kind of place, only larger, and with much the same pretty background of mountains. It is a monotonous country. We passed a number of big hotels on the way, apparently all guiltless of occupants, and the whole valley was laid out in lots to suit purchasers. Much of the land was already under cultivation.

As the large Raymond Hotel at Pasadena, the fashionable suburb of Los Angeles, was still closed, we put up at the Westminster Hotel, only opened a few months but quite comfortable. Everybody was talking about "Minister" West's foolish letter, and they looked upon the dishonourable means employed to obtain it as most praiseworthy; so "smart." The *Los Angeles Times* crowed about it much as our *Daily News* did of having secured some valuable piece of war news before any other newspaper had got it. The *Times* drew a most interesting distinction between "private" and "confidential." The letter to Mr. Sackville West promised that whatever answer he sent should be kept "private," and Mr. West marked his letters "private," and so "Mr. Murchison" (as the correspondent called himself) was at liberty to publish it; but had the word "confidential" been used, the *Times* would have considered it most dishonourable to have shown it to any one. The local Republican leaders were all delighted. I quote from the *Los Angeles Times*: Major Bonebrake "thinks it will have a good deal of influence in the result" of the election. Colonel Banbury said, "the richest thing you have struck;" while General Brierly remarked, "It's knocking the Democrats silly all along the line."

America is a wonderfully military country, one hardly ever meets a plain Mr. Probably not one of the three gentlemen interviewed by the *Times* had the slightest connection with the army. We had travelled with a San Francisco gentleman for some days, and had heard him addressed as "General," and saw his arrival at San Bernardino announced as that of "General," so I inquired why he was called General, as he was an insurance agent, and had never been in the army. The answer was, he was called so "by courtesy." The newest fashion is to call yourself or your friends "Judge." Probably military titles are becoming too common.

Two other quotations from the *Los Angeles Times* are rather good—"The *Pall Mall Gazette's exposé* of London immorality, the *Deutsche Rundschau's* publication of the late German Emperor's diary, and the *Los Angeles Times* Sackville West correspondence are the three great journalistic sensations of the present decade."

The other is remarkable for elegance of language :— "Thurman rose up on end yesterday in Ohio, and fairly snorted over the enterprise of the Pomona statesmen in springing upon an unsuspecting public the most beautiful sensation of the campaign."

Western American newspapers are very uninteresting. Often two pages will be devoted to a chronicle of the entertainments given by Mesdames Brown, Jones and

Robinson, the guests and their gowns; and long accounts of friendly societies' picnics. Another page will be taken by the *feuilleton* like a French paper, while less than half a page suffices for all European news. Baseball occupies a good deal of room, and there are curious announcements that such a town has "sold" an eminent player to another town. Often the articles are written in slang that is quite incomprehensible to foreigners, or, what is almost as bad, ordinary words used to convey new meanings, as for instance, in the following sentence from the *St. Louis Daily Globe Democrat*:—" As this country (America) is unexampled there is nothing to compare with it." The oddest newspaper we saw was presented to us by a fellow-traveller, who owned and edited it. It was about the size of the *Saturday Review*, was published weekly, and had but one subject—the wickedness of singing hymns when God had specially provided psalms for the purpose. All the crimes and misfortunes of humanity were attributed to our neglect of the Psalms.

We spent a day exploring Los Angeles, which appeared to be very prosperous and growing rapidly. The residential quarters are exceedingly pretty, each house having a garden planted with orange-trees, aloes, &c., and coming down to the edge of the road, from which it is separated only by a small curbstone, except in some streets where a stream of water about eighteen inches broad, flows between the pavement and the gardens. We noticed that the Los Angeles ladies are very pretty.

Sunday, October 28th.—We had engaged a trap to take us the grand round, and had been promised a spirited team and a driver who knew the country well and would point out everything. We got a driver who did not even know the way; and of our spirited team, one was broken-winded and very lame and the other could hardly keep on its legs. We started at 8.30, and drove first to Pasadena and up the hill occupied by the Raymond Hotel, to see the view from the terrace. The worst of this country is that there is only one view, the same at San Bernardino, Pasadena, and Los Angeles. From there, after much trouble to find the right road, we went to the Sierra Madre Villa, pleasantly situated on the slope of the mountain, with a good view and a garden. We had to wait here an hour for the horses to rest. As we drove away down the hill from the villa, one of them fell and nearly upset the trap. By-and-by we pulled up under a tree and ate our lunch of salt meat sandwiches, crackers, hard boiled eggs, and grapes. The fare never varies, and the driver always expects to share. This man was dull and uninteresting, in fact, he was half asleep. He told us he had to be up every morning at four o'clock to look after his horses, to drive all day, and to drive the 'bus to the train at night, not getting to bed until eleven o'clock. He got sixty dollars a month and a room. We generally found that wages were higher than with us, but the work much harder. One man does two men's work, and gets a man and a half's wages.

After losing our way several times, we reached

"Lucky" Baldwin's ranche, where there was nothing to see except some tumble-down sheds for stables, and a few fair horses. The whole place neglected and desolate looking. I could not learn that there was any special reason for Mr. Baldwin's nickname, except that he had made money, which is not uncommon in California.

From there we went to the San Gabriel Mission, stopping on our way at the charming San Gabriel Hotel to enjoy a lemon squash. The great feature of this hotel is that there is no bar, or drinking-place, an immense advantage for quiet people. This hotel also belongs to a company which owns an enormous tract of land, and hopes in time to build a town round it.

There was not much to see at the Mission. It is an old church built of brick and plastered, with a nice old-fashioned bell-tower. We looked inside and found a priest catechising some small folk in Spanish, which is still spoken by the old inhabitants.

Again we lost our way and found ourselves close to a large winery. The country roads are all loose soft sand, and are mended by putting down straw, which mixes with the sand and binds it together. The winery had used the grape stalks for the purpose. At last we hit upon a main road and reached the hotel about five o'clock. We should have liked to know if the driver received the extra dollar charged for the carriage because it was Sunday.

Tuesday, October 30*th.*—We left Los Angeles by the 9.40 a.m. train to San Pedro, and then went on board the tug which takes goods and passengers to the steamer. We waited one and a half hours for her some way out in the bay, but happily the sea was perfectly smooth. The sun went in about two o'clock, and after that it was very cold and dreary. Next day there was a strong ground-swell, which was too much for everybody on board. It was still very cold, but clear, so that we could see the beautiful coast, and when we arrived at San Francisco about 6.20 p.m., and passed through the Golden Gate, the scene was lovely. The city and the forts were brilliantly lighted up, the sunset had turned the sky to gold, and looking back, when we had passed through the Gate, we saw it as it gained its name—a fort on each side, and, through the opening, the glory of the sunset. It was one of the grandest sights in America.

The boat was about four hours late, so the baggage was not given out, though we landed before seven o'clock. The walk over the landing-stage was horrid, the hotel touters screaming and rushing at and over us like mad bulls, and hardly any lights, so that we all tumbled into holes and over dust heaps and planks.

We spent two more days in San Francisco, and had the pleasure of seeing the great Democratic demonstration. Some friends invited us to their corner room, from which we could see the procession come up Market Street and turn along Montgomery Street. We watched it for two and a half hours, and then retired, as it seemed likely to go on for some time. The prettiest things were the stands erected along the streets with red fires.

We could not see very well, as we were so far off and the light was so bad.

We took the ferry to Oakland, and went by train and car to Piedmont, a very pretty drive up hill, with a nice view over the great harbour. There is a restaurant at Piedmont, frequented in summer by the San Franciscans.

During our stay in California, the great divorce state, I watched the accounts of the divorce trials with much interest. They seemed to me to be very serious affairs. Only in one case was divorce granted for causes that would not have procured at least judicial separation in England. This exception was very remarkable. A white woman obtained a divorce on the sole ground that she had married, believing her husband to be a white man, and had discovered afterwards that he had black blood in him. The announcement was made in both the principal San Franciscan papers as an ordinary matter. Of course one hears tales of absurd divorces, but they may not be true. One *parvenu* millionaire, whose name is freely given, is said to have divorced his old wife, who had struggled through bad times with him, because he did not think her sufficiently elegant for his new position. This surely must be a joke, like the tale about the old negro who won 15,000 dollars in a lottery, so divorced his old wife and gave a white woman 3000 dollars to marry him; "For what," said he, "is wealth, without position in Society?"

It was on leaving San Francisco that we made the acquaintance of the American Ticket Brokers' Association. The main object of all American railways seems to be to avoid making money. For this purpose all baggage traffic was put into the hands of Wells, Fargo and Co., and similar firms, who take charge of it and pay the railroad companies so much a ton, but charge the passengers so much a pound. This was completely satisfactory so far as it went, but did not dispose of the passengers; so the different railways combined to issue absurd return tickets, unlimited as to time, which give choice of return by any route, and are only a trifle more expensive than single tickets. It is the same with long journey tickets, which are sold at greatly reduced rates.

We ignorantly bought single tickets from Chicago to San Francisco for 97½ dollars each, when for 100 dollars we might have had return tickets, which we could have used as far as Denver, and then sold to the Ticket Brokers' Association. We met a gentleman who had done so. These tickets took the traveller from Chicago to Tacoma, over the Northern Pacific, and down to San Francisco by the Shasta route. He might return to Chicago either by Salt Lake City, Denver, and the centre of America, or go south by the Southern Pacific as far as El Paso on the Mexican frontier, and back by any route he liked. Our only dealing with the Association was from San Francisco to Denver. We applied for tickets, and were seized by the Association agent, who bought us two tickets for New Orleans, *viâ* Denver, and other places we wished to visit. On reaching Denver we called at their office and sold the coupons we did not require at a price fixed by the agent in San Francisco—we saved 7½ dollars on each ticket.

I have the circular of the Association giving the official list of members for 1888. They have offices in 138 towns. The first purchaser gains by the transaction, the agency gains, and the second purchaser gains. Sometimes one ticket will pass through half a dozen hands. All this is so much loss to the companies.

Saturday, November 3rd.—We left San Francisco at 9.30 a.m. for Virginia City. It was a sunny, warm day, but after leaving Sacramento the line rises to a great height, and it got colder and colder, until a heavy snowstorm came on. The porter lighted the stove in the Pulman car, and burnt the evil-smelling coal so common in the States, so that we were almost suffocated, and were thankful to leave the train at midnight at Reno, where we got a bed at the little station hotel, which is quite clean and acceptable.

Next morning we were up early, and off by train to Virginia City, to see the celebrated silver-mines. We expected to have to spend a night there, but luckily met a gentleman in the train who told us we could see everything in the day, and return to Reno. Edward had asked for return tickets, but, being told they were only good for the day of issue, had not taken them. Our fellow-traveller told us they were the same price as the single tickets. In any European ticket office the clerk would certainly have told a stranger of this arrangement, and that the time allowed would be ample for seeing the mines.

The run to Virginia City was very interesting, up hill all the way, and probably prettier than usual on account of the snow which covered everything. It is a district of narrow gorges with rivers running through them which supply water-power for the quartz mills. Virginia City looks as if it had been thrown at the precipitous mountain side, and had stuck on as best it could.

Edward presented his letters of introduction to Mr. Lyman, of the Comstock Consolidated Mine, who settled for us to go down the mine at 1 o'clock, so we went off and had a good lunch at the very unpromising-looking International Hotel.

The descent proved to be a very serious business. First we had to change our clothes for costumes provided by the company, consisting merely of trousers and long blouses of blue serge, cap, thick boots and stockings. The only difference between us was that I wore my blouse outside, and tried to imagine it looked like a petticoat. A thick waterproof coat is worn until the low level is reached, where the heat is very great. We descended 1650 feet, and went through lofty passages nearly all supported by timber. Some of the supports were bent and curved by the enormous pressure of the earth above. They have to be constantly watched and renewed. Our guide pointed out in several places timbers that had been twelve years in position, and become quite hard. We brought away a piece of wood from the 1550 level that is as close and hard as a stone. It is an enormous mine. The last point of interest visited is the Sutro Tunnel, made to drain all the Comstock lode; it is many thousands of feet long, and contains a big stream.

The Comstock lode was discovered in 1859, and already 500,000,000 dollars have been taken out of it. It now yields four millions a year. This kind of mine is not so speculative as the old nugget-finding business. When a lode is discovered it can be tested to a certain extent, as to how far it goes, and how rich it is in metals.

On returning to the upper world we were turned into a luxurious dressing-room at the back of the office, with bath and hot towels, and gladly resumed our own garments. Then we were taken over the works to see the machinery, which differs in several respects from that at the Montana Mine. The Comstock people have an electrical process of separation.

There is no danger in silver-mines from foul and inflammable gases, as in coal-mines; but sometimes the old timbering takes fire. The water is taken off by the Sutro Tunnel, to which each mine pays it share. The water used for the hydraulic machinery is also conveyed away by the tunnel, so that they get an extra fall of 1700 feet.

We had a rush to catch our train back to Reno, but we just managed it, and so we were able to continue our journey by the midnight train to Ogden. We got lower berths in the Pulman car, and slept, notwithstanding the bitter cold. Next day we passed over a perfectly flat plain with a line of hills in the distance on each side. Usually this journey is very dusty and ugly, but the snow had remedied all that, and though monotonous it was really pretty. Edward saw a wolf cross the line. They abound in that country.

The platforms outside the cars were occupied by Indians, who have the privilege of riding free on this line, because it went through their reservation without paying them anything. They were dressed in the ordinary way except for their hats and that they wrapped themselves in blankets instead of overcoats. We could not induce them to talk.

We arrived at Ogden at 11 p.m., and put up at the little station hotel, just in time to secure the last bedroom. A lady and gentleman who followed us had to take a sitting-room. Next morning we left Ogden at 9.40 a.m., arriving at Salt Lake City at 11 a.m. We saw the Lake from the train, and, not far from the city, we passed some boiling springs, so close to the Lake that the railway had only just room to pass between them. There is a great bathing establishment on the Lake, which was closed for the winter. In summer great numbers go there for the salt-water bathing. The country between Ogden and Salt Lake City is well cultivated and covered by herds of fine cattle and horses.

We went at once to Walker House Hotel, which was very stuffy and disagreeable, quite a third-rate house. The Walkers were formerly Mormons, but have left the church; still I was surprised to see on sale in the hotel hall, tracts and pamphlets abusing the Mormons, and insulting photographs, and Mrs. Stenhouse's book. There is said to be a new and better hotel, called "Cullens."

Edward had a letter of introduction to Mr. Young, a son of Brigham Young, but he was away, so another eminent Mormon, Mr. B., and an old gentleman, Mr. A., one of the early believers, kindly took us to see the tabernacle and other objects of interest. The tabernacle is an immense building remarkable for its roof, 250 feet by 150 feet, in one span without any other support than the outer walls. The architect was Brigham Young, who invented the plan in the night, probably it was revealed to him in a dream. Wreaths of evergreens put up ten years ago still decorate the roof, because it was found they improved the acoustic properties of the hall, which seats 8000 people. We were taken to the gallery opposite the platform to hear a pin dropped in a hat, and the keeper whisper to us across the whole building. Both sounds came clearly to us, but I noticed that when he spoke aloud, the voice seemed blurred as it were, and the words were not distinct.

Mr. B. stated that every Sunday 25 per cent. of the whole population attended service in the temple. A lady told me that nothing can equal the miserable faces of the women of the congregation.

The unfinished Temple close by is a splendid edifice of white granite. This is to supersede the present Endowment House, if it is ever finished, and all the secret rites, to which Gentiles are not admitted, will be performed there, such as baptisms, marriages, &c., which they call the ordinances, so it is cut up inside into small apartments, which is a pity. The architecture is heavy, but imposing.

From there we went to the Gardo House, a very common-place villa, built for himself by Brigham Young, who did not live to occupy it. Our guides told us he meant to have "invited" his favourite wife Amelia to live with him there, and two rooms at the back of the house had been specially fitted up for the mother of his eldest son. The other wives would have remained over the way, at the Lion House, I suppose, with the numerous gables. We thought at first there was a gable for each wife, but that could not be the case, for there were only nine or ten gables.

The Gardo House is not worth visiting. The man in charge told us that, a few days before our visit, a lady tourist came alone, and asked to look round. He showed her into the drawing-room, and then addressed her thus, "Madam, how is it that you, a lady, dare venture thus alone into the power of a family of Mormons, of whom you have heard such dreadful accounts? Are you not afraid to come here, where there is none to help you?" The lady, no doubt thinking him mad, for he looks a complete lunatic, made at once for the hall door and fled.

Mr. B. then drove us to Fort Douglass, the United States military station, from which there is a beautiful view over the city and plains to the mountains, now finer than usual with the newly-fallen snow.

On our way back to the hotel we passed a polling

station, which reminded us that the Presidential election was going on. Utah not being a state, the election was only for local officers and the representative to Congress, who has not the same rights as a state representative. We stopped to see how the polling was carried on, and were allowed to go right into the booth. In California no one is allowed to go within 150 feet of it, except for the purpose of voting.

This was the process :—There are five election judges who correspond to our returning agents, and are nominated by the Government, but one must belong to the minority party. These five men sit at the back of a counter, on which are the ballot boxes. No one else is allowed there by the law, but, as a matter of fact, there were two others, one a policeman. By the ballot boxes are piles of small envelopes. The voter receives his voting-paper, which is printed, from the political agents, and brings it with him, and puts it into an envelope he takes from the pile, gums it up, and puts it in the box. There is no writing, no mark, no number of any kind, to distinguish one vote from another, so no scrutiny is possible. It seemed to us that there would be no difficulty in manipulating either papers or boxes.

Mr. A. was not allowed to vote because he was known to have two wives, though on account of his great age, he is not molested by the Government, who are now punishing polygamy by imprisonment, and have about 400 Mormons locked up. The President himself is in hiding. The difficulty seems to me to be that, legally, the Mormons are not married at all. They only go through their mysterious ceremony in the Endowment House, which I suppose has no legal weight.

During the drive I tried to have a little talk with Mr. A. about Mormonism, of which I knew absolutely nothing. My aim was to discover the important doctrine differing from other churches founded on the Bible, which induced the Mormons to cut themselves adrift from the rest of the world. Mr. A. could tell me of none. " Our principles," said he, " are all contained in the Gospels."

He preferred to tell me his own history. He is now over seventy years of age, and is evidently a man who would have fallen a prey to any religious excitement; he is the type of the religious fanatic. Mormonism happened to be the religious craze of the day, so he plunged into that. He came to Salt Lake City in 1852 from Manchester, accompanied by his wife, who was also a convert. Such was their haste to reach the promised land, that they started within a short time of his wife's confinement, which took place on board ship, and of course the baby died. As soon as they reached New York a child sickened, but they did not stop for that, on they went, and it died on the way. Leaving the poor little corpse unburied in the dead-house, they hurried on, and another, and then another child sickened and died, so that of seven children they lost five on their way to Zion. Mr. A. seemed to think this greatly to his credit, and that our Lord would be pleased that he had sacrificed his children. I did not like to remind him that Moloch was the god who liked to have children slain on his altar, but I did say that I should have thought God's curse was on the journey, and I should have hurried back at once. It was useless to ask for information why he did all this, he would continue his autobiography.

On arriving at Zion, his wife gave him a second wife, and they have "lived like sisters together, bringing up their families side by side." He had had seventeen children. I noticed that Mr. B., who was talking business with Edward, kept one eye on us as soon as religion was mentioned, and he often interrupted the conversation.

Next morning he called and offered to answer me any questions I wished to ask, so I asked if polygamy was an essential point in their religion. He said belief in it was, although not 10 per cent. of the Mormons practised it. A man must obtain permission from the President himself, and must show that he had means to support two or more families, and also that his character entitled him to the privilege. I reminded him of the projected settlement in Canada, where they had undertaken not to practise polygamy; he said they "would only take one wife to Canada, and leave the others in Utah."

They believe that Joseph Smith was inspired, and that their elders are inspired, not always, so as to be infallible, but occasionally, which must be an uncomfortable state of things, for who is to decide when a prophet is inspired and when not? Then he wandered off into vague talk about their belief that God was in the wind and the sunshine as much as in miracles, and that they could put no limit to His power, they could not say that He should no longer inspire men as of old. Evidently he was not going to tell us anything serious.

We visited the celebrated Co-operative Stores, which only appeared to differ from the Civil Service Stores in the curious particular, that prices were not marked in plain figures. I understand that the profits, which must be very large, go to the elders or shareholders, not like the real co-operative stores which divide them among the purchasers.

We went to the museum, a small place belonging to the Mormons, where they treasure a scrap of satin damask from the furniture in Windsor Castle, a bit of guimp from the Tuilleries curtains, an iron stove presented by Brigham Young to the first lady who became a plural wife, and other odds and ends.

I found a picture representing an angel in the usual white robes and wings, but with a beard like a prophet, and a man kneeling before him, so I asked for an explanation, which the keeper of the museum gave me fully. It was a portrait of the angel Moroni, or Mormon, who told Joseph Smith where to find the golden tablets of the Books of Mormon. The original picture was drawn from the description given by Smith and four or five others of the original Mormons who saw the angel. I did not know before that there had been an angel in the case, but the old fellow told me that Moroni was a prophet who lived in America A.D. 400, and wrote a book in strange characters on golden tablets, and buried it and died, apparently without doing anything particular. The book remained hidden until Joseph Smith found favour in the eyes of Moroni, whose angel appeared to him and pointed out the place of burial. Smith dug up the golden plates and translated them, and then the angel, with true American economy, took back the precious tablets. I began to laugh at the absurd tale, but I found that it really is part of the Mormon creed.

I found at the Walker Hotel a little paper giving the Thirteen Articles of Faith of the Mormon Church :—

"ARTICLES OF FAITH OF THE MORMON CHURCH.

" 1. We believe in God, the Eternal Father, and in His Son Jesus Christ, and in the Holy Ghost.

" 2. We believe that men will be punished for their own sins and not for Adam's transgression.

" 3. We believe that through the atonement of Christ, all mankind may be saved, by obedience to the laws and ordinances of the Gospel.

" 4. We believe that these ordinances are : First, faith in the Lord Jesus Christ ; second, Repentance ; third, Baptism by immersion for the remission of sins ; fourth, Laying on of hands for the Gift of the Holy Ghost.

" 5. We believe that a man must be called of God, by 'prophecy, and by the laying on of hands,' by those who are in authority, to preach the Gospel and administer in the ordinances thereof.

"6. We believe in the same organization that existed in the primitive church, viz. apostles, prophets, pastors, teachers, evangelists, &c.

"7. We believe in the gift of tongues, prophecy, revelation, visions, healing, interpretation of tongues, &c.

"8. We believe the Bible to be the Word of God, as far as it is translated correctly; we also believe the Book of Mormon to be the Word of God.

"9. We believe all that God has revealed, all that He does now reveal, and we believe that He will yet reveal many great and important things pertaining to the Kingdom of God.

"10. We believe in the literal gathering of Israel and in the restoration of the Ten Tribes. That Zion will be built upon this continent. That Christ will reign personally upon the earth, and that the earth will be renewed and receive its paradisic glory.

"11. We claim the privilege of worshipping Almighty God according to the dictates of our conscience, and allow all men the same privilege, let them worship how, where or what they may.

"12. We believe in being subject to kings, presidents, rulers and magistrates, in obeying, honouring and sustaining the law.

"13. We believe in being honest, true, chaste, benevolent, virtuous, and in doing good to *all men;* indeed, we may say that we follow the admonition of Paul, 'We believe all things, we hope all things,' we have endured many things, and hope to be able to endure all things. If there is anything virtuous, lovely or of good report or praiseworthy, we seek after these things."

The tenth article is very curious, and must be taken from the book of Mormon. There is surely no text in the Bible that can be twisted into a reference to America as the inheritance of the chosen people.

We left Salt Lake City on the 7th of November, and travelled with a gentleman from the Eastern States settled in Utah, and his mother, who had been on a visit to him, and they told us a good deal about the Mormons. Putting aside, as manifestly untrue, the horrible tales current in Salt Lake City, where of course there is a great deal of friction between the Gentiles and the Mormon population, there remains quite sufficient to show that they are very undesirable members of a nation. They will not allow the ordinary laws of the country to govern them. Their object is to be a community to themselves, governed by their own officers, or, as they say, the Church, which consists of the President and a body called, I think, Apostles. These men claim and obtain absolute power over the mass of the Mormons. If any disposition to rebel is shown, immediately an elder has a revelation which of course all believers are bound to obey. Formerly stronger measures were used. Officers called Destroying Angels would shoot down offenders in the streets, and it was on this account that Uncle Sam built Fort Douglass and keeps a whole regiment there. Even Mr. S. said that Salt Lake City would be more prosperous if it were not that there is a constant fear of the Mormons doing something violent.

The Mormons are still sufficiently in the majority to keep the City government entirely in their own hands. The young men are allowed to mix with the world, but the girls are kept in, and are taught that their only salvation is in marriage. The Mormon women are said to be very immoral, even Amelia, the Prophet's favourite wife, having sunk to the lowest depths. In families children cling to their own mothers, and are jealous of the other wives' families, so that there is great bitterness and heart-burning, and polygamy would die out of itself were it not that the heads of the church hold to it, as a means of fixing members they fear to lose. Our informant told us he had a friend who refused to go on a mission, thereby exciting the suspicions of the elders, who compelled him to take a second wife, much against his inclination.

Several important members have left the body, notably the Walkers, who provided for all their wives, and returned to decent life. The tithe, which is levied from all the community, is a stumbling-block to many. The large sums raised are paid to the Church, and are never accounted for, and it is the general belief that they go into private pockets, and that the Temple will never be completed because it forms a good excuse for the disappearance of the funds. It was commenced about 1850.

Polygamy is said to be more common in the country than in Salt Lake City itself. Peasants marry several wives, not because they want wives, but because they want field-labourers. A gentleman told us he had been in a hovel near Provo, where an old man lived with two wives and six grown-up daughters, two of these women, half-sisters, were to be married that week to a neighbour, as old as their father, who only wanted them to work on his farm. Rich Mormons, we were told, bought farms in different parts of the country, and established a wife on each farm, who managed it for her husband, he going to visit her when it was time to collect the profits.

It was three o'clock (November 7th) when we left Salt Lake City, and shortly after crossed a pretty little stream called the "River of Jordan." Our train was three and a half hours late, said to be a most unusual thing on this line. A broken axle on a goods' train had delayed the San Francisco express.

It was a brilliant starlight night and Castle Gate looked wonderfully grand. It is a bare rock sloping a little on one side, but perfectly perpendicular on the side fronting the railway, and quite on the edge of the line. It is 400 to 500 feet high, and only twenty to thirty feet broad. I believe there is a similar-shaped, but smaller, rock opposite. Some years ago a sailor, who was working on the road as foreman of a gang of plate-layers, undertook to go up it and plant the national flag on the top. It was considered an impossible feat, but one morning he went there with his gang, who were delighted to assist him, and somehow he got up and fulfilled his promise. The flag-staff is still there, but of course the flag has been torn to bits by the wind.

The Denver and Rio Grande Railroad is the most uncomfortable line we came across in our travels. The food in the buffet car was uneatable. There was actually only one egg on board. The berths are very uncomfortable on account of the narrow gauge. I tried an upper berth, but could not sleep. The cold was intense, as the porter let the fire go out. About five o'clock I got up, and took refuge in the first-class carriage, which was very warm.

Luckily, we got an excellent breakfast at Cimarron, and then, warmed and comforted, we settled ourselves on the platform at the back of the carriage to enjoy the grand scenery. The much-advertised observation car did not put in an appearance. It was a very fine sunny day, the snow five or six inches deep, and the cold so great that the Gunnison river was frozen quite across in several places, though it is a rapid stream.

As the train was so late, we arrived at the Black Cañon in broad daylight instead of at 5 a.m. We were disappointed with it. It was fine, but not equal to our expectations, but Marshall's Pass exceeded them. It is glorious. The train winds up the mountain-side for about two hours through magnificent scenery, all the grander for the covering of deep snow. As we emerged from every snow-shed, we could look down on the road we had just travelled, and sometimes we could see it double three or four times. The Ouray mountains form the background, and are seen from so many different points of view, that we could hardly believe it was always the same range. Many other fine mountains, whose names nobody knew, completed the picture. At the top of the Pass there is an immense snow-shed, in which the train halts for examination of wheels, &c., before commencing the descent, which is very steep, with many sharp curves. Everybody got out of the train, and marched about. The other passengers were much amused at my pocketing a splinter of wood off the shed to take home as a souvenir. One gentleman "guessed" he would take a rail home. I believe we were the only tourists in the train. We were fortunate in having a very pleasant conductor over this part of the line, who told us which way to look for views. The run down hill was very fine. The second engine, that had helped to pull us up, ran some way in front of us to make sure the line was in order. We could generally see it on the zigzags of the line running in the opposite direction to what we were going.

We arrived desperately hungry at Salida, where we found an excellent dinner. A German-American young lady called her father's attention to the energy with which we attacked the roast turkey. She was quite shocked by our voracity, but she had been living on the fat of the land at Salida for some days, while we had hardly had a well-cooked meal since leaving Vancouver.

Again we put on all our rugs, and settled ourselves to brave the cold at the back of the car for the sake of the grand Cañon of the Arkansas and the Royal Gorge. It was very cold, very smoky, and very dusty; but the scenery was worth the discomfort. The cañon is very pretty—the rocks come close to the river, and are very steep and grand, and broken into fine shapes ; but the Royal Gorge is overpowering. It is worthy of the Canadian Pacific, it is so sternly grand, the rocks so lofty and precipitous. There is only just room for rail (a single line, narrow gauge) and river ; indeed in one part the road is actually suspended over the river, and the colouring was very fine. The sun was in the west, and did not shine straight down the cañon, but caught a peak here, a boulder there, bringing out the rich red of the granite. This again is worth all the trouble of the whole journey. It is sublime.

Daylight just lasted long enough for us to see all the cañon. Soon after leaving it dusk came on, and we saw no more. We arrived at Colorado Springs about 7.30 p.m, and went to the Antlers Hotel, which is stuffy, badly managed, and the food wretched.

The excitement about the Presidential Election was very great everywhere. It was practically certain that Harrison was elected, although all the returns were not in, and his supporters were shaking hands and crowing lustily. Unfortunately, the man in charge of the luggage was a Republican, and showed his joy by pitching the boxes about wildly. The unfortunate Democrats were regretting not only their defeat, but their lost bets. A brakesman on the train had lost his gold watch, which he had staked against four silver ones, his thirty dollars overcoat just bought for the winter, his coat, hat, and shirt.

We met that day a curious example of American manners. When Edward went to the Pulman car lavatory in the morning he found three railway-men at their ablutions. They brushed their hair with the Pulman brush, and they used the Pulman soap and towels; the passengers had to wait until these men had finished.

Friday, November 9th.—We took a carriage and drove first to Manitou, a pretty village just at the foot of Pike's Peak. Here we tasted natural soda-water from the great spring, and then drove on to Ute Pass, as far as the Rainbow Falls, a nice little waterfall, which may catch a ray of sunshine for about five minutes during the day. The pass is a pretty rocky defile. From there we went to the Garden of the Gods, 500 acres of waste land with remarkable sandstone rocks. The most ordinary shape is the mushroom, the head being a different kind of stone from the stalk. The Tower of Babel, Jupiter, and the Cathedral are very large rocks. Unfortunately the Cathedral spires are not on the Cathedral, but some paces off, as if they had been brought there ready to put on when the Cathedral was completed. The Cathedral forms one side of the Beautiful Gate, and the Sentinel the other. After passing through it, we looked back on the wonderful scene. The sun was on the Gate, making the red sandstone rocks glow, and through them, as if in a frame, were the beautiful green slopes leading up to the snow-covered Pike's Peak. The sky was intensely blue. Altogether the combination of form and colour made a perfect picture. Close to the red Cathedral is a curious white rock.

We drove on to Glen Eyrie, where our driver assured us there was nothing to see, so, as we foolishly believed him, we missed the curious rock called the Major Domo. The drive back from Glen Eyrie is over a curious, natural embankment, from which the views, towards the mountains on one side, and over the immense plains on the other, are very fine.

Colorado Springs is a great health-resort—people come even from England. The air is so pure, dry and bracing, that people who settle here in good health, merely for business purposes, find it difficult to live anywhere else afterwards. We heard of a case of consumption stopped by the wonderful Colorado climate, but the poor fellow was obliged to remain there for the rest of his life. In the summer invalids go up to the parks, which are said to be very beautiful. The skies of Colorado are famous for their beauty, and certainly we have seen none finer except at Biarritz, where the sunsets are unrivalled. After making some purchases of the handiwork of the Navajo Indians, who live somewhere in the neighbourhood, we took the 4.10 p.m. train for Denver, passing the small Palmer Lake and the Castle Rock, which is very handsome, on the way, as well as many of the curious rocks of Monument Park. We arrived at Denver frightfully hungry; but owing to the hotel boy, a mere child, telling us that dinner went on until 8 o'clock, we reached the dining-room just too late, and could get nothing but supper. Why so large an hotel should stop dinner at 7.30 is a question I recommend to the consideration of the director who sent us there. Supper is a most disagreeable meal. We made a considerable disturbance. We interviewed the manager, but could not even get a plateful of soup. The Windsor is a good hotel, with exceptionally stupid and careless clerks, even for America.

Saturday, November 10th.—Fair, but very cold. We walked about the town, which has grown rapidly to a very fine large city, and bought some buffalo robes, which we had been searching for all our journey. They used to be very plentiful and cheap; but now all the buffaloes are killed, and the shopkeeper, an Englishman, named Taylor, said he did not expect he should get any more. We got also another Navajo Indian blanket. It is said the women stretch the warp from one tree to another, instead of in a loom.

After dinner we went to a friend's rooms, opposite the hotel, to see the great triumphal Republican torchlight procession. Before leaving the hotel we had the pleasure of hearing a performance on the drum by Major Hendershof, known as the Drummer Boy of the Rappahannock, accompanied by his son on a big drum, and a stout party on the flute. It was the first time we ever heard the drum as a solo instrument, and we were delighted with it. They came with the Leadville Republican Drum Band, which marched into the large hall of the hotel military fashion, and gave us several tunes. The favourite national air in the Northern States is "Marching through Georgia." It was always a great satisfaction to me to find that though the Northerners hate us much, they hate the South still more, and the

South have a very lively contempt for Northerners. Ireland and England are bosom cronies compared to the North and South.

The procession came up the main street, and turned along the cross street, and, as our friend's rooms were at the corner, we saw it splendidly. It took an hour and a half to pass. The procession was a curious mixture of politics and advertisements. First came, as part of the procession itself, two platoons of police on large white horses, then the Pioneer Corps Old Guard, a most exclusive club, which never exceeds twelve members, and wears bearskin hats and magnificent uniforms. Then came an unhappy democrat, who, in fulfilment of a bet, had to walk in the republican procession carrying a banner inscribed, "I am of the spoils"; he was enthusiastically cheered. Then came, according to the newspapers, a number of generals with their "aides" and staffs, colonels, majors, and commodores without end, probably all decent shopkeepers of Denver. Then clubs in quaint uniforms carrying banners with amusing inscriptions, "Grover, Grover, did you ever get left?" "Grover, Grover, get out of the clover." "Please pass the crow to Grover." This refers to a celebrated banquet in Chicago. Bets were made by twenty-four gentlemen that they would dine together after the election, and the twelve victors should feast on snipe, while the twelve vanquished should each consume a roast crow. Grover is Mr. Cleveland's christian name. Carts decorated with banners and lanterns came at intervals, sometimes entirely commercial, as, "Ask your grocer for Bluine;" sometimes wholly patriotic; sometimes a judicious mixture, as "Celebrate our Victory with Heidsieck's dry champagne, importer (name and address followed). The principal milliner had sent out a car with all her young ladies on board. A favourite emblem was the rooster, especially perched on the top of a broom wrapped in the national flag. Several carts contained men throwing fire about and fireworks. When they passed we had to shut the windows. One club called itself the " Devil's Own Crew," and was led by his Majesty. Many leading merchants of Denver rode in the procession. There was a coloured contingent, which is not a usual feature in republican demonstrations as the negroes are mostly democrats. Of course, there were several bands of music, and many amusing devices. On the following Monday at noon, there was to be another procession, which unfortunately we did not see. Several democrats had, in fulfilment of bets, to wheel victorious republicans in barrows down the main street. There seemed to be no end to the bets on the election, not only jokes like this, but money bets. A lady in the hotel had won a large sum through a New York broker in the ordinary business way.

There is a great deal to see round Denver by excursions of two or three days, but the weather was too cold for that kind of thing. In Denver itself there is little of interest. A gentleman took us to see some smelting works, which were interesting, and afterwards drove us round the residential part of the town, where there are many good houses and fine churches. Denver is the handsomest and most prosperous-looking town we saw after leaving Chicago, which it excels in beauty of situation. The long range of snow mountains in the distance is very fine.

Monday, November 12*th*.—We left Denver at 7.30 a.m. by the Fort Texas and Fort Worth line for Trinidad. We did this to escape a night in the cars, and also to see the country by daylight. We had reluctantly given up the Silverton excursion, on account of the snow. We were getting a little tired, too, of cañons and passes, and perpetual railway journeys.

The run to Trinidad was very beautiful. The Spanish Peaks and the Sangre de Christo range are well seen, and the grand Pike's Peak is hardly ever out of sight. The view from the top must be very extensive; but, unfortunately, we were six weeks too late to make the ascent, which is not difficult and is made on "burros," i.e. donkeys. Many Spanish words have got into the American language in the old Mexican provinces. The Grand Union Hotel at Trinidad was very dirty, and the food quite uneatable, but nobody ought to omit visiting Trinidad on that account. It is wonderfully well situated. A river runs through the middle of the town; on one side is Fisher's Peak, a mountain with a remarkable rock at the very top, shaped like an anvil, and on the opposite side are smaller hills, on one of which is a monument to the earliest pioneer, after whom it was named Simpson's Rest. Fisher was also one of the first settlers. The town appeared to be growing fast, and could boast already some large works and fine houses, but the old town is Mexican, with adobe buildings and curious beehive-shaped ovens in front of the houses. There are coal-mines close to the town, so coal is only one dollar per ton, while in San Francisco it was twenty-two dollars.

Tuesday, November 13*th.*—We were five minutes late for breakfast, so could not even get a poached egg, though it was only nine o'clock. We took another walk round the town and then came in and sat in our bedroom. Next door was the public sitting-room, which had been let to some travelling dentists. We smelt the ether, and heard the groans of the victim through the closed doors, and then the encouraging remark of the dentist, "All right, they are all out!" All!!!

By-and-by the porter came and said we must leave our room, it was let, but we might sit in the public room with the dentist, if we liked. We did not feel equal to that, so we went out again and walked to the station, buying six lemons for twenty cents on the way. We begged a glass of water, and astonished and amused the grocer very much by squeezing a lemon into the water and drinking it. It was quite a new idea to him. The glass was very dirty, but then everything in Trinidad was dirty. The streets were full of dead cats, dead rabbits, old hats and boots, bones, and tin cans.

We left Trinidad at 12.35, and were very glad to get a good dinner at Raton. We had a very disagreeable journey of twenty-seven hours to El Paso. The scenery is desolate and ugly, plains of sage brush, scrub and sand, with low hills in the distance. The only amusement was watching for the prairie dogs, of which we saw numbers sitting on their burrows, which look like very large ant-hills.

The car was very uncomfortable. Several passengers had their food with them and ate on board, a most objectionable practice, as the smell of food pervades the car, instead of meal-times being used for ventilation. I suppose it is economical, but it is dirty. There were two dreadful children on board. One, a puny, miserable-looking baby, that cried and moaned without ceasing for over twenty hours. At last I suggested to its mother she should retire to the ladies' lavatory with it for a time. "Ah!" she said, "I don't think it would do baby any good." "At any rate," said I cruelly, "it would be a great relief to the rest of us." Curiously enough, that baby ceased its lamentations and behaved quite well the rest of the way. The other was a fine merry boy, who would have been capital fun anywhere else, but he made a dreadful noise and played horses up and down the car with his nurse. His parents had taken the drawing-room, where they enjoyed peace, and left Friedrich in the car for our benefit. The sun was blazing, but the hot-water pipes in the car were kept too hot to touch all day, as if it had been very cold.

The cattle we passed looked very thin and weak; often we saw dead cows lying about, and often heaps of their bones. It has been a very bad season, no rain for eighteen months, and, therefore, no food for the cattle, which are entering the winter season in very bad condition. If it prove severe, the loss will be great.

El Paso is a pretty, prosperous little town, with a hideous new court-house, a very fair hotel, called the Grand Central, and large smelting works. Ore is brought in great quantities from Mexico, as well as from the States, because it is easier to work a mixture of different ores, than all from one mine. There is a heavy import duty on metals, but none on ore.

A tram-line, the only international line in the world, took us to Paso del Norte, just across the frontier. We visited the old church of adobe, or sun-dried brick, whitewashed. Inside, the church is very quaint, with a fine roof of semi-circular carved beams. There were many shops selling Mexican goods, and the whole place looked foreign, and the people dressed Mexican fashion and smelt of garlic. The Mexican Central Station is a very fine building. This is an English line. Americans never build handsome "depôts," as they call stations.

We left El Paso at 4 p.m. on November 15th, and had our luggage examined by a gorgeous person with a tall sombrero and a pistol, and no end of silver braid and buttons. He was perfectly polite and pleasant, as we found afterwards is the universal custom of Mexicans. Our plan had included visits to Chihuahua and Zacatecas; but Mr. Mackenzie, of the Mexican Central, advised us not to stop there, because it would be very cold as they are on very high ground, and the hotels are poor, so we went on to Querétaro. We found Friedrich on board the Pulman car, but he behaved better, being perhaps rather tired. Chihuahua looked very pretty from the train; it is two miles from the station. The country was much the same as in New Mexico as far as Zacatecas. We arrived there at 8.20 a.m. on November 17th.

Zacatecas is a great mining centre, and worthy of a visit. The mines are close to the line, so that we saw in one place horses trampling the ore, and in another we saw water being drawn from the mines in raw-hide buckets. It is said that labour is so cheap here that machinery does not pay. The town is surrounded by lovely hills and deep ravines, and is full of fine churches. From Zacatecas to Mexico the country is very pretty, and sometimes exceedingly beautiful. We spent all the morning at the back of the car. We reached Aguas Calientes, a very pretty place, about noon, and had a good meal there. The vegetation was a great delight to us. Every now and then a new plant appeared, first rare, then gradually becoming common. First came the magvey or aloe, a single plant here and there, but later there were great fields of it, as it is cultivated largely in Mexico. Then we caught sight of an "organ cactus," first a few spikes at long intervals, later on great hedges of it. The hills are finer as one gets south, and more varied in their shapes. We admired a curious bell-shaped peak, but could not learn its name. At Encarnacion there is a high trestle-bridge worthy of notice. At Silao we got a poor dinner, the only bad meal on the road.

The railway-station appears to be the favourite lounge of the people. Many bring baskets made of straw and horsehair, gloves, sweets, fruit, and other little things, to sell to the passengers. The "dulce de Celaya," a mixture of goats' milk and sugar, nicely flavoured, is very good.

There was a guard of soldiers at every station, who, if not useful, were very ornamental. After the long years of war, first against the Spanish Viceroys, then amongst themselves, and then the American and French invasions, numbers of men who had been soldiers took to the road as brigands, and plundered the trains and coaches, especially those carrying bullion. President Diaz took the matter in hand, and it is said that now the last highway robber has been shot.

The people are very good-looking, with the blackest hair and eyes, the whitest teeth, and the most picturesque rags ever seen.

We left the train at Querétaro at 10.35 p.m., after a journey of fifty-four and a half hours. We had telegraphed for a carriage, which met us at the station, and off we went in the dark, until we pulled up at a *porte-cochère* carefully shut and bolted. It was the Hotel del Ferro Carril. Our driver knocked hard until some one came, and they had a long conversation together before we were admitted. We then found ourselves in a small court-yard surrounded by a building one storey high, no light, except the lantern of the man who had admitted us, and the glorious stars. The man rushed off for a key, and showed us into a long, narrow room, with no window and tiled floor. He unrolled a hearth-rug, and put it by the bedside, and then rushed off again for the sheets and blankets. It was too small a room for two, so he had to fetch a second key and more blankets. Everything was very clean, but the mosquitoes took care we did not sleep. Perhaps, too, we were rather excited at finding ourselves at last in Mexico. People always pulled long faces when we said we were going to Mexico, and advised us to carry revolvers, and described the natives as nothing short of ogres, who spent all their time robbing and slaying the unwary traveller. The Americans cling particularly to these opinions; and, strange to say, the Mexicans have an equally bad opinion of the Americans. Often Mexicans have said to us, "We knew at once you were not Americans; we love the English." This dislike of the Mexicans to the Americans no doubt is caused mostly by the war, and partly also by the objectionable Americans who, having made their own country too hot to hold them, take refuge in Mexico, much as the English used to take refuge at Boulogne.

I have travelled a good deal in Europe, but I never met so pleasant a people as the Mexicans. Not only are they courteous to strangers, but to each other. Their politeness is Castilian, and their kindness quite Yorkshire. The merry fellow in rags that would disgrace a scarecrow, pulls off his hat to greet his lady friend whose chemise, petticoat, and reboso are not worth sixpence altogether. They have no awkward feeling of inferiority because you are richer than they, nor are they the least presumptuous. In short, they are thoroughbred, if such a term means anything. They have only one fault, they are dirty, which is not surprising, as water is so scarce that it is difficult often to get enough to drink. At one station on the line the women were actually waiting with large jugs to get water from the tender of the locomotive, it was so difficult to procure in the neighbourhood.

Sunday, November 18th.—We rose early, and having found our friend of the night before, made him understand that we wanted breakfast, so he took us through another court and into the dining-room, and gave us a very good breakfast. The coffee came in a tea-pot and the milk in a watering-can, and we drank it out of tumblers, and the waiter talked Spanish to us, which we did not understand, and we talked English to him which he did not understand, so we were very merry and enjoyed our meal immensely. Then we found the landlord, a courtly old gentleman, who had served under Maximilian and knew some French. He got a carriage for us and told the driver where to take us. It was a closed carriage, so we both perched on the seat by the driver, who was much amused and chattered away in his own tongue, pointing out all the great churches, &c. We admired his sombrero, so he stuck it on my head to see if I looked well in it.

First we went to the Cerro de las Campanas, or Hill of the Bells, where Maximilian and the two Mexican Generals, Mejia and Miramon were shot. Three small stone columns mark the spot; railings and brass plates have disappeared. Maximilian is generally regarded as rather an interesting person in England, but in Mexico they knew him too well, his cruelty, his vanity, and his weakness. His history was simply this. Being over head and ears in debt, and having quarrelled with his brother, the Emperor of Austria, he accepted the throne of Mexico, knowing well that it was only offered him by a faction. He bargained that he must have a handsome sum of money down, 3,000,000 dollars, with which he paid off the mortgages on his favourite residence, Miramar, and other pressing debts. Maximilian landed in Mexico on May 29th, 1864, and managed, by the help of the French army, under Bazaine, and the church, to keep up a kind of court in the city of Mexico; but the nation would not accept him. Juarez, the great President, never ceased to exercise authority, although once driven by the French as far as Paso del Norte. On October 3rd, 1865, Maximilian signed the decree, that in future all prisoners taken in arms against him should be shot as traitors, although at the time two-thirds of the country were in arms against him. Under this law, which he and the Empress Charlotte signed in a little boudoir off the ball-room between two dances, men were shot in cold blood after the engagements, sometimes twenty or thirty, sometimes hundreds at a time. When the American Civil War was ended, the United States put pressure on Napoleon to remove his troops, which he did willingly, seeing what a hopeless, never-ending contest it was.

After Bazaine's departure Maximilian took refuge in Querétaro, which, after a siege, was given up to the national army, and he was made prisoner and executed on June 19th, 1867.

It is said that Juarez would gladly have spared him, but the widows and orphans of the poor fellows murdered in obedience to that terrible Law of October 3rd, compelled the President to do justice. Since then the Republic has been firmly established, and the country has progressed rapidly. The present ruler, Porfirio Diaz, was one of Juarez' generals. His brilliant military exploits did much to dishearten the French, so Bazaine tried to induce him to betray the great President, and become ruler himself, but Diaz was not that kind of man.

The view from the Cerro over Querétaro and the neighbourhood is very lovely. The brilliant colouring of sky, verdure, white buildings, and tile-covered domes of churches, all shining in the delicious sunshine, the large haciendas or country-houses outside the town, and the lovely hills which surround it, made a glorious picture. A more unlikely place to stand a siege could not well be found, as the hills command it on all sides. From the Cerro we drove back to the town and through the picturesque streets, past Santa Clara, Santa Rosa and other fine churches, to the cathedral where a great service was going on, so we could not walk about. I went to the front and knelt among the worshippers, and received the blessing, and was asperged with holy water from the altar, but Edward was too severely Protestant for that, so he did not see the inside of the cathedral. Then we visited the Town Hall and saw the coffin in which Maximilian was first placed, and the stools with handsome satin cushions, but no backs, on which Mejia and Miramon sat at their trial. There was a portrait of Maximilian, a poor weak silly face. The Town Hall was a very nice building with large rooms. The driver pointed out to us the windows of the room the Emperor occupied during the siege, and also the windows of the room in which he was afterwards imprisoned in a convent. We visited another church in which were some curious wooden images, and then, as the driver seemed to think we had seen everything, we went back to the hotel and hunted up the landlord to ask him where we could buy opals. There are plenty of people about who come up to strangers and offer opals for sale, but they are poor things, just like cornelians.

The Mexican opal is not like the stone we call opal. There are some very like it, but they are not good. The best are red stones, transparent, with green fire, which when good are beautiful, but we never found a good one on sale. We saw two or three very fine ones worn by the owners. Then there are some that look like drops of water when held in the hand, and show all the prismatic colours, but these are too delicate to use. The colours would not show at any distance. There are yellow ones, which look like cairngorms, until the light catches them, and then they too show all colours. We were directed to a dealer in a back room, upstairs, in an ordinary house, nothing to show a dealer lived there. He had nothing really good, but we bought three at five dollars each (15s.), the Mexican dollar is worth only 3s. We then returned to the market-place, which was full of people, as Sunday is their market-day. There were fruit, rough but very pretty pottery, vegetables, meat, and other useful things on sale; but what astonished us was the quantity of toys, tiny jugs and crockery, little wooden things, tiny baskets of all shapes, the sweetest little things, which we were delighted to buy for a few pence, but what could the natives do with them?—and we were certainly the only strangers in Quérétaro. I saw many people in the poorest attire buy these things. It was new to us then, but we soon found that in Mexico, " Il n'y a de nécessaire que le superflu."

The natives never think of wasting money on clothes, anything does for clothes, an old sack is not at all an uncommon garment, but they buy ices, toys and cakes freely. It is the climate that does it, the delicious sunshine that is itself food and clothes, and makes mere existence a pleasure. There was fruit on the stalls that we never saw or heard of before, and as the good folks saw we did not understand the language, they ate them to show how good they were. It was great fun going round amongst them, they were all so merry, and jolly and friendly. Wherever we went a lad followed, trying to sell us a paper of small opals—we had bought one from him still embedded in a bit of rock. I was so lucky as to pick up a very old Spanish coin in good condition. It had been used as a hat decoration, and the owner wanted to change it for a modern quarter-dollar. He was offering it to a stall-keeper, who did not like the look of it, so I stepped in and made the exchange. I found I had really cheated the poor fellow, as the landlord told me it was a good old coin, and he would be glad to give me a dollar and a half for it.

We were very sorry to leave the market-place, but our train started at 11.35 a.m., so we went back to the hotel, and paid our very modest bill, and thanked the worthy landlord for his kindness. The lad with the opals was still with us, so the landlord bargained with him, and we bought them for about a third of what he first asked. Then we went to the station, where there was the funniest lot of people waiting to see the train come in. If it were not for the Atlantic Ocean we would certainly spend all our winters at Quérétaró.

There was no Pulman car on the train, but the first class was very comfortable, with only a few gentlemen on board. On leaving Quérétaro the train passes under one of the arches of the immense aqueduct, which is two miles long. The water is brought altogether five miles to supply the city. The first station is for the Hercules Cotton-Mills, a most important factory, and worthy of a visit. There are now many cotton-mills in Mexico which are very prosperous. The Indians (as the natives are always called, though they are not in the least like the Red Indians of North America) make very good workpeople, so long as their wages are paid regularly. If the wages are not forthcoming on the proper day, they are frightened at once, remembering how it was in the old unsettled times before the Republic was firmly established. The scenery was exceedingly pretty, and at every station there was an amusing crowd of merry picturesque people selling fruit, &c., or just begging. We got a capital dinner at San Juan del Rio. We just got a glimpse of a large church at Tula, but could not see anything of the Aztec remains, and unfortunately we never returned as we intended, to see this interesting old place. Daylight just lasted long enough for us to see the wonderful Tajo de Nochistongo, an immense ditch, commenced in 1607 to open a way through the mountains for the superfluous waters of the great Mexican table-land, which have no natural outlet. At first a tunnel was made, but that was perpetually coming to grief in one way or another, so it was finally decided to make this immense cut, which was completed in 1789. The greatest width is 630 feet, and its greatest depth 196 feet, and its length 67,537 feet. The railroad runs along the side of it, about fifty feet above the stream.

This great work did a good deal to drain the country, but there are still floods every year, and new works on a very large scale are being carried out at present. After passing through the Tajo we had a very fine sunset, and then a large round moon came out, but did not give much light, so we saw no more until we reached the city of Mexico at 7 p.m. Having been told that the Mexicans were great thieves, we were astonished to find that it is usual to hand over one's keys to a baggage collector, who passes the boxes through the Custom's-house and brings them on to the hotel. We had put a bag of money in a trunk, but nothing was missing. A bag of money sounds like great wealth, but it takes very few dollars to fill a bag, and even in the States one meets with little gold, some notes, but principally silver. In England one goes out shopping with money in one's pocket, and brings home one's purchases in a cart, but in the States one goes out with one's money in a cart, and returns with the purchases in one's pocket—thanks to the heavy coinage and the high prices of everything.

We went to the Hotel Yturbide, where we got a large room looking into a bit of garden with a tank of stagnant water. We had to go through this little garden on our way to the Café Anglais for dinner, as the restaurant in the hotel was closed. In the dim light we saw large creeping things going about in numbers. We picked our way through them carefully, but a Spanish lady passing, laughed at my precaution, and deliberately put her tiny foot on a horrible creature. We saw afterwards by daylight they were immense cockroaches about three inches long and two inches across, flat and black, with either claws or horns like stag-beetles.

Monday, November 19th.—We changed our hotel and got very good accommodation at the new Hotel Jardin, which has a restaurant on the premises. The hotel and the restaurant are generally separate businesses. The food was not very good, but then it was very cheap. Coffee and bread excellent, and plenty of milk. We paid a dollar each per day for breakfast, lunch, and dinner; and three and a half dollars for our apartment, which consisted of a small sitting-room and a large bedroom (with two beds) out of it. The hotel is an old monastery, overlooking a large garden. The Hotel Yturbide is a magnificent building, erected in the last century as a private residence, and used as a palace by the unfortunate Yturbide during his reign of a year. Yturbide was called the Liberator, because it was under his leadership that the long struggle of the Mexicans against the Spanish Viceroys was finally successful. His immense popularity turned his head, and he made himself emperor; but the people have a rooted objection to emperors, so they sent him into exile with a very handsome pension. After a short time he allowed himself to be persuaded to try to regain his throne, landed at Vera Cruz in 1824, was taken prisoner at once, and shot. Since 1855 the palace has been an hotel. We were told of several good restaurants in Mexico; but we were generally tired and glad to dine quietly at home. There was always something we could eat, and we could get poached eggs if we were not satisfied. We probably could have made arrangements with the restaurant-keeper to have fed us better if we had stayed any time.

The Mexican onyx, of which we think so much in England, must be very cheap, for I noticed both in the hotel, otherwise very simply furnished, and elsewhere, that it is used as commonly as marble with us.

The post-office is well managed. Every day a list is fastened up on the wall of letters *poste restante*, and of those insufficiently addressed. After examining the list one goes to the clerk and asks for one's letters, giving the day they arrived. Travellers must take note of a regulation which lost us many letters. After a month all unclaimed letters are opened and returned to the senders.

We had a delightful day loafing about the streets, which are full of handsome shops and wonderful old churches. The cathedral is worthy of the country. It is finely situated on the principal square, the Plaza Mayor, a very large open space with a garden called the Zocalo in the centre, and a band-stand where military bands play daily. The cathedral was commenced in 1573; it was the third church erected on this site, formerly occupied by the great Aztec Temple. It has two towers, from which there is a magnificent view of the whole table-land of Mexico. We loved the cathedral. Whenever we had half an hour to spare during our stay in Mexico we always made for the Plaza Mayor to look at it again, and every time it seemed to be more beautiful.

Tuesday, November 20*th.*—We went to the cathedral and visited the interior, which is very grand. The main altar is gaudy; but behind it, in the east end, is the glorious altar De los Reyes, all carved woodwork, gilt, and decorated with coloured statues and pictures, in a style named after its inventor, the Spanish architect Churrigverra, who flourished about 1690. Many of the side-chapels are richly adorned. The choir is very grand. Railings of tumbago, a mixture of gold, silver and copper, of enormous value, surround the choir, and make a pathway to the high altar. As we were peering through the doorway at the beautiful carved work of the stalls, a charming old ecclesiastic, evidently of authority, saw us and beckoned to us to come in. We tried very hard to have some conversation, but we could not get on well, though Spanish is an easy language, very like Italian. He asked us if we had cathedrals in England, and if we were Catholics, and he pointed out the beauties of the cathedral, of which he was evidently very proud, and had the old choir-books opened to show us the splendid illuminated letters and quaint pictures. On leaving he shook hands with us most kindly, and I dropped the best court curtsey I could manage, which I found afterwards was quite the correct thing for me to do.

Mexicans shake hands a good deal. I have seen a servant after bringing his master's luggage to the train, and taking his last orders, shake hands most cordially with him. He was a soldier servant, too, and his master an officer.

People who came to our assistance when we were unable to make ourselves understood always shook hands with us. The upper class mostly know French, and often strangers would stop and ask if they could help us when they saw we were in difficulties.

It is very amusing walking about Mexico, people offer you lottery tickets every minute, and there are delightful little stalls in the streets selling the oddest collection of odds and ends, from amongst which you sometimes can pick up an interesting old coin, or an old painting on copper. Sunday is the great day for these street-sellers, many of whom just spread their wares on the pavement. We often wondered who bought the glass stoppers without bottles, the fragments of brass and iron, umbrella tops, and similar valuables.

We found a nice old ivory figure in a little shop, amongst a lot of things of which not one was worth sixpence. I know well, for I looked into every hole and corner hoping to find another bit of ivory. I never found a good old Spanish fan, though I sought diligently for one. If I found an old fan it was not good—if good it was not old.

Doors and windows are generally open, and one can look in and see the dressmakers and tailors and cobblers at work, and the women making tortillas, the national dish. The tortilla-maker has a sloping slab of granite on four legs and a granite rolling-pin. She takes maize and crushes it without any preliminary grinding, mixing it with water until it becomes a soft paste. This is very hard work. Then she takes up a little bit, flattens it between her hands and pats it until it is quite thin like a pancake, and then it is cooked and eaten hot. Everybody seems happy and jolly, chattering like magpies, and delighted to see strangers. We sat in our window a long time watching a cabman and his wife have their dinner. She had brought it in a basket, and evidently she thought well of it and pressed him to eat, and when the husband had eaten as much as he wished of each dish she finished it. There were several courses, and they chattered the whole time.

Next day we again wandered about the city and visited the Academy, where there are some very fine old pictures, and just looked into the Museum, where the wonderful Aztec calendar stone, stone of sacrifice, &c., are kept. Mexico must have been very rich and magnificent in the old Spanish times. There are numbers of magnificent houses built round courtyards and decorated with fountains, statues, tiles and carvings. One house, built by the son or grandson of Cortez and La Marina, is entirely covered outside with tiles. The effect is curious and very handsome. The National Bank, the Mexican Railway Offices, and many other places of business occupy fine old houses formerly belonging to great Spanish families. The inner courtyard is still the favourite plan for a Mexican house, no doubt it is cool and pleasant in summer. The carriage is kept in it under the balcony which leads to the upper rooms, and sometimes the horses are groomed there. Plants stand about, and bird-cages, and sometimes a big dog.

There are almost as many churches as houses. It is said that some time ago the church owned two-thirds of all the wealth and land in the country, but as on several occasions they opposed the Republican Government and were found to be conspiring to overturn it, laws were passed depriving them of the power to own land at all, and abolishing convents and monasteries, and confiscating all their property, and forbidding the clergy to appear in the streets in distinctive dress. As the Mexicans are very devout Catholics it was thought the church would win the day, but the people stuck by the Government. Great streets were made right through the old ecclesiastical buildings, and when the priests excommunicated the workpeople who demolished them, they protected themselves by sewing relics and pictures of saints on to their garments and went on merrily. Often one sees a church turned into a warehouse or a railway station. What seems to me a great pity is that the oldest Catholic Church in Mexico, San Francisco, in which Cortez often heard mass, has been cut up into two Protestant places of worship, and part of the old church pulled down. San Domingo has escaped and is very large and handsome, the altars richly carved and gilded up to the roof, with coloured cherubs and faces introduced—the Churriguerresque style again. Santa Theresa is half destroyed. We never passed a church without looking in, there is generally something worth seeing, and often interesting services were going on with pleasant music.

Friday, November 23rd.—We started early to see the Monte de Piedad, which is on the Plaza Mayor. This is a national institution, founded by the Conde de Regla in 1775 to enable the poor to obtain loans on pledges at almost nominal rates of interest, and so keep them out of the hands of the usurers. At one time it was so highly thought of that family jewels and plate were deposited in the vaults, just for safe keeping during the troubled times, but President Gonzales having seized the funds and, some say, part of the property placed there, its credit was gone. It is now recovering from the blow, but there is nothing of any consequence in the vaults, as they are called, though they are upstairs rooms. Pledges remain unsold a year, then if interest is not paid on the loan, they are brought out, valued by specialists and put up to auction. If the price is not reached they remain a month exposed for sale in the large room on the ground floor, then the price is reduced and they are again put up to auction. This goes on until they are sold. Things go very cheap, but I never saw anything of real value sold there. We picked up a few little things cheap, but now there are so many dealers looking out for jewels, and so many English and American residents ready to buy curios, that things do not remain long unsold if they are really interesting. There are numbers of private pawnbrokers as well, who sometimes have very nice things to sell. We were told that the Mexicans have no prejudice against pawning their things. If a young lady wants a new ball dress she will pawn a necklace to get money for it. We never passed a pawnbroker without going to see what he had. Luckily for us they had not found out the value of old things, so we generally got what we wanted very cheap.

The flower-market is close to the Cathedral, and is full every morning of lovely bouquets, baskets, and devices in flowers at very low prices. On the other side of the Cathedral is the book-market; there we saw nothing remarkable, but probably that was owing to our ignorance. There were plenty of old books, but not illuminated or illustrated.

From the markets we went to the museum, and went through all the rooms. There are some wonderful pictures showing the progress of Cortez from the coast, said to be the very pictures sent to Montezuma at the time. There is Montezuma's feather-decorated shield, and ancient Aztec earthenware without end, some of it very elegant, both in form and decoration. The greatest treasure is a small obsidian vase or jug, wonderfully carved with the figure of a man, whose arms form the handles. There were some of the masks of different materials which puzzle antiquaries so much. They can never have been either useful or ornamental, and as the Spanish conquerors utterly destroyed every Aztec book and record, there is no means of finding out their purpose. In the gallery on the ground floor of the museum the Government has collected all the principal statues of the gods and great carvings, for fear they should be exported on the sly. Luggage leaving the country is always examined to prevent passengers taking any antiquities. The statues of the gods are all hideous; the most celebrated, the idol Huitzilopochtli, is evidently only a collection of attributes.

Teoyainiqui, the goddess of Death, and Chac-Mool, the god of Fire, are human figures. All the names are guess-work, and antiquarians differ among themselves about them. There is not a single beautiful figure; all are curious and many grotesque, but the decorative work is very fine. The feathered serpent, supposed to represent the god Quetzalcoatl, is really fine. This god, it is said, was believed by the Aztecs to have descended from heaven to live among them and teach them agriculture and many useful arts. After a time he left them and went into the mountains, bidding them keep alight the sacred fire until his return to reign over them, when he would come from the east on white wings.

Tradition described him as of a fairer complexion than the Aztecs, so when Cortez arrived from the east, a fair man compared to them, they took the white sails of his ships for the white wings, and many refused to fight against him, believing him to be Quetzalcoatl.

The Stone of the Sun, or Calendar Stone, is covered with beautiful carving, said to be hieroglyphics, very Egyptian in style. The Sacrificial Stone is decorated round the circumference, but the top is almost plain, with a hollow in the centre and a channel from it to the edge. This is said to have been for the blood of the human sacrifices; but if the thousands of victims we read of were really slain on this stone, is it not strange that there should not be the slightest stain on it?

As we wanted to finish all the "sights," we went on to the National Palace on the Plaza Mayor, where there is nothing of note except the picture of the "Cinco de Mayo," the battle on the 5th May, 1862, when the Mexicans, under General Zaragoza, obtained their first success over the French, so it has been ever since a great day with them. We were stopped by the guardian and shown into a handsome apartment until the governor's permission could be obtained, and after waiting some time an elegant little officer appeared, and deeply regretted that owing to the governor's absence we could not visit the palace. We explained that all we wanted was to see the picture. Not even that could be allowed, so we departed; but as we went towards the staircase, we saw an open door and we walked through it and found ourselves in the Hall of the Ambassadors, with the throne and the famous picture. We did not admire it very much after all. Then we went back to the Cathedral to visit the tiny Chapel de las Animas, which is embedded in the Cathedral. No one knows its origin, but it has been there for over 200 years.

We wanted to see the mint, and as La Mineria seemed a very likely translation, we walked to it, but found that was the School of Mines. The secretary kindly sent a man to show us round. He took us into the geological, astronomical, and mechanical rooms, and to the top of the building for the view. All Mexican roofs are flat. Then he took us to the library, which is in a fine old chapel. The altar had not been removed, but was used as a table, although the sacred pictures were still there. A young gentleman was busy with the plans for draining Mexico, which is always flooded after rain, being only very slightly higher than the Lake Texcoco. The streets were full of water, and many drains burst after a moderate rainfall during our visit; but in the rainy season, August, September, and October, the water in the streets is often two feet deep, and men make money by carrying people across them on their backs.

The young engineer kindly showed us the plans and explained them in French. There is to be a long canal going through the three lakes, and then a tunnel, conveying the water through the hills to the north of the city. Once through, the water is to be allowed to find its own way to the sea. Some people think that if all the water is drained away it will interfere with the foundations of the city and bring down some of the buildings.

After seeing so much, and as it was two o'clock, we felt we deserved our lunch, so we went back to the hotel and asked Johnny, the interpreter, to get us a carriage for the afternoon. Johnny is an amusing little fellow, a Mexican, who was brought up in the American Embassy, and speaks English. He got us a nice little victoria, one dollar per hour.

First we came to the Alameda, a pleasant, shady garden, where people walk on Sundays. At the back of it is the Plaza de Morelos, with a statue to the priesthero in the centre, and a lovely old church on each side. Then we went to the Panteone San Fernano, the cemetery where Juarez is buried. His tomb is a beautiful white marble monument by the brothers Islas, Mexicans. It represents Juarez lying dead, supported by a female figure of Mexico, over life-size. It is one of the finest statues we have ever seen. Guerrero, Zaragozo, whose monument bears the inscription Cinco de Mayo, and many of the heroes of the last war, are buried here, and I was surprised to see Mejia's tomb amongst them. Shot as a traitor, he is buried among the very men against whom he fought. The cemetery is very ugly and crowded, part of it under water, and the common folk buried on shelves, as in Italian cemeteries.

We drove to Atzcapotzalco, passing on the way two beautiful bits of architecture. The Casa de los Mascarones, or house of the masks, so called because there are faces amongst the elaborate ornamentation. It is occupied by some poor people who would not let us look inside. I fancy it was a girls' school. The beautiful façade is quite neglected, even grass growing in the cracks. The other was the fountain of the Fiddling Kings, also very elaborate. There used to be an immense aqueduct here, now half pulled down, taking water to Mexico, and this fountain evidently supplied the little village. No one knows who the Fiddling Kings were intended to represent, or anything about it. We drove past the village of Popotla, with a pretty old church, San Esteban, unfortunately with locked doors, and close to it the immense old trunk of the Arbol de la Noche Triste, the tree under which Cortez sat and wept after he had been driven out of Mexico, July 1st, 1520. The tree is still alive. The tears of Cortez must have preserved it, for there does not appear to be another old tree in the neighbourhood. At the next village, Tacuba, there was another fine old church, also locked up, and a large churchyard surrounded by a handsome wall of inverted arches, which is a common style in Mexico. At last we reached Atzcapotzalco, where, too, the large church was locked up. The wall of inverted arches surrounding this churchyard had a cow's horn inserted in each division, as if for a peg to fasten things to, and on each pinnacle where the arches met there was a statue or vase. The drive was very pleasant all the way, though the cottages we passed were, many of them, very poor and dirty, and the road was all holes and dust. There was a tram-line, the cars drawn by little mules that went very fast. We had to return the way we came.

Saturday, November 24th.—There had been heavy rain in the night, so that the streets were wet and dirty. We went to the Mercado (market) San Juan, where there was nothing interesting, but some way past it we found the lovely Salto del Agua, a fountain formerly the end of the Chapultepec Aqueduct. We wandered through some evil-smelling streets, and found the Collegio de San Ignacio, a beautiful building coloured pink, a favourite fashion here, and very pleasing. Even the Sagrario, which forms part of the Cathedral, is coloured pink.

On our return to the hotel we had a visit from a charming old Spanish gentleman, Señor de Garay, who talked to us for one and a half hours, telling us about Hidalgo, Morelos, and Juarez, for whom he has the greatest veneration. Señor de Garay has great faith in the future of Mexico and in the stability of the Republic. He told us that he had seen curious changes in nature take place here. The year of the cholera in Europe, the swallows that used to come in great numbers did not come at all, and every one said it was a sign of the approaching cholera. The cholera did not come, but the mosquitoes did, and although the swallows have reappeared lately (but not in large numbers), the mosquitoes have remained, and are very troublesome. There used to be swarms of rooks in the neighbourhood, but these have been killed off by the French and other foreign residents for sport, and they too have made an end of the hares which used to be very numerous. Mexicans will not eat hares, believing them to feed upon corpses. Three years ago, when the electric light was introduced, the enormous cockroaches made their appearance, and although the electric light has only existed three months in Morelia, the cockroaches are appearing there too. They had never been seen before anywhere. A pretty bird, very like a sparrow with a red breast, a sweet songster, now common, is a recent arrival in Mexico. He said several trees and plants grow now freely which were formerly unknown. The best way to make money, he thought, was to buy large haciendas, and cut them up into small farms, and sell to the tenants, or to the people from the neighbouring towns and villages, who will pay handsomely, as all have money saved, and there is a great desire among them to own land. Large haciendas, if away from the railways, can be bought very cheap.

Sunday, November 25th.—In the afternoon we went to the bull-fight, to see the Spanish company. It was a wretched affair. There were three fights going on that afternoon, so the seats were mostly empty. The bulls would not fight, and the men dare not go near them. If the bull turned his head there was a general scamper. At first there was some pretty work with the horses, who were not blinded, and were very plucky. The men kept the bull off and saved their horses for a time, but afterwards they just put them on to the bull to be gored. All the pretty play with the coloured cloaks was beyond the power of these cowardly fellows, and as for the poor bulls, all they asked was to live in peace, and go home to their wives and families. With much trouble, the first bull was made to understand that he was not among friends, but still he did not want to hurt anybody, so the matador, just arrived from Spain, approached to kill him. A disgusting butchery followed. The matador was so nervous that he dare not go near the bull; but at last he made an effort, and stuck his sword into the poor beast at random, right through his back under the bone. Then he got another sword and tried again. This time the poor thing fell, but it got up again, and walked about two or three minutes. Of course a clever matador kills the bull in a second. The second bull utterly declined to fight, so he was lassoed and taken out. The lassoing was very pretty. Two men came into the ring on horseback and cantered round. Then one of them threw his lasso over the bull's head and one fore foot; as he kicked, the other man threw his lasso over the hind legs, and threw him. After a couple of minutes the man holding his head jerked him to make him get up, while the other man slackened his lasso, and they trotted him out. It was such a wretched show we went away; there was not a bit of skill or pluck in the whole exhibition. We found some Americans also departing, and walked home together. They had been in Yucatan, and had seen the great ruins, and had been much pleased. The American Consul there, who is continuing the excavations, had been very kind to them.

Monday, November 26th.—I dreamt I was at a pig-fight, and, as the sounds continued when I woke, I rushed to the window, and saw three men struggling with a great fat pig. They had three fat fellows in a cart and three running about the road. The men seized one very fat pig, and staggered under its weight to the cart, into which they hoisted it after great efforts, piggy scolding vociferously all the time. It was better fun than the bull-fight.

After doing a little shopping at Corilla's, the best silversmith, and at the Monte de Piedad, we visited a lovely church called La Profesa, where we found some good paintings and some wonderful silver-work reliquaries framed like pictures. We visited the Mint, and, notwithstanding our ignorance of Spanish and theirs of anything else, they understood that we wanted to see the works, and so they showed us round most politely.

The Mexican silver dollar is a very pretty coin. On one side is the Cap of Liberty in a glory, and on the other side the national crest, an eagle sitting on a nopal or cactus, eating a snake, just as the Aztecs saw it when, on their descent from the north, it was a sign to them that that was the right place for them to settle and build their city.

We found great inconvenience resulting from the recent change in the coinage to the decimal system. The old real, worth $12\frac{1}{2}$ centavos, is still the popular unit of value, and now there is no coin answering to it. Half a real is called a medio, but the new five and ten cent pieces have no individual names. In the country districts the people look very suspiciously at the new coins.

We walked from the Mint to the Plaza de la Concordia, and into the pretty little church El Carmen, where some ceremony was going on. As we turned from the church door we caught sight for the first time of the glorious snow mountains Popocatepetl and Tztaccihuatl, both extinct volcanoes. We made off to the Cathedral at once, and up the tower to get the full view. It was glorious. All the city, the lakes, the plains, the Shrine of Guadalupe, and the great circle of mountains, all fine, though none equal to the two giants. Everything was clear and lovely. Mexico looks quite a small city, with an inordinate number of churches. Most of them have tiled domes, which look very bright in the sunshine. The straight Paseo de la Reforma, leading to Chapultepec, showed well, but the fortress palace was mostly hidden by the trees. The sunset threw a lovely pink glow on the snow mountains. Iztaccihuatl is called the "White Woman," because the snow-covered part is exactly the shape of a dead woman covered by a shroud. It was a glorious scene.

Tuesday, November 27th.—We got up at 4.45 a.m. and got breakfast at the station, at a stall—very fair coffee, with milk and bread. The train left at 6.30 for Puebla. Our kind friends of the Mexican Railroad had given us a private carriage at the end of the train, and there we sat in comfort, and enjoyed the beautiful scenery. The morning was very cold, but it brightened into a glorious day.

The Mexican Railroad leaves Mexico along the old causeway built in 1676 for the pilgrims to Guadalupe, with fifteen beautiful altars dedicated to the fifteen mysteries of the Rosary. About six or seven of these altars are still standing by the side of the railway. The line runs for some way by the shallow Lake Texcoco, passing Guadalupe, of which we got a good view. Then through the great fertile plain of Apam, mostly planted with magveys, cultivated for the sake of the juice, which is made into pulque, the national drink. We tasted it once only. It looks like thin milk, tastes like something nasty fermenting, and smells like yeast. It is said to be wholesome, and is rather intoxicating. The fibres of the plant are equal to hemp, and are used in many manufactures—thread, matting, &c. The Aztec mounds at San Juan Teotihuacan can be seen from the train.

At Apizaco we found a good lunch, and looking up from its consideration, saw a pleasant, genial, honest face that could only belong to an Englishman. It was Mr. Evans, the locomotive superintendent, who had been informed of our arrival and had come to greet us. It turned out he was an old Midland Railway man, so Edward and he soon found they had many mutual friends. He was married to an English lady, and had lived many years in the country very comfortably. He told us their servants had been with them over ten years. The Mexicans seem to make very good servants, kindly and attentive, and becoming attached to their employers like English servants.

At Apizaco we left the main line for the Puebla branch, which runs through beautiful scenery. Popocatepetl and Iztaccihuatl on the right, and the snow-covered Peak of Orizaba and the Malintzi on the left, while the countless beautiful churches, large haciendas, and the rich vegetation make a magnificent foreground. Soon after leaving Apizaco we passed a very pretty waterfall, name unknown. The railroads are everywhere used by the natives as high roads. There are very few trains in the day, and the ordinary roads are very bad, so riders and foot-passengers take the railroad. When a train appears they have to get off the line as best they can. Sometimes they have great difficulty, and have to plunge into thickets or scramble into the ditches. Often they are overtaken and killed. Before we knew that accidents were of common occurrence we used to be very much amused by their difficulties ; but afterwards we felt rather nervous. Happily, we never witnessed anything of the kind, but it seems numbers are run over in the year.

We arrived at Puebla at 11.45 a.m. and took the bus to the Hotel de las Diligencias ; very comfortable, with good food and pleasant servants.

After lunch we made our way with much difficulty to the Cholula tramway and had an hour's shaky ride to Cholula, passing an old aqueduct in ruins and a picturesque bridge with a fine gateway at each end. The Pyramid of Cholula, once surmounted by a temple to Quetzalcoatl, is now crowned by the church of Nostra Señora de los Remedios. The tram-car stops to set down passengers at the foot of the mound, and then goes on to some distant village. The ascent is by an easy winding road, attributed by some to the Aztecs and by some to the Spaniards. What a glorious country Mexico would have been if the Spaniards had never come! They knocked down and destroyed everything! The pyramid was once a dense mass of houses in terraces; now it would be difficult to believe it was not a natural mound, except that pieces are broken away and show how it is built up, mostly of lava and concrete. As we strolled to the top a lad followed us with a handful of ancient Aztec earthenware heads, spindle whorls, beads, and obsidian arrow-heads found amongst the débris. We bought them at last for a small sum. I picked a number of bits of arrow-heads out of the cutting made for the tram line. The little heads are a great puzzle to antiquarians. They abound all round the old Aztec cities, and no one knows what they were used for. They are all different, so perhaps it was their way of taking portraits.

The view from the top of the pyramid is very fine. After enjoying it for some time we went down into Cholula and made for a large Gothic-looking church, which turned out to be San Francisco, built in the sixteenth century, and containing a wonderful flat arch —so flat, it is a marvel that it stands. It was undergoing repairs, and so was the Capilla de los Naturales, an immense building erected in 1660 to accommodate the great number of Indians that flocked to the shrine. We were told by a Spanish gentleman that the district of Puebla contains no less than 200 churches! We walked round the plaza and then back to the car, and were jolted to Puebla, but landed a long way from our hotel. Having utterly lost our way, we applied to a young gentleman who was passing, and he actually walked all the way to the door and then waved his hat and shook hands with us. Unfortunately he only spoke Spanish. It was a perpetual source of regret to us that we could not speak Castellana. Dictionaries are not always to be relied on, as that evening Edward, having looked up blankets, went to the landlord and asked for "blanquilla." Our host consented cheerfully, and sent at once for a couple of eggs!

Wednesday, November 28th.—We went to the Cathedral and spent all the morning admiring it and the wonderful decorations of the interior. The Cathedral is built of dark grey stone with white ornaments, and is large, dark, and impressive outside, but inside all is gorgeous. The high altar, completed in 1819, is very large, most of it being of Puebla marble or onyx richly carved and gilt, and adorned with life-sized coloured statues of bishops. Beneath the altar is the sepulchre of the Bishops of Puebla, said to be very beautiful, but we missed seeing it. The choir is a miracle of inlaid woods, and has old books splendidly illuminated. Every confessional is elaborately carved, and all the side altars rich with ivory figures, silver reliquaries, and fine pictures. It was curious to find amongst all these riches occasional places where, from some cause or other, they had fallen short, so that instead of marble there was the commonest painted wood, and abominable daubs within a few feet of priceless old masters. The sacristy was full of old tapestry and inlaid furniture. Service was going on all the morning, with very sweet music.

After lunch we took a carriage and drove round the

city, which is full of fine old churches. It is said that there is a network of subterranean passages under the whole of Puebla, connecting the churches and monasteries with each other. This is said of many places in Mexico, and that people do not like venturing into them to explore them, when they are discovered by a monastery or church being pulled down. Of course our driver took us first to see the new Casa de la Maternidad, a fine building of which they are very proud, and the Penitentiary, which was in the unhappy condition that the old was pulled down, and the new not yet built, but after that he took us to the church of San Francisco, a very large handsome building decorated inside and out with priceless old tiles as beautiful as gems; some were quite pictures, one tile having on it a design of two birds and several flowers round them, the colouring remarkably brilliant. In this church is treasured an ugly doll with long hair, dressed doll fashion in rich satin and damask. It is the image of the Holy Virgin, presented by Cortez to his friend the Tlascallan chief. We stopped to look at the public laundry. There were two rows of washing-places, with a natural stream flowing between them, the whole roofed over. The women were chattering merrily over their work. We went through the market, where there was the usual display of pottery, fruit, vegetables, and baskets. Often in the markets we saw people selling scraps of cotton materials that had evidently been samples, and we wondered what use could be made of them. Afterwards we saw that they are used to patch clothes. We visited the pawnbrokers, but found nothing to suit us.

Puebla is an exceedingly pretty town, the principal square, in which the Cathedral stands, has arcades on three sides with good shops, and altogether the city looks prosperous and comfortable. We met here a contractor for part of the Inter-oceanic Railroad, who told us he paid labourers thirty-seven centavos a day, and stone-masons seventy-five centavos, and generally had to give them something every night on account.

Thursday, November 29th.—We retook possession of our comfortable carriage at eight o'clock, and started for Apizaco, and from there to Orizaba. It was as usual a delicious sunny morning, and all the big mountains were quite clear. We just caught a glimpse of the Pyramid of Cholula. At Apizaco we had a chat with an English railway official, who had spent nearly all his life in Mexico, and gave the natives an excellent character. We had a very pleasant run through a prosperous-looking country to Esperanza, where a nice young Englishman, Mr. Hollis, road-master on this portion of the line, met us, and told us he had been commissioned by Mr. Shirley, the traffic-manager, to run us down the celebrated incline on a hand-trolly, so that we might see it better than we could from the train. Mr. Hollis had only recently come from England with his young wife, neither of whom could speak Spanish. He took us to see her in their little house by the station, a lonely life for her without a single person to speak to in her husband's absence. Our car went on ahead of the trolly, which is a delightful conveyance. We sat in front, and Mr. Hollis at the back, working the break, and showing us the points of interest, and generally enjoying the rare pleasure of having English people to talk to. We were sorry to say good-bye to him at the end of the day's journey.

The incline begins at Boca del Monte where we got on to the trolly, and were soon tearing down the incline, slowing for the interesting bits, and often stopping altogether to admire the scenery and the engineering of the line, which are both wonderful and worthy of each other. The line is like a shelf on the mountain side, the gradient in some parts one in twenty, with many short tunnels and some giddy bridges, of which the most remarkable is called by the name of the engineer, "Winner's Bridge." It was a very curious feeling to stop on one of these bridges and look down on to the valley below, much like standing in a spider's web. From the line we looked straight down on to the roofs of Maltrata, in the lovely valley of La Joya, every field, road, and cottage marked as if on a map. About halfway down is a station called Alta Luz. Mr. Hollis told us that women, after offering their fruit and flowers for sale at Maltrata, will rush up a mountain path and be at Alta Luz as soon as the train, to offer their wares again. As we descended flowers became more plentiful. Unfortunately, I have never been able to remember the names of flowers, but I recognized many old hot-house friends. The gardenia grows freely and appears to be a great favourite.

From Maltrata the line goes straight across the valley and then enters a lovely ravine with a stream rushing through it. The ravine is so narrow that for some distance the line runs on a bridge above the stream. This is the Barranca del Infiernillo, or ravine of the little hell. After that the descent to Orizaba is so slight that we had to get men to push the trolly. At Nogales we passed a large and prosperous cotton factory belonging to Mr. Braneth, of the Mexican Railroad, and a marble quarry and works, belonging to two Americans called Brisbane, who are doing very well. When we arrived at the station we found the landlord of the Hotel de la Borda waiting for us. He is a German with an English wife, and his hotel is exceedingly comfortable and clean, and the food excellent. As it was too late to do much we went to the Plaza, where there is a pretty garden, and to the market-place.

The weekly market was just over and everybody packing up and going to church, so we went there too, and found a large crowd attending the evening service after the close of their busy day, before going home. They were very devout, and joined heartily in the responses.

Friday, November 30th.—We took a carriage and drove over the worst road we had seen, which is saying a great deal, to a wonderful waterfall. We passed through a large farm where we saw coffee, bananas, and many hot-house flowers growing almost wild. The oranges looked lovely in the sun. After driving some distance we left the carriage, and the driver guided us through fields to a point whence we looked down into the loveliest ravine. A stream ran down the centre between steep rocks, and just opposite us a second stream came leaping down the cliff in a series of falls of great height to join it; one waterfall falling into another. Across the ravine were the beautiful mountains, and all round us trees and flowers, with butterflies and great buzzards flying about, and over all the intense blue sky and the sunshine which maketh glad the heart of man. We stayed there a long time, and our cheery driver danced round us, picking flowers and finding good places whence to see the falls, and generally doing everything he could think of to give us pleasure, as is the custom of this delightful people. We drove back to the hotel by another road passing the lovely old church of San Gertrudis on the way.

We met Mr. Shirley close to the hotel, who said if we would wait another day he would take us down part of the way himself. Of course we accepted with joy. He walked through the town with us and kindly acted as interpreter. We found some nice old Spanish tortoiseshell combs adorned with gold-work and pearls at a pawnbroker's, and a lovely old coral bead and fine gold-work rosary. These we bought very cheap, but I had the curiosity to ask the price of a modern European ring that had been left by some traveller, and I was amused to find the pawnbroker wanted much more than it would have cost new. In another pawnshop I bought some pearls; the colour is good, but they are too badly shaped to be worth much. A great deal of coarse brown pottery is made in Orizaba, often very pretty, and I saw here two twisted glass bottles that a little more skill and better tools would have made "Venetian." Pottery is made everywhere, and is often very artistic, both in shape and decoration, but is rarely well enough baked to stand packing.

This is the great coffee-growing district. A gentleman at the hotel was buying quantities of it to ship to New Orleans. He told us that his broker had called his attention to a group of Indians who had brought into town eight asses laden with coffee which they sold for 160 dollars. The men were in rags. The broker said this money would be taken home and buried. An Indian never breaks into a dollar. He has no wants beyond what he supplies by his own and his family's labour, and the only purchase he makes is, at long intervals, a straw hat for a few coppers. This has been going on for generations, the secret of the deposit is handed down from father to son, and it is believed there are millions buried in the district. These Indians have a great objection to strangers coming amongst them. It is all very well for the day, but when night draws on they like the stranger to return home, as they are afraid he wants to discover their hidden treasures. In one Indian town the military have had to be called in twice, and use very severe measures, for the inhabitants murdered people who tried to settle among them. An American couple have started a little fruit and flower farm near Maltrata, but we were told they were sure to give it up shortly, so many *accidents* would happen to them.

It is curious how the Indians cling to the manners

and customs of their ancestors. Rich men will send their sons and daughters to be educated at the best establishments, but on their return they have to give up modern dress and ways, and wear the simple and not too burdensome native garb, and carry goods to market for sale.

We spent the afternoon wandering about the town, which is exceedingly prettily situated at the foot of the mountains, with a river running through it, and a pleasant alameda, or public garden, and pretty streets and lanes. Orizaba is the beginning of the hot country, so the vegetation is very luxuriant and beautiful. Mr. Shirley dined with us at the hotel, and told us a good deal about the natives, of whom he spoke very kindly. The Mexican Railroad pay higher wages than are usual because they like to keep their men. At Orizaba they pay 50 cents a day for a labourer, but down in the hot country they pay more, because it is difficult to work in the terrible heat. There is much swampy land on the low level, which is very unhealthy. The line near the coast is said to have cost a life for every sleeper. Out of 1400 foreign workmen, principally from New Orleans, only 250 went home again. This great mortality was mainly caused by the immoderate indulgence of the men in the native spirit, aguardiente, which is very cheap.

Saturday, December 1st.—Unfortunately our view from the trolly was spoilt by rain. Mr. Shirley took us as far as Fortin. About half-way we stopped and walked through a little tunnel by the side of the line into a beautiful glen. A large river falls about 100 feet, and then disappears underground, reappearing five miles off. It is a lovely spot, and can be reached no other way. Happily the rain cleared in time for us to see the Metlac bridge, which crosses a broad ravine, down which a stream flows, that, until last September, had never been known to be more than two or three feet high. It is a wrought-iron girder bridge carried on castiron columns substantially braced together (very like the Crumlin Viaduct in South Wales), and is built on a curve, radius 325 feet, the height is 95 feet. On the night of September 8th there was no rain at Metlac, but a waterspout must have fallen up in the hills, for 30 feet of water came rushing down the ravine, tearing up big trees, and dashing them like catapults against the bridge. The flood broke down 150 feet of the bridge, leaving the rest uninjured. The traffic then crossed this piece on a temporary wooden trestle roadway, but a new iron bridge was on its way from England, and is probably in its place now.

At Fortin Mr. Shirley presented us to Mr. Tomblin, who left England with his brother when agriculture was at its worst, and is doing well out in Mexico. They live with a charming Spanish gentleman, a bachelor, who owns an enormous coffee plantation, which they manage for him, and they all join in coffee buying and other speculations. It must be delightful for Señor Vivanco to have two bright young English fellows to live with him. Mr. Tomblin took us across a couple of fields to their house, and he and Señor Vivanco received us with the greatest kindness. Luckily our host spoke English well and French like a Parisian. Mr. Tomblin showed us all the process of coffee-drying. When first picked it is put in the sun to dry. We saw quantities on the flat roof. Then it is put through machines which knock off the outer husk and the inner husk and skin. When the inner skin is completely removed the coffee is called " washed." The sorting is not a matter of quality, but of shape. The round berries fetch a rather higher price than the flat ones, because they roast better. Then it is packed in sacks. We were mounted on lovely little Mexican horses to visit the plantations where there are 350,000 coffee-trees, shaded by 3,000,000 bananas. The combination of the small, dark green foliage and the crimson berries of the coffee plant, with the large drooping leaves of the bananas is very pretty. Señor Vivanco lent me his own dear little grey horse, but unfortunately he had no ladies' saddle, and the only thing to be found in the neighbourhood was an old child's saddle, with a tiny stirrup in the shape of a heart, and fastened on to the horse by one strap over a piece of carpet. I believe the horse was ashamed of both saddle and rider, for I had the greatest difficulty in keeping my perch; it could not be called a seat. The Mexican bridle is very easy to manage; the bit is cruel in a heavy hand, but insures instant obedience. The horses are very fresh and spirited, and did not seem troubled by the bits.

Mr. Tomblin said he would bring over some of the Mexican horses when he came to England and exhibit them. They descend from the Spanish barbs, and are beautifully formed, swift and active, with very easy paces, generally about fourteen hands high. We had a delightful ride, and on our return a delicious dinner, of which I will give the *menu*, as it was the only meal we got in the house of a Spaniard, though we got native dishes several times.

Soup with some kind of paste in it.

Omelette with a sauce of tomatoes and chillies.

Filet de bœuf.

Small gourds cut in halves, filled with some mixture of vegetables.

A Ragout.

Baked puff fritters, very crisp and light, with chilli sauce. Rice cake and custard. Pine-apple sliced in sugar. Oranges sliced in claret. Fruit pastes of all kinds, made in moulds like jellies. French wine and mezcal with the coffee, a spirit or liqueur made from aloes, but not the same kind of aloes that are used for pulque. We brought some mezcal home with us, and also some fruit paste, which is made largely in Mexico. Coffee was curiously served. Cold extract of coffee, made every morning in sufficient quantity for the day, was brought in a decanter, and a little poured into the cups, and boiling water added. Several times during the meal tortillas were brought and placed by each person, some cold and crisp, some hot, all very delicate and very nice. The common way of eating tortillas is to fold them up and use them as spoons, of course devouring them at the same time. They are named on this account "Spoons of Montezuma," because when a Spaniard, boasting one day of his king's magnificence, gave as an example of it that he had a clean spoon with each course, the Mexican answered, " My king is still more magnificent, for he has a new spoon with every mouthful." Señor Vivanco told me one servant was employed all day long making tortillas for his household. She prepared the corn, and made it into dough every afternoon, for use the following day.

The garden was very beautiful. There were roses, gardenias, large variegated-leaved plants grown at home in stoves, tulip-trees, which are so common that they are even used for hedges, orange-trees and a wonderful convolvulus with a beautiful flower, which when still a bud is exactly the shape and size of a duck. Señor Vivanco told me the natives were very pleasant people, and quite honest. He pointed out a man at the station who makes his living by selling bouquets. As this man lives at the station it is quite a common thing for people to leave large sums of money, which they wish to send off by train, in his care.

Mr. Shirley joined us again at the station, and went on to Vera Cruz with us. We saw the beautiful falls of the Atoyac from the train, and then passed for miles through a dense jungle. The vegetation was marvellous, all shapes, sizes and colours of trees, shrubs and grasses but very few flowers. It was not the right time of the year for them. In the old diligence days this part of the road was much dreaded, it was so unhealthy.

Captain Powell, of the Mexican Railroad, met us at

the station, and kindly walked with us to the Hotel Universal, where we got a good clean room. The chambermaid at this hotel did her work with a cigarette in her mouth, and an ugly dog following her. It was very smelly down stairs. Captain Powell told us there had been no case of yellow fever in Vera Cruz for exactly two years. The old town walls had been pulled down, and since then it had been more healthy. A Norther was on all the time we were in the Tierra Caliente, or Hot Land, as the low-lying districts near the sea are called, so we did not get any great heat. We had heard such conflicting accounts of Vera Cruz that we hardly knew whether it was safe to visit or not. Many told us we must arrange to arrive in the morning, and leave in the evening, so that we should not spend a night there for fear of the "Vomito," the yellow fever; but we found that positively it is looked upon as a health-resort by Mexicans, who go there for sea breezes.

Sunday, December 2nd.—Vera Cruz is a pretty little town with a Plaza Mayor, where the band plays, and where cocoa-nut palms grow. These were the first we had seen. The shops and the market were not particularly interesting, but the harbour and landing-stage were most amusing. The famous island fortress San Juan d'Ulloa is very near the main land, and affords some protection for the ships, but if a storm comes on their only safety is in flight to the sea. The government have begun to construct a breakwater, but probably were short of money, so after letting down blocks of stone sufficient to prevent ships leaving the harbour that way, they stopped the works. The great danger lies in the numerous reefs, visible in calm weather by the surf on them. There was a wreck lying to the south of the harbour, a French ship lost in the same storm that destroyed the Metlac bridge. The most amusing feature of Vera Cruz is certainly the zopilotes, or buzzards, who are the city scavengers, and swarm everywhere, walking about the streets and skurrying away on one leg, and with much wing action, when I poked them with my umbrella. They sit in groups on the balconies and housetops, and appear to have a good deal of conversation among themselves. They are the size of small turkeys, and black as night.

Mr. Shirley came for us and took us to see the great fortress. The governor was formerly in the employ of the Mexican railroad, so as Mr. Shirley was with us, he took us round himself and was very polite and pleasant. It is about twenty minutes' row to the island—a very pleasant journey through the shipping congregated there. As soon as we got inside the fort, a number of prisoners surrounded us, offering their handiwork for sale. We bought a good many of their carved cocoa-nuts and two cocoa-nut cups, exceedingly well done and most elaborate. They make them to get a little pocket-money for tobacco, &c. First we were taken to the governor's rooms, and then to the top of a tower to see the fine view of the city and surrounding country, all sand wastes, and the distant hills, and seawards we could distinguish the dangerous reefs on which so many vessels have come to grief.

Then the governor took us over the prison. We visited the kitchen, and saw the food preparing for the prisoners. It smelt very nice. They have two dishes for dinner, one a strong meat soup, with lumps of meat and vegetables in it, the other a savoury mess of vegetables, with oil or fat and a large piece of bread. At breakfast and supper they have coffee, bread, and the favourite national dish, frijoles or beans, without which no Mexican meal is complete. The prisoners wear striped garments. There is no capital punishment in Mexico, but ninety-nine years' imprisonment is the severest legal sentence. We were told that some of the men were there for dreadful crimes. There is a law which compensates to a great extent for the want of the death penalty, that is:—one that a prisoner shall be immediately shot down if he attempt to escape. Prisoners particularly obnoxious to the government are generally got rid of under this law while being conveyed from one prison to another. Men convicted of minor offences are often sent into the army instead of to prison. The present governor of San Juan has done all he can to improve the condition of the prisoners, but the dungeons are beyond his power to make really fit for habitation He has done a good deal by breaking through the immense walls and putting in doors and windows, such as they are, mere slits in the enormously thick masonry. Formerly the only communication with the dungeons was a hole in the roof. The prisoner was let down with ropes, and food and water given him the same way. Light and air there were none, except through this hole.

The governor showed us small dungeons in which political prisoners used to be confined alone. Santa Anna had locked up, or rather buried, Juarez in one. There was no break in the walls, except the hole in the roof. By-and-by Juarez got the upper hand and put Santa Anna in the dungeon, but when quiet times came he forbade the use of them altogether, and most of them were destroyed. We went into the dungeons now used, which are very dark and damp and unsavoury. It is by the light of those bits of windows, or miserable candles, that the prisoners do the fine carving. They soon spoil their eyesight. Very often the prisoners mutiny and try to escape, but they have never yet been successful. Generally a soldier is found to help them, who steals the keys, probably killing the officer who keeps them. He lets out the prisoners and they lock up the soldiers, and try to kill the officers and the governor. There has been one mutiny under the present governor. He and another officer took refuge in the tower, which has a narrow winding staircase, and defended themselves with a handspike. All the other officers were killed, and then forty prisoners got on a raft to go to the land. A cannon-ball sunk the raft, and those who managed to swim ashore were seized as soon as they reached land and shot at once.

In the afternoon we took cars all round the town (for there is no Mexican town without tramways). It was a pretty drive, past the Bull-ring and the old fortifications and many new houses. We had a pleasant evening with the Shirleys, who have a little house close to the sea, where they bring the children for change of air. Here, again, our ignorance of Spanish was very vexatious, for Mrs. Shirley's jolly little son could not speak English. We spent the night in our carriage as the train started for Jalapa at such an unearthly hour in the morning. Mr. Shirley lent us sheets and blankets, so that we had very comfortable beds, but oh, the mosquitoes !

Monday, December 3rd.—Our untiring benefactor, Mr. Shirley, sent his man with coffee for us just before the train started at 4.30. We got up comfortably, and were ready to change to the mule cars at Paso de San Juan at 6.8.

The gradients are too steep for locomotives to run to Jalapa, and there is not sufficient traffic to make a better line pay. The new inter-oceanic railroad is to pass through Jalapa on its way to the coast. We were favoured with a small car and a pair of mules belonging to the manager of the line, Colonel Thrirkill, and started before the others. There were seven relays, and each time much persuasion, kicking and pushing were required to get the mules harnessed and started. They always wanted to go another way, but once started, they gave no more trouble. It was amusing to watch them jump over the holes, and where the road was bad, from sleeper to sleeper. The line is 54 miles long from the junction, the steepest gradient 8 in 100, and the total rise, 4562 feet. Going up one does not see the country so well as coming down, and the day was misty, but even then the journey was charming, on account of the beautiful trees and flowers, and numbers of large butterflies and humming-birds with whom we made acquaintance for the first time. There were great lizards eighteen inches long—splendid fellows, quite harmless. Our driver tried to catch one for me as it was rushing into its hole, but unfortunately the tail broke off in his hand. We arrived at Jalapa at four o'clock, an hour before the other cars, having had a delicious Mexican meal at Rinconada, besides excellent coffee and bread at a little refreshment-room at one of the first villages we came to. Colonel Thrirkill met us and insisted on our going to his house, which we did with very great pleasure. Nothing is more delightful on a long journey than to escape from the hotels, and be once more in a well-ordered home, with a friend at the head of the table; and Colonel Thrirkill was the most delightful host. He had been in the great American Civil War, and told us about the desperate struggle the South made against the North, before she was crushed by superior wealth and numbers. Colonel Thrirkill had had an open fireplace built in his sitting-room, probably the only one in Mexico. The fire was delightful as it was cold in the evenings.

We took a walk round the town which is prettily situated on a slope, with a good market-place and club, and one or two churches. The oldest church has been pulled down by the government on the pretext that it was so decayed it was falling down of itself, but I daresay the real reason was that great treasures were said to be hidden there. Many iron pots were discovered embedded in the walls, but all were empty. The owner of a neighbouring house was more fortunate. Some accident brought a bit of his wall down, and he found a treasure in coin, silver spoons and dishes, &c., worth 30,000 dollars. The pawnbrokers were quite uninteresting.

Tuesday, December 4th.—It rained all day, so the expedition Colonel Thrirkill had planned to take us to Cautepec, could not come off. I enjoyed the fire all day, but the gentlemen ventured out to a tobacco manufactory, employing 600 or 700 hands, where they bought some cigars. Tobacco grows well in Mexico, and is often sold for Havana.

Wednesday, December 5th.—It was a magnificent day but very cold at first, quite a hard frost. We started for Vera Cruz at 6.30, Colonel Thrirkill going with us. The mist had all cleared away, and the immense mountains at the back of Jalapa, the Cofre de Perote and the Peak of Orizaba, looked glorious in the sunshine. On the way down we often got magnificent views as far as the sea and over the surrounding country. On the north a line of hills extends right into the sea, and there is only one path over them to the next valley, and that is so bad that, though mules go over with baggage, it is not considered safe for people to ride. The natives carry travellers up and down on their backs. They are so strong they will run up the steep ascent even when carrying a stout German who owns a vanilla plantation there. This German has become very rich by cultivating the vanilla. It is easy to grow the bean, but very difficult to dry it properly, neither too quickly nor too slowly. He dries them in blankets by a method of his own.

Colonel Thrirkill pointed out to us by the roadside several trees on which men had been hung for plundering the diligences in the old times. They were hung on the spot where they committed the crime. One tree had had forty-nine men hung on it after a great highway robbery; among them were a man, his five sons and two nephews. After an execution the branch used is always cut off. We asked if he had ever been shot at, he said only once, not by a brigand but by a man he had prosecuted for stealing. He was caught and sent to San Juan d'Ulloa.

A wonderful bean grows here covered with tiny, almost invisible prickles. Boys collect them in quills and amuse themselves by blowing them abroad, in church, or wherever there is a crowd. They enter the skin and instantly cause intense irritation which lasts twenty-four hours. It was suggested we should bring some home to disperse our opponents' meetings at the next general election.

The mules brought us down very quickly, they can do twenty-four miles an hour. The natives are quite as active as the mules. They will leave the junction with the car and arrive at Jalapa before it, going across country and not stopping, like the car, fifty minutes for refreshments.

We had a capital dinner at the Hotel Diligencias, and took coffee in front of the Hotel Universal, and then said good-bye to our good friends, Colonel Thrirkill and Mrs. Shirley, and once more retired to our car.

Thursday, December 6th.—The train started very early for Mexico, but our man managed to get us a little coffee, and after dressing quietly we got more coffee and bread, both excellent, at Paso del Macho. It was a lovely morning, and the mountains and trees and the Atoyac waterfall, everything was at its best. At Cordova we laid in a stock of fruit at absurdly low prices. A large basket of capital oranges, basket included, 2 reals (10d.), 17 bananas also 2 reals, but this price was far too high; a pine-apple, very sweet and juicy, cost us a medio (2½d.), we might have had two for the price but did not want another, and natives would have got three. The granadita is one of the nicest Mexican fruits. It is shaped like an egg with a hard rind, and the inside is like a gooseberry. There were many quite new to us. On one occasion we caused great amusement in the restaurant at Hotel Jardin, by bringing home a fruit that looked like a green hedgehog. After considering it with great interest during lunch, we proceeded to cut it up and eat it, our opposite neighbour chattering to us in Spanish the whole time, It was very nasty, and Johnny coming in just then was called up by our friend to explain that it was not a fruit at all, but a vegetable and should only be eaten cooked. This was what he had been trying to tell us all the time. We had it at Colonel Thrirkill's as a vegetable, and liked it much better.

The day being very bright and clear we saw to

advantage the splendid scenery that was partly hidden by rain on our downward journey. It turned cold before we reached Mexico.

Friday, December 7th.—Professor Gardner came to lunch with us, and told us of a delightful curiosity-shop, where we got some beautiful things, a wonderful old ivory amongst them the like of which has been rarely seen at Christie's. We paid many visits to the funny little shop.

Next day we visited the Castle of Chapultepec. The drive there is very pretty. It is along the Paseo de la Reforma, the fashionable promenade, two miles long and very wide, with trees on each side of the drive, and again at the side of the wide footpaths. There are handsome stone seats, where there were often picturesque groups of natives, flirting or gossiping. At the city end is an equestrian statue of Charles IV., said to be very fine, and further on a beautiful monument to Columbus by the French sculptor, Cordier. In the next glorieta (or open space) is a work by a native artist Jiminez, a monument to Guatimotzin, the last Aztec king, who was tortured to death by Cortez, in the hope that he would reveal hidden treasures. Many heroic legends are associated with his name. This pleased me most. It is decorated with fine bas-reliefs of historical scenes, and at the top is a very spirited statue of the hero in the act of throwing a dart. There are six glorietas, and eventually all are to be adorned with statues of national heroes. Juarez is to come next. It is interesting to note that the native Mexican element is overpowering the Spanish. Juarez and Diaz both sprang from the old Aztec stock without any Spanish intermixture.

At the end of the Paseo, which is perfectly straight, stands the great rock on which the castle is built. It is divided into two portions, the military school and the palace, which is very commonplace inside, much as if Gillow had been turned in to do as he liked, except the rooms furnished and decorated by Maximilian which are far below Gillow's standard. The views from the broad marble terraces are very fine. It must be a delightful residence. At the foot of the great rock is a magnificent grove of monster cypress-trees, older than history. The grey moss which hangs from every bough gives them a hoary appearance, but they are quite vigorous. A monument commemorates the saddest incident of the American invasion. When the American army marched on Mexico city, they were compelled to take Chapultepec, which is a fortress as well as a palace and a military academy. The cadets turned out to defend the place and fought splendidly, and almost every one of these poor lads was killed.

We drove back to Mexico too early to meet the fashionable world who assemble here every afternoon in closed carriages. So genteel is this promenade that fashionable families, if unable to attend in person, send their carriages with closed windows to represent them. Gentlemen go on horseback, and a Mexican gentleman on horseback is indeed a thing of beauty. He wears a short coat or jacket, tight-fitting trousers, adorned from waist to boots with a double row of silver buttons, large spurs inlaid with silver, which look formidable, but are really harmless, as the rowels do not end in points, and a large felt sombrero with silver or gold decorations. These sombreros often cost immense sums of money. The saddles are very large, of embossed or embroidered leather, with endless flaps and dangling appendages, and silver ornaments and enormous stirrups. Behind the rider is strapped the bright-coloured serape, hanging down to the level of the stirrups. The beautiful little horses look almost too small for so much splendour. The serape is the national garment for men of every degree. It is about eight feet long and four feet wide, with a hole in the middle to put the head through. This hole is seldom used, it is generally draped across the shoulders. The women of the lower classes invariably wear the reboso, the same shape as the serape, but of thin blue and black cotton. They put them over their heads. Anything more picturesque and less convenient could not well be imagined as there is nothing to keep it in its place. Ladies have quite discarded them, though formerly they had charming silk ones, which are now becoming scarce and valuable.

We went to the Cathedral as usual, and found it magnificently decorated with blue and silver damask, and hundreds of lighted candles, in honour of the feast of the Immaculate Conception. It seemed to be a great social festivity, as we met numbers of bouquets evidently on their way to be presented to friends, and confectioners' boys carrying cakes, as if many afternoon teas were going on. It is a mystery to me why artists do not come out here and paint the glorious scenery and the handsome people who are wonderfully graceful and picturesque in their bright-coloured rags. It would be such a delightful change from the eternal views of Venice by sunlight, moonlight, early morning, sunset, &c., &c.

Sunday, December 9th.—We went by tramcar to Guadalupe to visit the celebrated shrine. Unfortunately the great church was closed for repairs. The Virgin of Guadalupe is the patroness of the native Mexicans, while the Virgin de los Remedios belongs specially to the Spaniards. The good people seem to look upon them as quite distinct and rival divinities. The reason of the national devotion to the shrine of Guadalupe is that it contains the miraculous picture of the Holy Virgin, presented by her to a native Mexican, while our Lady de los Remedios is merely a Spanish importation. The legend is this:—A poor man called Juan Diego, very pious, was on his way to mass one morning in December, 1531, when the Blessed Virgin appeared to him and told him to go to the Bishop, and say she wished a church to be built in her honour on the site of an ancient Aztec temple. The Bishop Zumarraga refused to believe his tale, so he went back, and told the Holy Virgin, and she commanded him to meet her there again on the following Sunday. Again she appeared to him and again the Bishop refused to accept his message, unless he could bring some proof that he was divinely commissioned. The Bishop seems to have been impressed to some extent, for he sent people to watch Juan Diego, but as soon as he reached the hill where the vision appeared, they lost sight of him. Our Lady told him to come next day, and he should receive the necessary proof. Next day, however, he was kept at home by his uncle's illness, which got so much worse that the following day he had to fetch the priest to confess the dying man, and, so that he might not be delayed by the vision, he took another road. When crossing a barren rock, the Holy Virgin met him and told him his errand was needless, for his uncle was quite recovered. She then commanded him to go once more to the Bishop, and as proof she caused to spring out of the rock a rose-tree in full bloom. He was to pluck the roses, wrap them in his serape, and show them to no one until he reached the Bishop. When the vision disappeared a miraculous spring gushed from the rock, which retains marvellous powers of healing to this day. When Juan Diego opened his serape to give the roses to the Bishop, he found that a picture of the Holy Virgin, as she appeared to him, was painted on the rough cloth. Of course the Bishop hesitated no longer, but built the chapel and put in it the miraculous picture. Strange to say, artists have recently been allowed to examine it, and cannot discover how it is done. It is neither oil nor water-colours, nor any known medium.

On leaving the car we found ourselves on the large square in front of the big church. Dozens of gambling tables, with all manner of games of chance, stood about the square, which was crowded with dirty people. We saw some Indians sweeping down the bit of pavement where they had spent the night under a straw matting.

There were many Indians about who looked more like the Red Indians of the States than any we had seen before in Mexico. The great church being closed, service was going on in a side chapel. A bystander assured me the picture over the altar really was the *ritratto miraculoso*, but I think it can only have been a copy.

We went to the holy spring which is enclosed in a pretty little chapel. People not only drink the water but take it away in bottles for friends unable to come. It is very good water, and so plentiful that an eminent engineer would like to use it for supplying the city with drinking water, but fears ecclesiastical opposition. I meant to drink some, but after seeing what dirty people let down the cup into the water, drew it up, drank some and threw back what they left, I thought I would forego my share of the promised blessings. Then we mounted the steps to the small chapel "del Cerrito," of the little hill. The chapel has nothing worthy of notice except its fine position and the view from the terrace in front of it, but half-way up is a very curious representation in stone of the mast of a ship with sails spread. It is said to contain a real mast and sails and to have been erected by some sailors who being in imminent peril at sea, vowed to consecrate their ship to the Blessed Virgin of Guadalupe if she would save them. The storm immediately abated, and on reaching shore the sailors dragged their ship, according to their vow, across the great mountains and set it up here. The whole of Guadalupe is on the hill side, and is a very conspicuous and beautiful object from any part of the great tableland.

Monday, December 10*th.*—We got up at five o'clock, breakfasted at the station, and started at seven o'clock by the National Railway for Toluca. It was a hard frost but the sun soon came out and the day was very hot. We arrived at Toluca at 9.30 a.m. It was a very pretty run. The line winds through the hills, following a stream for some miles, then turning down a more convenient valley, until it reaches the edge of the immense plain on which Toluca is situated. Then it runs along a terrace about 200 feet above the plain and the views are very fine. The plain is as flat as a board, and beyond it rise the mountain and the great snow-topped extinct volcano Xinanticatl.

Toluca is a pretty town, very prosperous-looking and full of churches. There is a calvario on a hill close by, from which one can see all over the plains. All Mexican towers are prettily built, with open spaces and arcades, and stalls selling cheap goods. Pillow lace is made at Toluca very like torchon lace. I got several pieces, but one particular bit I wanted was on the pillow of a woman in the market. She had already made several yards, but it was an order, and nothing would induce her to let me have it. The Church must be enormously rich here. Although there were fine churches at every corner, we saw two new ones in the process of construction, both very important buildings. There is in the church of El Carmen the first organ made in America. It is a queer-looking thing, with the pipes in a box and the bellows outside. We regretted having stopped a whole day at Toluca, for there is nothing particular to see and our time was getting short. The Hotel Gran Sociedad was very good.

Tuesday, December 11*th.*—We took the 9.35 a.m. train for Morelia. About half an hour after leaving Toluca we passed the Cerro del Señor, a high hill with a church at the very top, formerly a place of pilgrimage. About one o'clock we came to a real cañon, very pretty, though on a tiny scale compared to those in the States. It twists and turns with the course of the river, and smaller cañons branch off, affording lovely views. All at once the train rushes into the open, and the glorious panorama of the valley of Solis lies before the traveller. After crossing this valley, and through another range of hills, the valley of the Lerma is reached, and for miles the track runs by the side of the big river. Great old trees grow in the water. The province of Michoacan is the richest in Mexico; there are mines of silver and gold, great grazing-districts covered with herds of splendid cattle and horses, much cultivated land, which gives often two crops a year, and in the hotter part there are forests of valuable trees, both for ornamental woods and precious dyes.

Acambaro is the junction for Morelia. Here we had to change trains, as so far we had been on the main line for the north. After leaving Acambaro, and crossing another range of mountains, the third in the day, we reached the valley of Morelia and the beautiful lake of Cuitzeo. The sun set soon after we reached the lake, turning the mountains rose colour and the sky into gold. It was exceedingly beautiful. We reached

Morelia about seven o'clock, and, by the advice of the guard, we took the tram-car and he took our baggage-ticket to give to a cargadore, or carrier, to bring to the hotel. It never came. Hotel Oseguerra was clean and comfortable, but the food very bad.

On our way a fussy little man had attached himself to us, who was the English agent for Singer's sewing-machines in Morelia. He was very kind in helping us, and after dinner he called to take us to see the illuminations in honour of the festival of Guadalupe.

We walked down the street to the fine promenade leading to the Sanctuary of Guadalupe. Strings of coloured lamps were hung across the road, and the promenade and park at the end of it were crowded. We noticed numbers of soldiers in the crowd, for this is the district where the Church and reactionary party have most power, and it is well garrisoned to prevent a rising. The church called the Sanctuary was a blaze of light, and crowded to suffocation.

Close to it is a large open space, where hundreds of people were lying about, and cooking their food or buying it of the many stall-keepers. These were country folk, come to take part in the greatest religious festival of the year. They were going to spend the night there in the open air.

Wednesday, December 12*th.*—Of course our first care was to look up our box. We found it safe enough at the station, and by-and-by we met the station-master, who was seeking us to take us to the governor to complain. It seems there is a Custom-house officer at the station, who ought to examine all the luggage that comes in, but rarely does so; only now and then, at long intervals, he insists on visiting a box. Unluckily, ours took his fancy, and nothing would induce him to let it be sent to us. We accompanied the station-master to the governor's, and he made a speech and the governor made a speech, all in Spanish, and we bowed respectfully whenever they pointed to us, and finally shook hands with everybody in the room, and the station-master was satisfied and we got our box; but we had lost a couple of hours over the affair.

Our new friend of the sewing-machines was waiting for us in the full glory of the Mexican costume, spurs, silver buttons, and all. The effect was decidedly marred by a pair of *pince-nez*. He got the keys of the cathedral towers for us, and we went up at once and got a splendid view of the town and surrounding country. Morelia is beautifully situated on a small hill rising out of the wide plain. Though a small town, it is the principal one of the district and has a large market. The streets are straight, crossing each other at right angles, and whichever way one looks there is a glimpse of green fields and trees at the end of them.

The cathedral is large and imposing outside; inside the best thing was the carving of the choir railings and seats and the organ. We visited many of the churches including the little old church of the Santa Cruz, formerly the cathedral. There was nothing particular in any of them.

The Monte de Piedad, a branch of the great establishment in Mexico, contained nothing interesting. The two markets were almost empty. There were a few stalls protected from the sun by great straw umbrellas. The shops were closed on account of the feast. Our friend urged us to stay over the next day, which was market-day, to see all the country people come in. We should have liked to do so, but we had seen in the guide-book that the market at Patzcuaro was particularly interesting, and rich in fancy work in ivory and the famous Uruapan ware. We much regretted afterwards that we had not taken his advice. After mid-day dinner we went again to the fine old causeway leading to the sanctuary. It is paved, and on each side is a handsome stone wall with a continuous line of seats. We noticed that the barracks were placed in the old monastery actually adjoining the sanctuary.

There is a pretty garden in what is supposed to be the old Aztec style, with curious stone carvings, and past the church is the fine aqueduct, 100 years old, and a wood with shady walks. The most charming bit of all is the old Glorieta, with a large fountain in the centre and comfortable seats all round. We remained there a long time watching the people, many of whom had brought provisions and were evidently spending the whole day there.

We visited the cathedral once more, and left Morelia at 7.10 p.m. for Patzcuaro, which we reached at 9.15. The only hotel by the lake is Hotel Ibarra, in an old hacienda. It is very dirty and objectionable in every way, ut the journey must not be given up on that account.

Thursday, December 13*th.*—A very fine day. At 7.30 a.m. we went on board the steamer *Mariano Jimenez*—such a ghost of a steamer, everything worn out and broken and hardly hanging together. For some time we were drenched by the steam from the engines, which poured through every crevice. The captain, engineer, pilot and a third of the crew was a very nice young fellow who lodged in the hotel. We took our lunch with us, a large dish of cold chicken and another of tongue. Unfortunately, the chicken was smothered in garlic and the tongue soaked in vinegar, so we had only the hard-boiled eggs to eat after all.

The Lake of Patzcuaro is exceedingly beautiful, with many islands, and surrounded by hills that at one end are very lofty. There are thousands of ducks and coot, and some gentlemen staying at the hotel had gone out in a little boat to shoot them. To their great mortification they hardly got a bird. Afterwards, the reason for their want of luck was discovered. The natives, who go about in canoes *à la* Robinson Crusoe, just tree-trunks hollowed out, and oars like spoons, have a great hunt every Wednesday. Hundreds of boats come out and act in concert, forming a large circle, to drive all the birds together, then they shoot what they can with a kind of javelin, and form another circle round those that escape the first. They continue this hunt all day, so naturally the birds are very wild on Thursday.

We stopped at a village across the lake, called Sinzunzan, where there is a very old church, with the oldest and biggest olive-trees I ever saw in the churchyard. We measured one that was thirty feet in girth. Here is treasured a very large picture by Murillo, a gift from the King of Spain when the church was rich and important. It is said that Church, the American artist, offered a million dollars for this great work, which represents the entombment of our Lord, but nothing could induce the natives, who are very proud of their picture, to part with it. When at one time they thought it was going to be sold and sent away, they mounted guard round the church to prevent its removal. It is very powerfully painted, but, so far as one can see in the dim light of the sacristy, it is very dull, sober colouring for Murillo. There was a very early picture in the church itself, with a kind of shutter to close over it and only leave the faces exposed. At the back of the main altar there was some fine hammered silver work, also very old.

On our way back to the boat we entered a cottage to see the pretty common pottery made. The woman made it very rapidly. The clay is red and takes a fine glaze, and they make very pretty, as well as funny shapes, and decorate them with black and white, and scratch designs on them. We bought six pieces for seventeen cents.

After a very pleasant day on the lake we got back to the hotel at 5.30, and had a very bad supper. We afterwards met a Mr. Roberts from New Orleans, conductor on the Guadalahara railway, who had been in this neighbourhood and had learnt that there was a great Aztec king, named Calzontzin, who had ruled over the Sinzunzan district, buried in the village, and great treasures were supposed to be buried with him. Mr. Roberts and some of his friends clubbed together to dig up his Majesty, and, after going some feet into the ground, the labourers came to enormous stone slabs, which were raised, and under them was found the body of the king, very well preserved, but it fell to pieces as soon as it was touched. There were no treasures with him, and when they wished to dig deeper the Government interfered, so all their money was wasted. Mr. Roberts gave me a fragment of the old king's clothes, two of his teeth, a little head like those we got at Cholula, and some horn rings and one of silver, from chains of rings that were with the body. All these things were taken from the grave. If we had known when at Sinzunzan, we would have visited the spot.

Friday, December 14th.—We set off with our pockets full of money for the Patzcuaro weekly market, of which the guide-book had promised such great things. We found absolutely nothing to buy! It was a large market, but only of fruit, vegetables, matting, common pottery, and imported manufactured articles. A man took us to his house to show us some very elaborate feather-work pictures, large landscapes. They were curious, but very ugly. The colours of the feathers were not suitable for landscapes. We walked the two and a half miles from the lake to the town, as it was a terrible road to drive over, and the only available carriage was broken, and tied up with string in all directions. The Americans at the hotel charged us strictly not to return after dark, which was hardly likely as we started at 8.30 a.m., and they advised us anyhow to take a gun. One might as well take a gun along the Bayswater Road. A merrier, friendlier people I never saw. They were all laughing and chattering as they passed in shoals along the road, and most of them greeted us, and remarked that we were "Ingles." It was delightful to see how amiable and courteous they were with each other. The way a Mexican dismisses a beggar is characteristic of the people. He does not say, "Go away, you lazy rascal; you ought to be made to work," but he smiles sweetly upon the beggar, and says, "Perdonite, por Dios," ("Forgive me, for the love of God.") The effect is the same, but with less friction. We had a most amusing walk to the town, and on our return the glorious view over the lake made up for the absence of the people. There is nothing in the town specially worthy of a visit, though it is pretty, as all the towns are, and the hotel seemed better than ours. After our return we sat a long time on the balcony of the hotel watching the people return from the market and embark in their primitive canoes for home. Patzcuaro Lake is wonderfully pretty, and well worth the discomfort one has to put up with. Probably a better hotel will be started now that the line is open.

Saturday, December 15*th.*—We had a starlight walk to our train, which started at 5 a.m. It was very cold until the sun came out. After that the day was delightful. Had it not been for the kindness of the conductor,

Mr. Murray, a Canadian, we should not have got away, for the luggage-clerk said our box had come too late, it ought to have been there an hour before. We had to wait at Acambaro from 10.30 to 4.35. We walked through the very pretty town, and visited some churches, the finest and handsomest being San Francisco, which contains two large fine Chinese vases in the sacristy, one converted into a filter. The rest of the time we spent sitting on the benches that surrounded the fountain in the large garden of the Plaza Mayor, watching the people fetch water for their household consumption. All the water is carried by hand. Every town has its own peculiar fashion of carrying water, that is the professional water-carrier. The poor people fetch their own, children often bringing quite large jars to fill that seem much too heavy for them to carry. Each person drank what he wanted before filling the great earthen-ware vessels of all shapes and sizes. Though we did not see a person in Acambaro who appeared to have a penny to spare, there was an ice-vendor very busy. The cry, "Nieve; Nieve," is rarely silent in Mexican towns.

We got on to Celaya that evening, and put up at Hotel Solis. I think we should have done better at the other hotel; we could not well have done worse. Our room was about twenty-five feet square, and had no window or ventilation of any kind, except the door, which was not very large. The smell was most unpleasant. Edward dragged my bed close to the door, which we left open, so I slept quite well. We walked round the town after supper, and saw some magnificent churches, one especially looked very fine in the moonlight. The streets were full of people selling fruit and food of different kinds, and each little stall had a light made by a small fire in a brazier stuck on the end of a strong stick. These fires quite lighted up the streets, and made a warm glow on the lower part of the churches, while the cold blue light of the moon illuminated the upper part, and caught the tiles on the domes.

Sunday, December 16th.—Owing to the stupidity of the hotel servant, we were up far too early, and had to wait a long time for our train. We tried to get some coffee at the station, but found it too bad to drink. This is far from the coffee-growing country.

We arrived at Irapuato at 6.30 a.m., and had to wait two hours for the Guadalahara train, so we took the tram-car to the town, which is some way from the station, and tried to get some coffee in the market, which was being held in the great open space opposite the big church, and in the broad, principal street. The coffee was very bad, so we went to the Hotel del Ferro Carril, where we got a very fair meal. It appeared to be a much better hotel than that at Celaya, and is kept by a Havana Englishman. The town is full of beautiful churches, and is worthy of a longer visit than we made. Strawberries are said to be ripe here all the year round. We bought some at the station which were not fit to eat.

The journey to Guadalahara is not interesting, mostly over flat low-lying land. We got a very bad lunch in the middle of the day in a hut made out of old sleepers. The natives crowded round to watch the animals feed, and peered in through every crack and cranny in the walls. This line is only just completed; it was opened last May, and is a source of great excitement and astonishment to the natives. When we arrived at Guadalahara at 6 p.m., the station was densely packed with well-to-do people, who had come to see the train arrive. Half a mile out carriages and gentlemen on horseback were waiting to see the wonder. We had quite a struggle to get away. We engaged a man to take our box to a cab, but he set off direct to the hotel with it at a tremendous pace, and we had to tear after him, for when one of these men gets a load to carry he runs, and the heavier it is the faster he goes. We were delighted to meet an hotel servant, and set him to pursue the box, while we followed quietly. The dust was dreadful. The hotel was quite good—Hotel Cosmopolita.

Monday, December 17th.—The official in charge of the station lent us one of their people, a Mexican, who spoke English, to show us round and interpret for us. Our first excursion was to San Pedro, along the fashionable drive. Guadalahara is a social centre, many country people have houses there, and come in for the wet season. The self-taught artist, Panduro, lives at San Pedro, and it is also the centre of the pottery manufacture for which Guadalahara is famous. It excels all other native pottery, and is remarkable for its brilliant colouring and decorations in silver and gold. We bought a quantity of it for 25 dollars. Panduro works in clay, but he does not make vases and jars. He makes figures, water-carriers, men on horseback, groups,

&c., and his fame is principally owing to his portrait busts, which are three or four inches high, and very clever. He did Edward and me; both excellent likenesses. Panduro is a very intelligent-looking man, with full dark eyes, and a heavy crop of dark hair. He was at work in a shed when we arrived, but he took us to his bedroom for Edward's first sitting. It was a large room, beautifully clean. His serape spread on the bed for a quilt, and a picture of Our Lady of Guadalupe on the wall. In working he holds the lump of clay in his left hand and fashions it with his fingers, and with small bits of wood and iron sharpened to a point. Another excellent figure-maker is Pedro Zumiga.

There is no hotel at San Pedro, so we went into a little eating-house for lunch, where the woman was busy cooking and sending out meals, with the help of a servant. She only had a fire in a brazier, on which they put everything to cook in little pots and squatted by it, keeping up the fire with fans, and when there was nothing else to cook the servant made tortillas. Seeing we were people of note, and should require delicacies out of the ordinary way, she sent for some meat, curious fragments of some unknown animal, and eggs and sugar, and set to work to prepare our meal. It was all very nasty and very amusing. Unfortunately the husband came in quite drunk, and was put in a chair, where he went off to sleep at once. After finishing our shopping, we took the tram-car back to Guadalahara. After dinner we went to the Plaza Mayor, where the band was playing.

Tuesday, December 18*th.*—Every day during our short stay in Guadalahara, Panduro came in and worked on the busts. He had recently returned from a two months' visit to Mexico City, where he had been employed by President Diaz at 100 dollars a month and all expenses, to make busts of his family and friends. There was some talk of sending him to the French exhibition.

Guadalahara is a very handsome town, but looks too new to be so interesting as many others. It is extremely prosperous, being the centre of a rich district. The climate is said to be perfection, and certainly was so during our visit. It is warmer than Mexico City, being 700 feet lower. Our Mexican friend took us round the shops and to the prison, which is very large, accommodating 1100 prisoners. The building is very peculiar, and is made to suit the system of government, which is strictly Republican. On the ground-floor are long corridors, having on each side cells, fifteen feet by twenty feet. Each prisoner has a cell to himself. These corridors meet in three large courtyards, one for those who are awaiting their trial, one for men, and one for women. In the daytime the prisoners work together, and they are turned into the courtyards for an hour every evening for recreation. On this level there are no paid officials whatever. Order is kept by managers chosen from amongst the prisoners, generally men of a better class than the bulk or of more respectable antecedents. These managers are armed with clubs. If they do well, they get their term of imprisonment curtailed. One of the managers was a gentleman who had been rudely treated and struck by a police officer. He waylaid him next day and killed him. He was taken, tried, and sentenced to a long term of imprisonment. On the flat roof that covers the cells and forms long terraces commanding the courtyards and windows, and quite inaccessible from below, are stationed sentinels with loaded guns, who would shoot down at once any prisoner who attempted to escape, or was beyond the control of the managers. There were only twenty-five paid men in all the prison. Work is done by the prisoners and sold for their benefit. We bought a serape and some fire-fans, and we were shown some wonderful straw work sombreros, that were going to the Paris Exhibition. A charming old gentleman walked round the roofs with us and explained all this.

As we walked back from the prison we passed a very old Spanish church falling to ruins, and also San Felipe, which we entered, and a beautiful old church of the Capuchinas with a fine tower. This is the loveliest object in Guadalahara. After dinner we again went to hear the music on the plaza and found it illuminated in honour of the anniversary of some victory gained over the French by the Governor, whose palace forms one side of the plaza. Another side is occupied by the very ugly modern cathedral with towers like extinguishers.

We noticed several times in the town and in the courtyard of our own hotel, a curious pavement made of bones.

Wednesday, December 19*th.*—We visited the Orphanage, a large building where a number of orphans are brought up, the girls completely, the boys until the age of twelve, when they are transferred to the School of Artisans. All the children looked very happy and well cared for, and the bright, pleasant young lady who showed us round, told us she had been a pupil and was now a teacher, and knew nothing of the outside world. The children are taught, besides the ordinary subjects, photography, lithography, music, advanced drawing, and the most wonderful embroidery. They were making wonderful things for the Paris Exhibition.

Thursday, December 20*th.*—Our train left at 8 o'clock a.m., and arrived at Irapuato at 5.20 p.m. Some priests travelled by our train, one, a charming old gentleman, was seen off by about a dozen friends. It amused us much to watch their farewells. Besides much handshaking, they embraced him just like people do on the stage, no attempt at kissing at all, but first the right arm over the shoulder and the left arm on the waist, and then the left arm over the shoulder and the right arm on the waist. There was a lady amongst the friends who took leave the same way, but it was the most delicate, graceful ghost of an embrace, they just touched each other with the tips of their fingers. We took our lunch with us to avoid the horrid meal we had had in coming, and as we got plenty of delicious fruit on the way, we did well. We dined comfortably at the Hotel del Ferro Carril at Irapuato, and afterwards walked back to the station by starlight, joined the express at 7.40, and were fortunate in getting good berths. We arrived in Mexico at 7.15 next morning, and drove at once to the hotel for breakfast. We spent the whole day shopping and packing.

The plaza was full of booths and hawkers selling sweets, candied fruits, toys of all kinds, and great paper boxes of curious shapes, meant to be filled with bonbons, and hung up at Christmas parties as a kind of Aunt Sally, to be shied at. When broken, of course the sweets fall all over the floor, and the children scramble for them. Some were ballet-girls, some devils, balloons, fish, and the prettiest of all were ships in full sail. There was a great crowd, and numbers of boys with baskets, anxious to be hired to carry home purchases. A lady told me that on the Jour des Morts there was a similar market, but all the wares represented skeletons, coffins, death's-heads, or something pertaining to death or burial. Children were sucking sugar skulls, and the stall-keepers cried, "Fresh skeletons!" She gave me a skeleton ice-seller, wonderfully made in paper, for which she had paid a real.

Saturday, December 22nd.—We walked about the lovely city, feeling very sorrowful that we had to leave it so soon, and might never see the glorious cathedral again. We took the tram-car to Tacubaya, with which we were disappointed, as all the vaunted gardens are enclosed by high walls. We saw the Arbol Benito, under which a holy priest rested long years ago, and blessed it, that it should never lose its leaves, but be for ever green. I am sorry to say it was shedding its leaves rapidly, and was not green at all; but the fountain which sprang from the ground at the bidding of the priest is still there, so the tale must be true.

Sunday, December 23rd.—Again we visited the arcades, and bought some silver buttons and clasps, and some tiny wooden boots, exquisitely carved by an Indian, who picks up the old boots thrown into the street and copies them in miniature. We went up the cathedral tower again, and admired the lovely mountains that seemed close to us, the air was so clear.

Monday, December 24th.—By the kindness of Mr. Foot, of the Mexican Railroad, we were run down to San Juan Teotihuacan at 9.30 to see the wonderful Aztec remains, instead of having to take the only regular train in the day, which starts about 5 a.m., and would have given us a very long time to wait before we could return. A gentleman connected with the railway, who spoke Spanish, went with us. As there is no inn at San Juan, we took lunch with us, but nothing could induce the manager of the restaurant to lend us knives and forks; he said we might never come back. It was in vain that Johnny reminded him that we were leaving all our luggage in the hotel; he would not trust us. On our return we found him very penitent, and anxious to make friends again. He would come to us at almost every meal, and converse in Spanish in the most affable way, though he knew we could not understand what he said. We were an hour in the train, and then got into a wonderful old carriage that was waiting for us at the station, and drove over a rough road, over big stones and across beds of streams, all guiltless of water except one, where a little tiny brook trickled down a great ravine that would hold a roaring torrent in the rainy season. This stream was the Teotihuacan, and had a handsome new bridge across it. There were great hedges of organ cactus, and numbers of aloes and prickly pears. We passed a fine old church, much out of repair, and a few small cottages, each guarded by a savage dog. We had to take a long round to get to the Pyramid of the Moon, which we climbed in the heat of the day, and found it a very stiff pull, over loose stones and what had once been a path. The mound is built up principally of lime, concrete, and lava, and soon falls to pieces when meddled with. A large cavern had been dug into the rock to see if it contained any tombs, and a deep hole was discovered, but, having been left for some time, the roof had fallen in and the whole of it was choked up. The ground is covered with bits of broken crockery and obsidian arrowheads. People came to sell beads, little heads, and such things for a few coppers. Two large carvings offered us were very ugly, and coarse, and indistinct. The opinion of antiquarians is that each of these mounds was crowned by a temple, and the road, still plainly discernible, called the Pathway of the Dead, connected the two, while the immense city was built all round them.

The view from the top of the mound is very pretty and very curious, for the maguey fields are so different from anything one is accustomed to, and have a speckled appearance at a distance. I was disappointed with the Pathway of the Dead, which did not come up to the pictures of it. It is not a straight road from one mound to the other, it is straight for a long way, but not as far as the Pyramid of the Moon. At the top of the mound is a little altar with a wooden cross.

We scrambled down the other side and soon came to the colossal head forming a table, the whole one block of soft granite about five feet square. There is a gutter across the table, which is supposed to show that it was a sacrificial stone; but there is not the faintest stain of blood. We sat down by the stone to eat our lunch, and soon three friends gathered round us, and shared our meal. One was a man who squatted down beside us, and picked the carcase of the turkey. He found and carefully treasured the tinfoil off our bottle of wine. The other two were children, a funny little boy, and a sweet little girl, who was in charge of some goats. All we gave her she wrapped up in her reboso, and when we asked her where she was going to take it, she said, "A mi Mamma." I tried to get her to eat a tempting little cake, but she would not touch it, all must be taken to mamma. All three had a little store of clay heads and obsidian to sell. By the way it is a mystery how the ancient Mexicans procured so much obsidian. It is not much found in the country, if at all. We had a very pleasant lunch, and were much amused to see how the man refrained from pressing his goods upon us until we had purchased the children's. They were no relatives of his at all. We noticed this good feeling wherever we met the Indians selling things. They never seemed to care much whose wares we bought; nobody ever quarrelled or tried to get the better of the others. It was the same at the stations, and with the hawkers in the streets.

Many excavations have been made in the smaller mounds, and steps and foundations of houses have been discovered.

We had a rough climb up the Pyramid of the sun and down the other side. The mounds are high, the Moon 150 feet, and the Sun 216 feet, and there is not any road. Then we rejoined the carriage, and made off quickly to the station to catch the freight train, which landed us back in Mexico at 4.15. We had had a delightful day.

Christmas Day.—We could not help feeling a little homesick, especially as the whole of the hotel went to visit friends except ourselves. We had the restaurant to ourselves at dinner. A man came selling strawberries as we were at breakfast, so we bought some for a real, 5*d.*, just to say we had eaten fresh strawberries, grown out of doors, on Christmas Day. They had no flavour. We went to service in the cathedral in the morning, but there was nothing special, and in the plaza the people were busy pulling down the stalls, and taking them away. Evidently Christmas Day is not so much considered in Mexico as in England. Christmas Eve is the special occasion for family parties. In the afternoon we went to Guadalupe, hoping to find the great church open, but it was still closed.

Wednesday, December 26th.—An English firm had lent us their carpenter to help us to pack our purchases, and already he had spent hours measuring and making boxes, and putting in bits of wood he called "tavolas," to keep things apart. While Edward went off to get money and tickets, &c., the carpenter and I had quite a field-day. We managed to understand each other quite well somehow. He was very intelligent and obliging. At last, after great planning, and fixing, and fitting, and arranging, the fifth box was finished, and the dear man, who had been kindness and patience itself, took the hammer in his hand to put in the first nail of the last lid. "In the name of God," said he reverently as he struck the nail. It took me altogether about ten hours and quantities of cotton-wool to pack the large ivory figure alone. That very morning we secured the little ivory chorister boy we had bargained for so long in the Plaza San Domingo.

Thursday, December 27th.—It was a foggy morning, so we did not see Popocatepetl and Iztaccihuatl any more, but we got a glimpse of the cathedral towers as we drove to the station to take the Central Railway as far as Celaya. We saw our driver in the crowd that met the train at Quérétaro, and exchanged greetings. At Celaya we only had time to get across from one station to the other, to take the national line to San Miguel d'Allende, where we arrived in the dark, and left next morning before day, so we saw nothing of it, but we had a pleasant evening with Mr. Ferrars, who put us up in his nice little house there.

Friday, December 28th.—We were at the station at 4.40 a.m., only to find the train was two hours behind time. We waited in the station-master's office where there were five men asleep around the stove; the conductor on a camp-bed, two men on the floor, one on the table, and one on a box. Two more unfortunate travellers soon joined the party. When the train arrived we could not get into the Pulman car because the people had not got up yet, and the first-class was very uncomfortable, being crowded with second-class passengers, because there was no second-class car on the train. It is advisable in Mexico always to take second-class tickets if you do not wish to go in the Pulman car, for either there is no first-class car and all the travellers are put in the second-class, or there is no second-class and everybody goes in the first. This is often the case on American railways, too.

We arrived one and three-quarter hours late at San Luis Potosi, where Mr. Wharf met us, and took possession of us, and made life pleasant for us during our stay at San Luis. There was a great crowd to see the train come in, as there was at Guadalahara, because here, too, the line has only been opened a short time. We enjoyed our visit to San Luis immensely. It was delightful to have pleasant friends to talk to, and go about with. Mr. Wharf was the manager of that branch of the Central Railway, and lived at San Luis with his family, and there was also the engineer of the line to Tampico, Mr. Schmidt and his wife, who were kind to us. The hotel was poor, so Mr. and Mrs. Wharf insisted on our taking all our meals with them, which was very pleasant and home-like.

San Luis is a very prosperous town, increasing

rapidly, and likely to become a large place, as both the National and Central Railways go through it. There are some very fine old churches. The Cathedral is handsome outside, but poorly decorated inside, and the façade of the Church of El Carmen is exceedingly rich, with carved columns, and a very fine tower. Near the top of the façade is a curious attempt to represent clouds in carved stone. There is a very large alameda near the station, and a large market where I bought a napkin, decorated with drawn work, from an old woman's cake-basket. I offered her a dollar for it and though that was quite a large sum for her, she was unwilling to sell because it would disturb her little show of biscuits. At last her friends persuaded her to make the effort. The Plaza on which the Cathedral and hotel are situated is very pretty.

The pawnbrokers were delightful. I got several nice things, amongst them an old carved ivory fan. I asked the man the price, and I understood him to say *doce* (twelve), so knowing that one must always bargain in Mexico, I was just going to say, "Too dear, I will give you ten and a half," when Mrs. Wharf remarked, she did not think two (*dos*) dollars was a high price for it, so I altered my remark, and said, "Too dear, I will give give you one and a half for it." I got it for one and three-quarters. *Dos* pronounced "doss," and *doce*, pronounced "docee," sound much alike.

The next day we spent the same way, roaming about the town and visiting the churches. We saw the people fetching water from a fountain, and while we watched them they completely emptied the basin, although it was playing all the time. Waterworks are to be constructed shortly to supply the city, by an eminent English engineer. Like Guadalahara, San Luis enjoys a perfect climate, and it is said is becoming quite a health-resort. It is more interesting in itself, and the surrounding country prettier than Guadalahara. The sun comes out day after day with unfailing regularity, and even the wet season is healthy and pleasant. Wonderful embroidery is made in this neighbourhood, especially drawn work.

Sunday, December 30*th.*—We left San Luis at 9.50 a.m., our kind friends seeing us off. We had a dreary journey through an ugly flat country, stopping perpetually because something had gone wrong with the locomotive; at one time we stuck on a curve for an hour and a half. We got no dinner, because instead of arriving at Saltillo at 7 o'clock, we did not get there until 11 p.m. We went to bed at last in despair, and the porter brought us some black coffee at midnight.

Monday, December 31*st.*—We arrived at Nuevo Laredo, where we got breakfast, an 9.15. The Mexican customs examination was nominal, and the American officer examined the boxes quite quietly, not upsetting anything.

We felt very doleful about leaving Mexico, which is, of all countries, the most beautiful and the pleasantest to travel in. The pure bracing air and heavenly sunshine make one feel happy and ready to enjoy everything. I never saw a happier-looking people.

Numbers of Englishmen are settling in Mexico, which is full of minerals, especially on the west, while the fertility of the country is extraordinary. The English get on well with the natives, and find them very satisfactory workpeople, anxious to learn, and not afraid of work. Often the English marry Mexican ladies, who are very pretty and devoted to home life.

Part of the Central Railway having been washed away, the men worked most energetically to get it put right, going on as long as daylight lasted. We asked the contractor what he paid for overwork. "We pay them for all they work over twenty-four hours a day," he said.

We had a dreary journey from Laredo to San Anton. The day was dull and rainy, and the country ugly and flat. As usual, the train was late, so the Southern Pacific train had gone on without us, and we had to spend the night at San Anton. The Menger Hotel is a large second-class house with first-class prices.

Tuesday, January 1st.—The new year came in cold and dull. We started in the morning for New Orleans. We could get no Pulman car until we reached Houston, where a capital dinner was set before us; but we had only time to pay for it, not to eat it.

We arrived at New Orleans early next morning. It is a disagreable entrance like San Francisco; one has to leave the train and go on a ferry-boat. There is some talk of building a bridge to enable trains of all lines to run into the city. The St. Charles Hotel is very good. We had unpleasant, rainy, cold weather all the time we were in New Orleans, which is a dreadfully damp place. The country is perfectly flat as far as one can see, and very ugly. In fine weather New Orleans is probably a very pleasant city, but it looked very ugly and dirty to us. The main street, Canal Street, is immensely broad, 200 feet, and must have been very pretty when there was an avenue of trees down the middle of it; but now that the avenue is replaced by a tram-line, the beauty has departed.

The old French Cathedral and the buildings on each side of it in Jackson Square are very handsome and interesting; they are so totally different from anything else in America. It is strange to pass from the bustling streets, full of black folk, to this peaceable, lonely spot, like a bit of an old French town. Another survival of the French times is the expression "Creole," taken to signify anything first-class; for instance, the *ménu* at breakfast included "Creole eggs," which I ordered, hoping to discover a new dish, but the waiter explained it only signified they were best quality. No doubt it acquired this signification when the Creoles monopolized all the good things. We walked to the jetty, which seemed to be covered with cotton ready for shipping. Negroes everywhere, rather short and poor-looking. The policemen even there were Irish. We spoke to one, and he answered us in a lovely brogue.

We took the car to the great cemeteries to see the monuments to the Confederate Generals. The finest is that to General Andrew Johnson, an equestrian statue of great spirit. There were fresh bouquets and wreaths on the tomb. When I was subsequently buying photographs of New Orleans I could not find one of this statue, but the photographer said he would get one for me somehow and send it to England, and he did so. He would not be paid for it; he seemed pleased at our admiration for it, and for Southern pluck. Most of the graves are very costly, being small houses to contain the coffins, as the ground is too wet for them to be buried.

Thursday, January 3rd.—Another cold, rainy day. Mr. Corthell, the eminent engineer, who is to build the new bridge over the Mississippi, took us with him in a tug up the river to the place where it is to cross, and then down to where a carpet was being made of trees, brushwood, &c., held together by iron bands and wire, 18 inches thick, 200 feet wide, and 300 feet long, to lie upon the side of the river-bank up to low-water mark, and along the bottom, which is 150 feet deep. It was to be kept in place by heavy stones, in order to protect the bank, which the river continually carries away, 120 feet having been carried away in one year. What the Mississippi takes from one bank it gives to the other, to the detriment of both. A gentleman of the party, a town commissioner, told us he remembered when the river extended over the space now occupied by the jetty whence we started, and three blocks of houses up to the Custom House. The carpet costs 12 dollars per foot, and is confidently expected to prevent further trouble. We passed a number of wooden barges, like long boxes, with square ends, each containing 1000 tons of coal, brought all the way from Pittsburg—2600 miles—on the river, at the rate of 1½ dollars a ton. One steamer can bring thirty of these barges down stream, but the current is so strong that only a quarter of them can be taken back empty. The rest are sold for 25 dollars each for firewood, though they cost 700 to make. We saw, also, the flat boats that bring fruit from Honduras and the hot countries to New Orleans, whence it is sent north by train, and the curious cotton steamers, with the cabins supported on columns, and all the deck covered with cotton-bales. These steamers used to do a large passenger trade before the railways were made. The river itself is only admirable for its great size. The water is muddy, and the banks flat. We were shivering in the cold east wind, and very glad to get on shore and find a cab to take us through the drenching rain to the hotel, where a good dinner soon warmed us.

That afternoon and next day, also cold and wet, we spent arranging for our homeward journey. We found that none of the big boats of any line were running to suit us, so we took a cabin on the s.s. *Fulda*, of the Nord-deutscher Lloyd. We left New Orleans at 5.30 p.m. by the Illinois Central, and after a dreary journey we arrived at Cairo at 6 p.m. next day, five hours late, so it was too dark to see the bridge for whose sake we had come so far out of our way. We reached St. Louis about midnight, and put up at the excellent Southern Hotel, especially recommended in the advertisement as "fireproof," which seems to be a favourite description of anything superior in St. Louis. I suppose conflagrations are common there.

The pride of St. Louis is the fine bridge built by Captain Eads over the great river. The city is very large, smoky, and prosperous, quite new and handsome, and utterly uninteresting.

We left by the 8 p.m. train next day for New York by the Vandalia route, very rough and shaky. When a carriage was added to the train it was done with such force that we thought it was a collision. At Pittsburg we were transferred to the Pennsylvania Central, which is a first-class line. From there we ran at night through a country of forges and coke-ovens, and immense towns flaring with natural gas. It was a fine sight in its way.[1]

Tuesday, 8th January.—We arrived at New York at 8.40 a.m., and had once more the weary business of crossing the ferry, which makes the entrance to so many American cities unsightly and disagreeable. We were busy all day arranging for our departure, and only found time to visit Tiffany's shop, of which one hears so much. We were much disappointed with it. It is like a large bazaar, and though things were very nice, they were no better than half-a-dozen big London jewellers, and there were no large pieces of silver. Things were of the wedding present description. Edward dined with some friends, so I had to go down alone, and to my horror, was placed by the head waiter to do gooseberry at a small table where a gentleman was entertaining a very pretty, sweet-looking girl. He was

[1] The district since drowned by the bursting of the great reservoir.

an author, and she had read his book and they talked literature. "Do you like Tennyson?" "Oh so much. Do you like Emerson?" "Oh yes, I have read everything he wrote. Do you like Longfellow?" As long as they kept to this style of criticism they did very well, but at last they got to Shakespeare, whose Antony and Cleopatra seems to contain the "To be or not to be" speech, in the American version. Then the gentleman struggled valiantly with Antony's speech about an honourable man; he was sure there was something about an honourable man in it, and the lady remarked that Shakespeare was a great friend of her father, and often dropped in to tea. This was too much for the author, so he changed the subject.

As I listened to the conversation going on around me, I gathered that nearly every one present lived permanently at the hotel, which seems to be quite a little social world in itself. Between eight and nine o'clock a number of ladies went away from the hotel, evidently to some kind of entertainment, for they were most expensively and elegantly dressed in bright or very light colours, but with bonnets. I suppose they must have been going to the theatre or concerts. The ideas of American ladies on dress are very different from ours. It is only lately that they have generally adopted low dresses at all, but now they wear them more than we do. A lady who gives an afternoon at home, wears a low-necked dress and so do her daughters, and the young ladies who are asked to help to entertain, but the guests come in bonnets and cloaks. It must either be very hot for them, or very cold for the hostess.

Wednesday, January 9th.—We went on board the *Fulda* at 11 a.m., and started punctually at noon. Our cabin was very comfortable; and the whole boat clean and well ventilated, the food remarkably good and the servants very attentive. The first night was very rough, and only six passengers appeared for breakfast next morning, but after that we all got quite well, and then it was I learnt the truth of the sailor's proverb about "the appetite of a first-class passenger." The weather was delightfully warm and sunny, and though the sea was very rough, no one was the worse for it of all the 120 passengers. The *Fulda* seemed to be such a little cockle-shell of a boat compared to the *Umbria*, and of course went much more slowly. We landed at Southampton on the 17th January, and reached London at nine o'clock the same evening. Some day, when the new steamers make the voyage across the Atlantic a pleasure instead of the dreary business it is now, we hope to return to sunny Mexico and its merry, courteous people.

LONDON:
PRINTED BY GILBERT AND RIVINGTON, LIMITED,
ST. JOHN'S HOUSE, CLERKENWELL ROAD.

A Catalogue of American and Foreign Books Published or Imported by MESSRS. SAMPSON LOW & CO. *can' be had on application.*

St. Dunstan's House, Fetter Lane, Fleet Street, London,
October, 1889.

A Selection from the List of Books

PUBLISHED BY

SAMPSON LOW, MARSTON, SEARLE, & RIVINGTON,

LIMITED.

Low's Standard Novels, page 17.
Low's Standard Books for Boys, page 18.
Low's Standard Series, page 19.
Sea Stories, by W. CLARK RUSSELL, page 26.

ALPHABETICAL LIST.

ABBEY and Parsons, Quiet life. From drawings; the motive by Austin Dobson, 4to.

Abney (W. de W.) and Cunningham. Pioneers of the Alps. With photogravure portraits of guides. Imp. 8vo, gilt top, 21s.

Adam (G. Mercer) and Wetherald. An Algonquin Maiden. Crown 8vo, 5s.

Alcott. Works of the late Miss Louisa May Alcott:—
  Aunt Jo's Scrap-bag. Cloth, 2s.
  Eight Cousins. Illustrated, 2s.; cloth gilt, 3s. 6d.
  Jack and Jill. Illustrated, 2s.; cloth gilt, 3s. 6d.
  Jo's Boys. 5s.
  Jimmy's Cruise in the Pinafore, &c. Illustrated, cloth, 2s.; gilt edges, 3s. 6d.
  Little Men. Double vol., 2s.; cloth, gilt edges, 3s. 6d.
  Little Women. 1s. } 1 vol., cloth, 2s.; larger ed., gilt
  Little Women Wedded. 1s. } edges, 3s. 6d.
  Old-fashioned Girl. 2s.; cloth, gilt edges, 3s. 6d.
  Rose in Bloom. 2s.; cloth gilt, 3s. 6d.
  Shawl Straps. Cloth, 2s.
  Silver Pitchers. Cloth, gilt edges, 3s. 6d.
  Under the Lilacs. Illustrated, 2s ; cloth gilt, 5s.
  Work: a Story of Experience. 1s. } 1 vol., cloth, gilt
  ——— Its Sequel, "Beginning Again." 1s. } edges, 3s. 6d.
 ——— *Life, Letters and Journals.* By EDNAH D. CHENEY. Cr. 8vo, 6s.
 ——— See also "Low's Standard Series."

Alden (W. L.) Adventures of Jimmy Brown, written by himself. Illustrated. Small crown 8vo, cloth, 2s.
 ——— *Trying to find Europe.* Illus., crown 8vo, 5s.

A

Alger (*J. G.*) *Englishmen in the French Revolution,* cr. 8vo, 7s. 6d.
Amateur Angler's Days in Dove Dale: Three Weeks' Holiday in 1884. By E. M. 1s. 6d.; boards, 1s.; large paper, 5s.
Andersen. Fairy Tales. An entirely new Translation. With over 500 Illustrations by Scandinavian Artists. Small 4to, 6s.
Anderson (*W.*) *Pictorial Arts of Japan.* With 80 full-page and other Plates, 16 of them in Colours. Large imp. 4to, £8 8s. (in four folio parts, £2 2s. each); Artists' Proofs, £12 12s.
Angling. See Amateur, "Cutcliffe," "Fennell," "Halford," "Hamilton," "Martin," "Orvis," "Pennell," "Pritt," "Senior," "Stevens," "Theakston," "Walton," "Wells," and "Willis-Bund."
Arnold (*R.*) *Ammonia and Ammonium Compounds.* Translated, illus., crown 8vo, 5s.
Art Education. See "Biographies," "D'Anvers," "Illustrated Text Books," "Mollett's Dictionary."
Artistic Japan. Illustrated with Coloured Plates. Monthly. Royal 4to, 2s.; vol. I., 15s.; II., roy. 4to., 15s.
Ashe (*R. P.*) *Two Kings of Uganda; Six Years in E. Equatorial Africa.* Crown 8vo, 6s.
Attwell (*Prof.*) *The Italian Masters.* Crown 8vo, 3s. 6d.
Audsley (*G. A.*) *Handbook of the Organ.* Imperial 8vo, top edge gilt, 31s. 6d.; large paper, 63s.
—— *Ornamental Arts of Japan.* 90 Plates, 74 in Colours and Gold, with General and Descriptive Text. 2 vols., folio, £15 15s.; in specially designed leather, £23 2s.
—— *The Art of Chromo-Lithography.* Coloured Plates and Text. Folio, 63s.

*B*ACON (*Delia*) *Biography, with Letters of Carlyle, Emerson,* &c. Crown 8vo, 10s. 6d.
Baddeley (*W. St. Clair*) *Tchay and Chianti.* Small 8vo, 5s.
—— *Travel-tide.* Small post 8vo, 7s. 6d.
Baldwin (*James*) *Story of Siegfried.* 6s.
—— *Story of the Golden Age.* Illustrated by HOWARD PYLE. Crown 8vo, 6s.
—— *Story of Roland.* Crown 8vo, 6s.
Bamford (*A. J.*) *Turbans and Tails.* Sketches in the Unromantic East. Crown 8vo, 7s. 6d.
Barlow (*Alfred*) *Weaving by Hand and by Power.* With several hundred Illustrations. Third Edition, royal 8vo, £1 5s.
Barlow (*P. W.*) *Kaipara, Experiences of a Settler in N. New Zealand.* Illust., crown 8vo, 6s.
Bassett (*F. S.*) *Legends and Superstitions of the Sea.* 7s. 6d.

THE BAYARD SERIES.

Edited by the late J. HAIN FRISWELL.

Comprising Pleasure Books of Literature produced in the Choicest Style.

"We can hardly imagine better books for boys to read or for men to ponder over."—*Times*.
Price 2s. 6d. each Volume, complete in itself, flexible cloth extra, gilt edges, with silk Headbands and Registers.

The Story of the Chevalier Bayard.
Joinville's St. Louis of France.
The Essays of Abraham Cowley.
Abdallah. By Édouard Laboullaye.
Napoleon, Table-Talk and Opinions.
Words of Wellington.
Johnson's Rasselas. With Notes.
Hazlitt's Round Table.
The Religio Medici, Hydriotaphia, &c. By Sir Thomas Browne, Knt.
Coleridge's Christabel, &c. With Preface by Algernon C. Swinburne.
Ballad Poetry of the Affections. By Robert Buchanan.
Lord Chesterfield's Letters, Sentences, and Maxims. With Essay by Sainte-Beuve.
The King and the Commons. Cavalier and Puritan Songs.
Vathek. By William Beckford.
Essays in Mosaic. By Ballantyne.
My Uncle Toby; his Story and his Friends. By P. Fitzgerald.
Reflections of Rochefoucauld.
Socrates: Memoirs for English Readers from Xenophon's Memorabilia. By Edw. Levien.
Prince Albert's Golden Precepts.

A Case containing 12 Volumes, price 31s. 6d.; or the Case separately, price 3s. 6d.

Beaugrand (C.) Walks Abroad of Two Young Naturalists. By D. SHARP. Illust., 8vo, 7s. 6d.

Beecher (H. W.) Authentic Biography, and Diary. Ill. 8vo, 21s.

Behnke and Browne. Child's Voice: its Treatment with regard to After Development. Small 8vo, 3s. 6d.

Bell (H. H. J.) Obeah: Negro Superstition in the West Indies. Crown 8vo, 2s. 6d.

Beyschlag. Female Costume Figures of various Centuries. 12 reproductions of pastel designs in portfolio, imperial. 21s.

Bickerdyke (J.) Irish Midsummer Night's Dream. Illus. by E. M. COX. Crown 8vo, 1s. 6d.; boards, 1s.

Bickersteth (Bishop E. H.) Clergyman in his Home. 1s.
—— *Evangelical Churchmanship.* 1s.
—— *From Year to Year: Original Poetical Pieces.* Small post 8vo, 3s. 6d.; roan, 6s. and 5s.; calf or morocco, 10s. 6d.
—— *The Master's Home-Call.* N. ed. 32mo, cloth gilt, 1s.
—— *The Master's Will.* A Funeral Sermon preached on the Death of Mrs. S. Gurney Buxton. Sewn, 6d.; cloth gilt, 1s.
—— *The Reef, and other Parables.* Crown 8vo, 2s. 6d.
—— *Shadow of the Rock.* Select Religious Poetry. 2s. 6d.
—— *Shadowed Home and the Light Beyond.* 5s.
—— See also "Hymnal Companion."

Biographies of the Great Artists (Illustrated). Crown 8vo, emblematical binding, 3s. 6d. per volume, except where the price is given.

Claude le Lorrain, by Owen J. Dullea.
Correggio, by M. E. Heaton. 2s. 6d.
Della Robbia and Cellini. 2s. 6d.
Albrecht Dürer, by R. F. Heath.
Figure Painters of Holland.
Fra Angelico, Masaccio, and Botticelli.
Fra Bartolommeo, Albertinelli, and Andrea del Sarto.
Gainsborough and Constable.
Ghiberti and Donatello. 2s. 6d.
Giotto, by Harry Quilter.
Hans Holbein, by Joseph Cundall.
Hogarth, by Austin Dobson.
Landseer, by F. G. Stevens.
Lawrence and Romney, by Lord Ronald Gower. 2s. 6d.
Leonardo da Vinci.
Little Masters of Germany, by W. B. Scott.
Mantegna and Francia.
Meissonier, by J. W. Mollett. 2s. 6d.
Michelangelo Buonarotti, by Clément.
Murillo, by Ellen E. Minor. 2s. 6d.
Overbeck, by J. B. Atkinson.
Raphael, by N. D'Anvers.
Rembrandt, by J. W. Mollett.
Reynolds, by F. S. Pulling.
Rubens, by C. W. Kett.
Tintoretto, by W. R. Osler.
Titian, by R. F. Heath.
Turner, by Cosmo Monkhouse.
Vandyck and Hals, by P. R. Head.
Velasquez, by E. Stowe.
Vernet and Delaroche, by J. Rees.
Watteau, by J. W. Mollett. 2s. 6d.
Wilkie, by J. W. Mollett.

IN PREPARATION.

Barbizon School, by J. W. Mollett.
Cox and De Wint, Lives and Works.
George Cruikshank, Life and Works.
Miniature Painters of Eng. School.
Mulready Memorials, by Stephens.
Van de Velde and the Dutch Painters

Bird (*F. J.*) *American Practical Dyer's Companion.* 8vo, 42s.

—— (*H. E.*) *Chess Practice.* 8vo, 2s. 6d.

Black (*Robert*) *Horse Racing in France: a History.* 8vo, 14s.

—— See also CICERO.

Black (*W.*) *Penance of John Logan, and other Tales.* Crown 8vo, 10s. 6d.

——See also " Low's Standard Library."

Blackburn (*Charles F.*) *Hints on Catalogue Titles and Index* Entries, with a Vocabulary of Terms and Abbreviations, chiefly from Foreign Catalogues. Royal 8vo, 14s.

Blackburn (*Henry*) *Art in the Mountains, the Oberammergau* Passion Play. New ed., corrected to date, 8vo, 5s.

—— *Breton Folk.* With 171 Illust. by RANDOLPH CALDECOTT. Imperial 8vo, gilt edges, 21s.; plainer binding, 10s. 6d.

—— *Pyrenees.* Illustrated by GUSTAVE DORÉ, corrected to 1881. Crown 8vo, 7s. 6d. See also CALDECOTT.

Blackmore (*R. D.*) *Kit and Kitty.* A novel. 3 vols., crown 8vo, 31s. 6d.

—— *Lorna Doone. Édition de luxe.* Crown 4to, very numerous Illustrations, cloth, gilt edges, 31s. 6d.; parchment, uncut, top gilt, 35s.; new issue, plainer, 21s.

—— *Novels.* See also " Low's Standard Novels."

Blackmore (R. D.) Springhaven. Illust. by PARSONS and BARNARD. Sq. 8vo, 12s.; new edition, 7s. 6d.

Blaikie (William) How to get Strong and how to Stay so. Rational, Physical, Gymnastic, &c., Exercises. Illust., sm. post 8vo, 5s.

—— *Sound Bodies for our Boys and Girls.* 16mo, 2s. 6d.

Bonwick. British Colonies. Asia, 1s.; Africa, 1s.; America, 1s.; Australasia, 1s. One vol., cloth, 5s.

Bosanquet (Rev. C.) Blossoms from the King's Garden: Sermons for Children. 2nd Edition, small post 8vo, cloth extra, 6s.

—— *Jehoshaphat; or, Sunlight and Clouds.* 1s.

Bowden (H.; Miss) Witch of the Atlas: a ballooning story, Crown 8vo, 6s.

Bower (G. S.) and Spencer, Law of Electric Lighting. New edition, crown 8vo, 12s. 6d.

Boyesen (H. H.) Modern Vikings: Stories of Life and Sport in Norseland. Cr. 8vo, 6s.

—— *Story of Norway.* Illustrated, sm. 8vo, 7s. 6d.

Boy's Froissart. King Arthur. Knightly Legends of Wales. Percy. See LANIER.

Bradshaw (J.) New Zealand as it is. 8vo, 12s. 6d.

—— *New Zealand of To-day*, 1884-87. 8vo, 14s.

Brannt (W. T.) Animal and Vegetable Fats and Oils. Illust., 8vo, 35s.

—— *Manufacture of Soap and Candles, with many Formulas.* Illust., 8vo, 35s.

—— *Manufacture of Vinegar, Cider, and Fruit Wines.* Illustrated, 8vo.

—— *Metallic Alloys. Chiefly from the German of Krupp* and Wildberger. Crown 8vo, 12s. 6d.

Bright (John) Public Letters. Crown 8vo, 7s. 6d.

Brisse (Baron) Menus (366). A *ménu*, in French and English, for every Day in the Year. 2nd Edition. Crown 8vo, 5s.

Brittany. See BLACKBURN.

Browne (G. Lennox) Voice Use and Stimulants. Sm. 8vo, 3s. 6d.

—— and Behnke *(Emil) Voice, Song, and Speech.* N. ed., 5s.

Brumm (C.) Bismarck, his Deeds and Aims; reply to " Bismarck Dynasty." 8vo, 1s.

Bruntie's Diary. A Tour round the World. By C. E. B., 1s. 6d.

Bryant (W. C.) and Gay (S. H.) History of the United States. 4 vols., royal 8vo, profusely Illustrated, 60s.

Bryce (Rev. Professor) Manitoba. Illust. Crown 8vo, 7s. 6d.

—— *Short History of the Canadian People.* 7s. 6d.

Bulkeley (Owen T.) Lesser Antilles. Pref. by D. MORRIS. Illus., crown 8vo, boards, 2s. 6d.

Burnaby (Mrs. F.) High Alps in Winter; or, *Mountaineering in Search of Health.* With Illustrations, &c., 14s. See also MAIN.
Burnley (J.) History of the Silk Trade.
—— *History of Wool and Woolcombing.* Illust. 8vo, 21s.
Burton (Sir R. F.) Early, Public, and Private Life. Edited by F. HITCHMAN. 2 vols., 8vo, 36s.
Butler (Sir W. F.) Campaign of the Cataracts. Illust., 8vo, 18s.
—— *Invasion of England, told twenty years after.* 2s. 6d.
—— *Red Cloud;* or, *the Solitary Sioux.* Imperial 16mo, numerous illustrations, gilt edges, 3s. 6d.; plainer binding, 2s. 6d.
—— *The Great Lone Land; Red River Expedition.* 7s. 6d.
—— *The Wild North Land; the Story of a Winter Journey* with Dogs across Northern North America. 8vo, 18s. Cr. 8vo, 7s. 6d.
Bynner (E. L.) Agnes Surriage. Crown 8vo, 10s. 6d.

CABLE (G. W.) *Bonaventure: A Prose Pastoral of Acadian Louisiana.* Sm. post 8vo, 5s.
Cadogan (Lady A.) Drawing-room Plays. 10s. 6d.; acting ed., 6d. each.
—— *Illustrated Games of Patience.* Twenty-four Diagrams in Colours, with Text. Fcap. 4to, 12s. 6d.
—— *New Games of Patience.* Coloured Diagrams, 4to, 12s. 6d.
Caldecott (Randolph) Memoir. By HENRY BLACKBURN. With 170 Examples of the Artist's Work. 14s.; new edit., 7s. 6d.
—— *Sketches.* With an Introduction by H. BLACKBURN. 4to, picture boards, 2s. 6d.
California. See NORDHOFF.
Callan (H.) Wanderings on Wheel and on Foot. Cr. 8vo, 1s. 6d.
Campbell (Lady Colin) Book of the Running Brook: and of Still Waters. 5s.
Canadian People: Short History. Crown 8vo, 7s. 6d.
Carbutt (Mrs.) Five Months' Fine Weather in Canada, West U.S., and Mexico. Crown 8vo, 5s.
Carleton, City Legends. Special Edition, illus., royal 8vo, 12s. 6d.; ordinary edition, crown 8vo, 1s.
—— *City Ballads.* Illustrated, 12s. 6d. New Ed. (Rose Library), 16mo, 1s.
—— *Farm Ballads, Farm Festivals, and Farm Legends.* Paper boards, 1s. each; 1 vol., small post 8vo, 3s. 6d.
Carnegie (A.) American Four-in-Hand in Britain. Small 4to, Illustrated, 10s. 6d. Popular Edition, paper, 1s.
—— *Round the World.* 8vo, 10s. 6d.
—— *Triumphant Democracy.* 6s.; also 1s. 6d. and 1s.
Chairman's Handbook. By R. F. D. PALGRAVE. 5th Edit., 2s.

Changed Cross, &c. Religious Poems. 16mo, 2s. 6d.; calf, 6s.
Chess. See BIRD (H. E.).
Children's Praises. Hymns for Sunday-Schools and Services. Compiled by LOUISA H. H. TRISTRAM. 4d.
Choice Editions of Choice Books. 2s. 6d. each. Illustrated by C. W. COPE, R.A., T. CRESWICK, R.A., E. DUNCAN, BIRKET FOSTER, J. C. HORSLEY, A.R.A., G. HICKS, R. REDGRAVE, R.A., C. STONEHOUSE, F. TAYLER, G. THOMAS, H. J. TOWNSHEND, E. H. WEHNERT, HARRISON WEIR, &c.

Bloomfield's Farmer's Boy.	Milton's L'Allegro.
Campbell's Pleasures of Hope.	Poetry of Nature. Harrison Weir.
Coleridge's Ancient Mariner.	Rogers' (Sam.) Pleasures of Memory.
Goldsmith's Deserted Village.	Shakespeare's Songs and Sonnets.
Goldsmith's Vicar of Wakefield.	Tennyson's May Queen.
Gray's Elegy in a Churchyard.	Elizabethan Poets.
Keats' Eve of St. Agnes.	Wordsworth's Pastoral Poems.

"Such works are a glorious beatification for a poet."—*Athenæum.*

Christ in Song. By PHILIP SCHAFF. New Ed., gilt edges, 6s.
Chromo-Lithography. See AUDSLEY.
Cicero, Tusculan Disputation, I. (Death no bane). Translated by R. BLACK. Small crown 8vo.
Clarke (H. P.) See WILLS.
Clarke (P.) Three Diggers: a Tale of the Australian Fifties. Crown 8vo, 6s.
Cochran (W.) Pen and Pencil in Asia Minor. Illust., 8vo, 21s.
Collingwood (Harry) Under the Meteor Flag. The Log of a Midshipman. Illustrated, small post 8vo, gilt, 3s. 6d.; plainer, 2s. 6d.
—— *Voyage of the "Aurora."* Gilt, 3s. 6d.; plainer, 2s. 6d.
Collinson (Sir R.; Adm.) H.M.S. "Enterprise" in search of Sir J. Franklin. 8vo.
Colonial Year-book. Edited and compiled by A. J. R. TRENDELL. Crown 8vo, 6s.
Cook (Dutton) Book of the Play. New Edition. 1 vol., 3s. 6d.
—— *On the Stage: Studies.* 2 vols., 8vo, cloth, 24s.
Cozzens (F.) American Yachts. 27 Plates, 22 × 28 inches. Proofs, £21; Artist's Proofs, £31 10s.
Craddock (C. E.) Despot of Broomsedge Cove. Crown 8vo, 6s.
Crew (B. J.) Practical Treatise on Petroleum. Illust., 8vo, 28s.
Crouch (A.P.) Glimpses of Feverland: a Cruise in West African Waters. Crown 8vo, 6s.
—— *On a Surf-bound Coast.* Crown 8vo, 7s. 6d.
Cumberland (Stuart) Thought Reader's Thoughts. Cr. 8vo., 10s. 6d.
—— *Queen's Highway from Ocean to Ocean.* Ill., 8vo, 18s.; new ed., 7s. 6d.

Cumberland (S.) Vasty deep : a Strange Story of To-day. New Edition, 6s.

Cundall (Joseph). See " Remarkable Bindings."

Cushing (W.) Initials and Pseudonyms. Large 8vo, 25s.; second series, large 8vo, 21s.

Custer (Eliz. B.) Tenting on the Plains; Gen. Custer in Kansas and Texas. Royal 8vo, 18s.

Cutcliffe (H. C.) Trout Fishing in Rapid Streams. Cr. 8vo, 3s. 6d.

DALY (Mrs. D.) Digging, Squatting, and Pioneering in Northern South Australia. 8vo, 12s.

D'Anvers. Elementary History of Art. New ed., 360 illus., 2 vols., cr. 8vo. I. Architecture, &c., 5s.; II. Painting, 6s.; 1 vol., 10s. 6d.

—— *Elementary History of Music.* Crown 8vo, 2s. 6d.

Davis (Clement) Modern Whist. 4s.

—— *(C. T.) Bricks, Tiles, Terra-Cotta, &c.* N. ed. 8vo, 25s.

—— *Manufacture of Leather.* With many Illustrations. 52s.6d.

—— *Manufacture of Paper.* 28s.

—— *(G. B.) Outlines of International Law.* 8vo. 10s. 6d.

Dawidowsky. Glue, Gelatine, Isinglass, Cements, &c. 8vo, 12s.6d.

Day of My Life at Eton. By an ETON BOY. New ed. 16mo, 1s.

Day's Collacon : an Encyclopædia of Prose Quotations. Imperial 8vo, cloth, 31s. 6d.

De Leon (E.) Under the Stars and under the Crescent. N.ed., 6s.

Dethroning Shakspere. Letters to the Daily Telegraph; and Editorial Papers. Crown 8vo, 2s. 6d.

Dickinson (Charles M.) The Children, and other Verses. Sm. 8vo, gilt edges, 5s.

Dictionary. See TOLHAUSEN, " Technological."

Diggle (J. W.; Canon) Lancashire Life of Bishop Fraser. 8vo, 12s. 6d.

Donnelly (Ignatius) Atlantis; or, the Antediluvian World. 7th Edition, crown 8vo, 12s. 6d.

—— *Ragnarok : The Age of Fire and Gravel.* Illustrated, crown 8vo, 12s. 6d.

—— *The Great Cryptogram : Francis Bacon's Cipher in the so-called Shakspere Plays.* With facsimiles. 2 vols., 30s.

Donkin (J. G.) Trooper and Redskin : N.W. Mounted Police, Canada. Crown 8vo, 8s. 6d.

Dougall (James Dalziel) Shooting: its Appliances, Practice, and Purpose. New Edition, revised with additions. Crown 8vo, 7s. 6d.

"The book is admirable in every way. . . . . We wish it every success."—*Globe.*
"A very complete treatise. . . . . Likely to take high rank as an authority on shooting."—*Daily News.*

Doughty (H.M.) Friesland Meres, and through the Netherlands.
Illustrated, crown 8vo, 8s. 6d.
Dramatic Year: Brief Criticisms of Events in the U.S. By W.
ARCHER. Crown 8vo, 6s.
Dunstan Standard Readers. Ed. by A. GILL, of Cheltenham.

EARL (H. P.) Randall Trevor. 2 vols., crown 8vo, 21s.

Eastwood (F.) In Satan's Bonds. 2 vols., crown 8vo, 21s.
Edmonds (C.) Poetry of the Anti-Jacobin. With Additional
matter. New ed. Illust., crown 8vo, 7s. 6d.; large paper, 21s.
Educational List and Directory for 1887-88. 5s.
Educational Works published in Great Britain. A Classified Catalogue. Third Edition, 8vo, cloth extra, 6s.
Edwards (E.) American Steam Engineer. Illust., 12mo, 12s. 6d.
Eight Months on the Argentine Gran Chaco. 8vo, 8s. 6d.
Elliott (H. W.) An Arctic Province: Alaska and the Seal
Islands. Illustrated from Drawings; also with Maps. 16s.
Emerson (Dr. P. H.) English Idylls. Small post 8vo, 2s.
—————— *Pictures of East Anglian Life.* Ordinary edit., 105s.;
édit. de luxe, 17 × 13½, vellum, morocco back, 147s.
—————— *Naturalistic Photography for Art Students.* Illustrated.
New edit. 5s.
—————— *and Goodall. Life and Landscape on the Norfolk*
Broads. Plates 12 × 8 inches, 126s.; large paper, 210s.
Emerson in Concord: A Memoir written by Edward Waldo
EMERSON. 8vo, 7s. 6d.
English Catalogue of Books. Vol. III., 1872—1880. Royal
8vo, half-morocco, 42s. See also "Index."
English Etchings. Published Quarterly. 3s. 6d. Vol. VI., 25s.
English Philosophers. Edited by E. B. IVAN MÜLLER, M.A.
Crown 8vo volumes of 180 or 200 pp., price 3s. 6d. each.

Francis Bacon, by Thomas Fowler. | Shaftesbury and Hutcheson.
Hamilton, by W. H. S. Monck. | Adam Smith, by J. A. Farrer.
Hartley and James Mill. |

Esmarch (F.) Handbook of Surgery. Translation from the
last German Edition. With 647 new Illustrations. 8vo, leather, 24s.
Eton. About some Fellows. New Edition, 1s.
Evelyn. Life of Mrs. Godolphin. By WILLIAM HARCOURT,
of Nuneham. Steel Portrait. Extra binding, gilt top, 7s. 6d.
Eves (C. W.) West Indies. (Royal Colonial Institute publication.) Crown 8vo, 7s. 6d.

FARINI (G. A.) Through the Kalahari Desert. 8vo, 21s.

Farm Ballads, Festivals, and Legends. See CARLETON.

Fay (T.) Three Germanys; glimpses into their History. 2 vols., 8vo, 35s.
Fenn (G. Manville) Off to the Wilds: a Story for Boys. Profusely Illustrated. Crown 8vo, gilt edges, 3s. 6d.; plainer, 2s. 6d.
—— *Silver Cañon.* Illust., gilt ed., 3s. 6d.; plainer, 2s. 6d.
Fennell (Greville) Book of the Roach. New Edition, 12mo, 2s.
Ferns. See HEATH.
Fitzgerald (P.) Book Fancier. Cr. 8vo. 5s.; large pap. 12s. 6d.
Fleming (Sandford) England and Canada: a Tour. Cr. 8vo, 6s.
Florence. See YRIARTE.
Folkard (R., Jun.) Plant Lore, Legends, and Lyrics. 8vo, 16s.
Forbes (H. O.) Naturalist in the Eastern Archipelago. 8vo. 21s.
Foreign Countries and British Colonies. Cr. 8vo, 3s. 6d. each.

Australia, by J. F. Vesey Fitzgerald.	Japan, by S. Mossman.
Austria, by D. Kay, F.R.G.S.	Peru, by Clements R. Markham.
Denmark and Iceland, by E.C.Otté.	Russia, by W. R. Morfill, M.A.
Egypt, by S. Lane Poole, B.A.	Spain, by Rev. Wentworth Webster.
France, by Miss M. Roberts.	Sweden and Norway, by Woods.
Germany, by S. Baring-Gould.	West Indies, by C. H. Eden,
Greece, by L. Sergeant, B.A.	F.R.G.S.

Franc (Maud Jeanne). Small post 8vo, uniform, gilt edges:—

Emily's Choice. 5s.	Vermont Vale. 5s.
Hall's Vineyard. 4s.	Minnie's Mission. 4s.
John's Wife: A Story of Life in South Australia. 4s.	Little Mercy. 4s.
	Beatrice Melton's Discipline. 4s.
Marian; or, The Light of Some One's Home. 5s.	No Longer a Child. 4s.
	Golden Gifts. 4s.
Silken Cords and Iron Fetters. 4s.	Two Sides to Every Question. 4s.
Into the Light. 4s.	Master of Ralston. 4s.

*** There is also a re-issue in cheaper form at 2s. 6d. per vol.

Frank's Ranche; or, My Holiday in the Rockies. A Contribution to the Inquiry into What we are to Do with our Boys. 5s.
Fraser (Bishop). See DIGGLE.
French. See JULIEN and PORCHER.
Fresh Woods and Pastures New. By the Author of "An Amateur Angler's Days." 1s. 6d.; large paper, 5s.; new ed., 1s.
Froissart. See LANIER.
Fuller (Edward) Fellow Travellers. 3s. 6d.
—— See also "Dramatic Year."

GASPARIN (Countess A. de) Sunny Fields and Shady Woods. 6s.
Geary (Grattan) Burma after the Conquest. 7s. 6d.
Geffcken (F. H.) British Empire. Translated by S. J. MACMULLAN. Crown 8vo, 7s. 6d.

Gentle Life (Queen Edition). 2 vols. in 1, small 4to, 6s.

THE GENTLE LIFE SERIES.

Price 6s. each ; or in calf extra, price 10s. 6d.; Smaller Edition, cloth extra, 2s. 6d., except where price is named.

The Gentle Life. Essays in aid of the Formation of Character.
About in the World. Essays by Author of "The Gentle Life."
Like unto Christ. New Translation of Thomas à Kempis.
Familiar Words. A Quotation Handbook. 6s.; n. ed. 3s.6d.
Essays by Montaigne. Edited by the Author of "The Gentle Life."
The Gentle Life. 2nd Series.
The Silent Hour. Essays, Original and Selected.
Half-Length Portraits. Short Studies of Notable Persons. By J. HAIN FRISWELL.
Essays on English Writers, for Students in English Literature.
Other People's Windows. By J. HAIN FRISWELL. 6s.; new ed., 3s. 6d.
A Man's Thoughts. By J. HAIN FRISWELL.
Countess of Pembroke's Arcadia. By Sir P. SIDNEY. 6s.; new ed., 3s. 6d.

Germany. By S. BARING-GOULD. Crown 8vo, 3s. 6d.
Gibbon (C.) Beyond Compare: a Story. 3 vols., cr. 8vo, 31s. 6d.
Giles (E.) Australia twice Traversed: five Expeditions, 1872-76. With Maps and Illust. 2 vols, 8vo, 30s.
Gillespie (W. M.) Surveying. Revised and enlarged by CADEY STALEY. 8vo, 21s.
Goethe. Faustus. Translated in the original rhyme and metre by A. H. HUTH. Crown 8vo, 5s.
Goldsmith. She Stoops to Conquer. Introduction by AUSTIN DOBSON ; the designs by E. A. ABBEY. Imperial 4to, 42s.
Gordon (J. E. H., B.A. Cantab.) Electric Lighting. Ill. 8vo,18s.
—— *Physical Treatise on Electricity and Magnetism.* 2nd Edition, enlarged, with coloured, full-page, &c., Illust. 2 vols., 8vo, 42s.
—— *Electricity for Schools.* Illustrated. Crown 8vo, 5s.
Gouffé (Jules) Royal Cookery Book. New Edition, with plates in colours, Woodcuts, &c., 8vo, gilt edges, 42s.
—— Domestic Edition, half-bound, 10s. 6d.
Grant (General, U.S.) Personal Memoirs. With Illustrations, Maps, &c. 2 vols, 8vo, 28s.
Great Artists. See "Biographies."

Great Musicians. Edited by F. HUEFFER. A Series of Biographies, crown 8vo, 3s. each:—

Bach.	Handel.	Rossini.
Beethoven.	Haydn.	Schubert.
Berlioz.	Mendelssohn.	Schumann.
English Church Composers. By BARRETT.	Mozart. Purcell.	Richard Wagner. Weber.

Groves (J. Percy) Charmouth Grange. Gilt, 5s.; plainer, 2s. 6d.

Guizot's History of France. Translated by R. BLACK. In 8 vols., super-royal 8vo, cloth extra, gilt, each 24s. In cheaper binding, 8 vols., at 10s. 6d. each.

"It supplies a want which has long been felt, and ought to be in the hands of all students of history."—*Times.*

———————————— *Masson's School Edition.* Abridged from the Translation by Robert Black, with Chronological Index, Historical and Genealogical Tables, &c. By Professor GUSTAVE MASSON, B.A. With Portraits, Illustrations, &c. 1 vol., 8vo, 600 pp., 5s.

Guyon (Mde.) Life. By UPHAM. 6th Edition, crown 8vo, 6s.

HALFORD (F. M.) *Floating Flies, and how to Dress them.* New ed.t., with Coloured plates. 8vo, 15s.

———— *Dry Fly-Fishing, Theory and Practice.* Col. Plates, 25s.

Hall (W. W.) How to Live Long; or, 1408 *Maxims.* 2s.

Hamilton (E.) Fly-fishing for Salmon, Trout, and Grayling; their Habits, Haunts, and History. Illust., 6s.; large paper, 10s. 6d.

Hands (T.) Numerical Exercises in Chemistry. Cr. 8vo, 2s. 6d. and 2s.; Answers separately, 6d.

Hardy (A. S.) Passe-rose: a Romance. Crown 8vo, 6s.

Hardy (Thomas). See "Low's Standard Novels."

Hare (J. L. Clark) American Constitutional Law. 2 vls., 8vo, 63s.

Harper's Magazine. Monthly. 160 pages, fully illustrated, 1s. Vols., half yearly, I.—XVIII., super-royal 8vo, 8s. 6d. each.

"'Harper's Magazine' is so thickly sown with excellent illustrations that to count them would be a work of time; not that it is a picture magazine, for the engravings illustrate the text after the manner seen in some of our choicest *éditions de luxe.*"—*St. James's Gazette.*

"It is so pretty, so big, and so cheap.... An extraordinary shillingsworth— 160 large octavo pages, with over a score of articles, and more than three times as many illustrations."—*Edinburgh Daily Review.*

"An amazing shillingsworth ... combining choice literature of both nations."— *Nonconformist.*

Harper's Young People. Vols. I.-V., profusely Illustrated with woodcuts and coloured plates. Royal 4to, extra binding, each 7s. 6d.; gilt edges, 8s. Published Weekly, in wrapper, 1d.; Annual Subscription, post free, 6s. 6d.; Monthly, in wrapper, with coloured plate, 6d.; Annual Subscription, post free, 7s. 6d.

Harris (Bishop of Michigan) Dignity of Man: Select Sermons. Crown 8vo, 8s. 6d.

Harris (W. B.) Land of African Sultan: Travels in Morocco. Illust., crown 8vo, 10s. 6d.; large paper, 31s. 6d.

Harrison (Mary) Complete Cookery Book. Crown 8vo.
―――― *Skilful Cook.* New edition, crown 8vo, 5s.
Harrison (W.) Memorable London Houses : a Guide. Illust. New edition, 18mo, 1s. 6d.
Hatton (Joseph) Journalistic London : with Engravings and Portraits of Distinguished Writers of the Day. Fcap. 4to, 12s. 6d.
―――― See also LOW'S STANDARD NOVELS.
Haweis (Mrs.) Art of Housekeeping : a Bridal Garland. 2s.6d.
Hawthorne (Nathaniel) Life. By JOHN R. LOWELL.
Heldmann (B.) Mutiny of the Ship "Leander." Gilt edges, 3s. 6d.; plainer, 2s. 6d.
Henty. Winning his Spurs. Cr. 8vo, 3s. 6d. ; plainer, 2s. 6d.
―――― *Cornet of Horse.* Cr. 8vo, 3s. 6d.; plainer, 2s. 6d.
―――― *Jack Archer.* Illust. 3s. 6d. ; plainer, 2s. 6d.
Henty (Richmond) Australiana : My Early Life. 5s.
Herrick (Robert) Poetry. Preface by AUSTIN DOBSON. With numerous Illustrations by E. A. ABBEY. 4to, gilt edges, 42s.
Hetley (Mrs. E.) Native Flowers of New Zealand. Chromos from Drawings. Three Parts, 63s.; extra binding, 73s. 6d.
Hicks (E. S.) Our Boys: How to Enter the Merchant Service. 5s.
―――― *Yachts, Boats and Canoes.* Illustrated. 8vo, 10s. 6d.
Hinman (R.) Eclectic Physical Geography. Crown 8vo, 5s.
Hitchman. Public Life of the Earl of Beaconsfield. 3s. 6d.
Hoey (Mrs. Cashel) See LOW'S STANDARD NOVELS.
Holder (C. F.) Marvels of Animal Life. Illustrated. 8s. 6d.
―――― *Ivory King: Elephant and Allies.* Illustrated. 8s. 6d.
―――― *Living Lights : Phosphorescent Animals and Vegetables.* Illustrated. 8vo, 8s. 6d.
Holmes (O. W.) Before the Curfew, &c. Occasional Poems. 5s.
―――― *Last Leaf : a Holiday Volume.* 42s.
―――― *Mortal Antipathy*, 8s. 6d. ; also 2s. ; paper, 1s.
―――― *Our Hundred Days in Europe.* 6s. Large Paper, 15s.
―――― *Poetical Works.* 2 vols., 18mo, gilt tops, 10s. 6d.
―――― See also " Rose Library."
Howard (Blanche Willis) Open Door. Crown 8vo, 6s.
Howorth (H. H.) Mammoth and the Flood. 8vo, 18s.
Hugo (V.) Notre Dame. With coloured etchings and 150 engravings. 2 vols., 8vo, vellum cloth, 30s.
Hundred Greatest Men (The). 8 portfolios, 21s. each, or 4 vols., half-morocco, gilt edges, 10 guineas. New Ed., 1 vol., royal 8vo, 21s.
Hymnal Companion to the Book of Common Prayer. By BISHOP BICKERSTETH. In various styles and bindings from 1d. to 31s. 6d. *Price List and Prospectus will be forwarded on application.*

ILLUSTRATED Text-Books of Art-Education. Edited by
EDWARD J. POYNTER, R.A. Illustrated, and strongly bound, 5s.
Now ready:—

PAINTING.

Classic and Italian. By HEAD. | **French and Spanish.**
German, Flemish, and Dutch. | **English and American.**

ARCHITECTURE.

Classic and Early Christian.
Gothic and Renaissance. By T. ROGER SMITH.

SCULPTURE.

Antique: Egyptian and Greek.
Renaissance and Modern. By LEADER SCOTT.

Inderwick (F. A.; Q.C.) Side Lights on the Stuarts. Essays. Illustrated, 8vo, 18s.

Index to the English Catalogue, Jan., 1874, *to Dec.,* 1880 Royal 8vo, half-morocco, 18s.

Inglis (Hon. James; "Maori") Our New Zealand Cousins. Small post 8vo, 6s.

—— *Tent Life in Tiger Land: Twelve Years a Pioneer Planter.* Col. plates, roy. 8vo, 18s.

Irving (Washington). Library Edition of his Works in 27 vols., Copyright, with the Author's Latest Revisions. "Geoffrey Crayon" Edition, large square 8vo. 12s. 6d. per vol. *See also* "Little Britain."

JACKSON. New Style Vertical Writing Copy-Books. Series 1, Nos. I.—XII., 2d. and 1d. each.

—— *New Series of Vertical Writing Copy-books.* 22 Nos.

—— *Shorthand of Arithmetic: a Companion to all Arithmetics.* Crown 8vo, 1s. 6d.

Japan. See ANDERSON, ARTISTIC, AUDSLEY, also MORSE.

Jerdon (Gertrude) Key-hole Country. Illustrated. Crown 8vo, cloth, 2s.

Johnston (H. H.) River Congo, from its Mouth to Bolobo. New Edition, 8vo, 21s.

Johnstone (D. Lawson) Land of the Mountain Kingdom. Illust., crown 8vo. 5s.

Julien (F.) English Student's French Examiner. 16mo, 2s.

—— *Conversational French Reader.* 16mo, cloth, 2s. 6d.

—— *French at Home and at School.* Book I., Accidence. 2s.

—— *First Lessons in Conversational French Grammar.* 1s.

—— *Petites Leçons de Conversation et de Grammaire.* 3s.

—— *Phrases of Daily Use.* Limp cloth, 6d.

KARR (H. W. Seton) Shores and Alps of Alaska. 8vo, 16s.

Keats. Endymion. Illust. by W. ST. JOHN HARPER. Imp. 4to, gilt top, 42s.

Kempis (Thomas à) Daily Text-Book. Square 16mo, 2s. 6d.;
interleaved as a Birthday Book, 3s. 6d.
*Kennedy (E. B.) Blacks and Bushrangers, adventures in North
Queensland.* Illust., crown 8vo, 7s. 6d.
*Kent's Commentaries: an Abridgment for Students of American
Law.* By EDEN F. THOMPSON. 10s. 6d.
*Kerr (W. M.) Far Interior: Cape of Good Hope, across the
Zambesi, to the Lake Regions.* Illustrated from Sketches, 2 vols.
8vo, 32s.
*Kershaw (S. W.) Protestants from France in their English
Home.* Crown 8vo, 6s.
King (Henry) Savage London; Riverside Characters, &c.
Crown 8vo, 6s.
Kingston (W. H. G.) Works. Illustrated, 16mo, gilt edges,
3s. 6d.; plainer binding, plain edges, 2s. 6d. each.

Ben Burton. | Heir of Kilfinnan.
Captain Mugford, or, Our Salt | Snow-Shoes and Canoes.
and Fresh Water Tutors. | Two Supercargoes.
Dick Cheveley. | With Axe and Rifle.

*Kingsley (Rose) Children of Westminster Abbey: Studies in
English History.* 5s.
Knight (E. J.) Cruise of the "Falcon." New Ed. Cr. 8vo,
7s. 6d.
Knox (Col.) Boy Travellers on the Congo. Illus. Cr. 8vo, 7s. 6d.
Kunhardt (C. B.) Small Yachts: Design and Construction. 35s.
—— *Steam Yachts and Launches.* Illustrated. 4to, 16s.

LANGLEY (S. P.) New Astronomy. Ill. Cr. 8vo. 10s. 6d.
Lanier's Works. Illustrated, crown 8vo, gilt edges, 7s. 6d.
each.

Boy's King Arthur. | Boy's Percy: Ballads of Love and
Boy's Froissart. | Adventure, selected from the
Boy's Knightly Legends of Wales. | "Reliques."

Lansdell (H.) Through Siberia. 2 vols., 8vo, 30s.; 1 vol., 10s. 6d.
—— *Russia in Central Asia.* Illustrated. 2 vols., 42s.
—— *Through Central Asia; Russo-Afghan Frontier, &c.*
8vo, 12s.
Larden (W.) School Course on Heat. Third Ed., Illust. 5s.
Laurie (A.) Conquest of the Moon: a Story of the Bayouda.
Illust., crown 8vo, 7s. 6d.
Layard (Mrs. Granville) Through the West Indies. Small
post 8vo, 2s. 6d.
Lea (H. C.). History of the Inquisition of the Middle Ages.
3 vols., 8vo, 42s.

Lemon (M.) Small House over the Water, and Stories. Illust. by Cruikshank, &c. Crown 8vo, 6s.

Leo XIII.: Life. By BERNARD O'REILLY. With Steel Portrait from Photograph, &c. Large 8vo, 18s.; *édit. de luxe*, 63s.

Leonardo da Vinci's Literary Works. Edited by Dr. JEAN PAUL RICHTER. Containing his Writings on Painting, Sculpture, and Architecture, his Philosophical Maxims, Humorous Writings, and Miscellaneous Notes on Personal Events, on his Contemporaries, on Literature, &c.; published from Manuscripts. 2 vols., imperial 8vo, containing about 200 Drawings in Autotype Reproductions, and numerous other Illustrations. Twelve Guineas.

Library of Religious Poetry. Best Poems of all Ages. Edited by SCHAFF and GILMAN. Royal 8vo, 21s.; cheaper binding, 10s. 6d.

Lindsay (W. S.) History of Merchant Shipping. Over 150 Illustrations, Maps, and Charts. In 4 vols., demy 8vo, cloth extra. Vols. 1 and 2, 11s. each; vols. 3 and 4, 14s. each. 4 vols., 50s.

Little (Archibald J.) Through the Yang-tse Gorges: Trade and Travel in Western China. New Edition. 8vo, 10s. 6d.

Little Britain, The Spectre Bridegroom, and *Legend of Sleepy Hollow.* By WASHINGTON IRVING. An entirely New *Édition de luxe*. Illustrated by 120 very fine Engravings on Wood, by Mr. J. D. COOPER. Designed by Mr. CHARLES O. MURRAY. Re-issue, square crown 8vo, cloth, 6s.

Lodge (Henry Cabot) George Washington. (American Statesmen.) 2 vols., 12s.

Longfellow. Maidenhood. With Coloured Plates. Oblong 4to, 2s. 6d.; gilt edges, 3s. 6d.

—— *Courtship of Miles Standish.* Illust. by BROUGHTON, &c. Imp. 4to, 21s.

—— *Nuremberg.* 28 Photogravures. Illum. by M. and A. COMEGYS. 4to, 31s. 6d.

Lowell (J. R.) Vision of Sir Launfal. Illustrated, royal 4to, 63s.

—— *Life of Nathaniel Hawthorne.* Sm post 8vo. [*In prep.*

Low's Standard Library of Travel and Adventure. Crown 8vo, uniform in cloth extra, 7s. 6d., except where price is given.
1. **The Great Lone Land.** By Major W. F. BUTLER, C.B.
2. **The Wild North Land.** By Major W. F. BUTLER, C.B.
3. **How I found Livingstone.** By H. M. STANLEY.
4. **Through the Dark Continent.** By H. M. STANLEY. 12s. 6d.
5. **The Threshold of the Unknown Region.** By C. R. MARKHAM. (4th Edition, with Additional Chapters, 10s. 6d.)
6. **Cruise of the Challenger.** By W. J. J. SPRY, R.N.
7. **Burnaby's On Horseback through Asia Minor.** 10s. 6d.
8. **Schweinfurth's Heart of Africa.** 2 vols., 15s.
9. **Through America.** By W. G. MARSHALL.
10. **Through Siberia.** Il. and unabridged, 10s.6d. By H. LANSDELL.
11. **From Home to Home.** By STAVELEY HILL.
12. **Cruise of the Falcon.** By E. J. KNIGHT.

Low's Standard Library, &c.—continued.
- 13. **Through Masai Land.** By JOSEPH THOMSON.
- 14. **To the Central African Lakes.** By JOSEPH THOMSON.
- 15. **Queen's Highway.** By STUART CUMBERLAND.

Low's Standard Novels. Small post 8vo, cloth extra, 6s. each, unless otherwise stated.

JAMES BAKER. **John Westacott.**

WILLIAM BLACK.
   A Daughter of Heth.—House-Boat.—In Far Lochaber.—In Silk Attire.—Kilmeny.—Lady Silverdale's Sweetheart.—Sunrise.—Three Feathers.

R. D. BLACKMORE.
   Alice Lorraine.—Christowell, a Dartmoor Tale.—Clara Vaughan.—Cradock Nowell.—Cripps the Carrier.—Erema; or, My Father's Sin.—Lorna Doone.—Mary Anerley.—Tommy Upmore.

G. W. CABLE. **Bonaventure.** 5s.

Miss COLERIDGE. **An English Squire.**

C. E. CRADDOCK. **Despot of Broomsedge Cove.**

Mrs. B. M. CROKER. **Some One Else.**

STUART CUMBERLAND. **Vasty Deep.**

E. DE LEON. **Under the Stars and Crescent.**

Miss BETHAM-EDWARDS. **Halfway.**

Rev. E. GILLIAT, M.A. **Story of the Dragonnades.**

THOMAS HARDY.
   A Laodicean.—Far from the Madding Crowd.—Mayor of Casterbridge.—Pair of Blue Eyes.—Return of the Native.—The Hand of Ethelberta.—The Trumpet Major.—Two on a Tower.

JOSEPH HATTON. **Old House at Sandwich.—Three Recruits.**

Mrs. CASHEL HOEY.
   A Golden Sorrow.—A Stern Chase.—Out of Court.

BLANCHE WILLIS HOWARD. **Open Door.**

JEAN INGELOW.
   Don John.—John Jerome (5s.).**—Sarah de Berenger.**

GEORGE MAC DONALD.
   Adela Cathcart.—Guild Court.—Mary Marston.—Stephen Archer (New Ed. of "Gifts").**—The Vicar's Daughter.—Orts.—Weighed and Wanting.**

Mrs. MACQUOID. **Diane.—Elinor Dryden.**

HELEN MATHERS. **My Lady Greensleeves.**

DUFFIELD OSBORNE. **Spell of Ashtaroth** (5s.).

Mrs. J. H. RIDDELL.
   Alaric Spenceley.—Daisies and Buttercups.—The Senior Partner.—A Struggle for Fame.

W. CLARK RUSSELL.
   Frozen Pirate.—Jack's Courtship.—John Holdsworth.—A Sailor's Sweetheart.—Sea Queen.—Watch Below.—Strange Voyage.—Wreck of the Grosvenor.—The Lady Maud.—Little Loo.

Low's Standard Novels—continued.
FRANK R. STOCKTON.
　Bee-man of Orn.—The Late Mrs. Null.—Hundredth Man.
Mrs. HARRIET B. STOWE.
　My Wife and I.—Old Town Folk.—We and our Neighbours.—
　Poganuc People, their Loves and Lives.
JOSEPH THOMSON. Ulu: an African Romance.
LEW. WALLACE. Ben Hur: a Tale of the Christ.
CONSTANCE FENIMORE WOOLSON.
　Anne.—East Angels.—For the Major (5s.).
　French Heiress in her own Chateau.

See also SEA STORIES.

Low's Standard Novels. NEW ISSUE at short intervals. Cr. 8vo, 2s. 6d.; fancy boards, 2s.
BLACKMORE.
　Clara Vaughan.—Cripps the Carrier.—Lorna Doone.—Mary Anerley.
HARDY.
　Madding Crowd.—Mayor of Casterbridge.—Trumpet-Major.
HATTON. Three Recruits.
HOLMES. Guardian Angel.
MAC DONALD. Adela Cathcart.—Guild Court.
RIDDELL. Daisies and Buttercups.—Senior Partner.
STOCKTON. Casting Away of Mrs. Lecks.
STOWE. Dred.
WALFORD. Her Great Idea.

To be followed immediately by
BLACKMORE. Alice Lorraine.—Tommy Upmore.
CABLE. Bonaventure.
CROKER. Some One Else.
DE LEON. Under the Stars.
EDWARDS. Half-Way.
HARDY.
　Hand of Ethelberta.—Pair of Blue Eyes.—Two on a Tower.
HATTON. Old House at Sandwich.
HOEY. Golden Sorrow.—Out of Court.—Stern Chase.
INGELOW. John Jerome.—Sarah de Berenger.
MAC DONALD. Vicar's Daughter.—Stephen Archer.
OLIPHANT. Innocent.
STOCKTON. Bee-Man of Orn.
STOWE. Old Town Folk.—Poganuc People.
THOMSON. Ulu.

Low's Standard Books for Boys. With numerous Illustrat'ons, 2s. 6d.; gilt edges, 3s. 6d. each.
　Dick Cheveley. By W. H. G. KINGSTON.
　Heir of Kilfinnan. By W. H. G. KINGSTON.
　Off to the Wilds. By G. MANVILLE FENN.
　The Two Supercargoes. By W. H. G. KINGSTON.
　The Silver Cañon. By G. MANVILLE FENN.
　Under the Meteor Flag. By HARRY COLLINGWOOD.
　Jack Archer: a Tale of the Crimea. By G. A. HENTY.

Low's Standard Books for Boys—continued.
   The Mutiny on Board the Ship Leander. By B. HELDMANN.
   With Axe and Rifle on the Western Prairies. By W. H. G. KINGSTON.
   Red Cloud, the Solitary Sioux: a Tale of the Great Prairie. By Col. Sir WM. BUTLER, K.C.B.
   The Voyage of the Aurora. By HARRY COLLINGWOOD.
   Charmouth Grange: a Tale of the 17th Century. By J. PERCY GROVES.
   Snowshoes and Canoes. By W. H. G. KINGSTON.
   The Son of the Constable of France. By LOUIS ROUSSELET.
   Captain Mugford; or, Our Salt and Fresh Water Tutors. Edited by W. H. G. KINGSTON.
   The Cornet of Horse, a Tale of Marlborough's Wars. By G. A. HENTY.
   The Adventures of Captain Mago. By LEON CAHUN.
   Noble Words and Noble Needs.
   The King of the Tigers. By ROUSSELET.
   Hans Brinker; or, The Silver Skates. By Mrs. DODGE.
   The Drummer-Boy, a Story of the time of Washington. By ROUSSELET.
   Adventures in New Guinea: The Narrative of Louis Tregance.
   The Crusoes of Guiana. By BOUSSENARD.
   The Gold Seekers. A Sequel to the Above. By BOUSSENARD.
   Winning His Spurs, a Tale of the Crusades. By G. A. HENTY.
   The Blue Banner. By LEON CAHUN.

New Volumes for 1889.
   Startling Exploits of the Doctor. CÉLIÈRE.
   Brothers Rantzau. ERCKMANN-CHATRIAN.
   Young Naturalist. BIART.
   Ben Burton; or, Born and Bred at Sea. KINGSTON.
   Great Hunting Grounds of the World. MEUNIER.
   Ran Away from the Dutch. PERELAER.
   My Kalulu, Prince, King, and Slave. STANLEY.

Low's Standard Series of Books by Popular Writers. Sm. cr. 8vo, cloth gilt, 2s.; gilt edges, 2s. 6d. each.
   Aunt Jo's Scrap Bag. By Miss ALCOTT.
   Shawl Straps. By Miss ALCOTT.
   Little Men. By Miss ALCOTT.
   Hitherto. By Mrs. WHITNEY.
   Forecastle to Cabin. By SAMUELS. Illustrated.
   In My Indian Garden. By PHIL ROBINSON.
   Little Women and Little Women Wedded. By Miss ALCOTT.
   Eric and Ethel. By FRANCIS FRANCIS. Illust.
   Keyhole Country. By GERTRUDE JERDON. Illust.
   We Girls. By Mrs. WHITNEY.
   The Other Girls. A Sequel to "We Girls." By Mrs. WHITNEY.
   Adventures of Jimmy Brown. Illust. By W. L. ALDEN.
   Under the Lilacs. By Miss ALCOTT. Illust.
   Jimmy's Cruise. By Miss ALCOTT.
   Under the Punkah. By PHIL ROBINSON.

Low's Standard Series of Books by Popular Writers—continued.
An Old-Fashioned Girl. By Miss ALCOTT.
A Rose in Bloom. By Miss ALCOTT.
Eight Cousins. Illust. By Miss ALCOTT.
Jack and Jill. By Miss ALCOTT.
Lulu's Library. Illust. By Miss ALCOTT.
Silver Pitchers. By Miss ALCOTT.
Work and Beginning Again. Illust. By Miss ALCOTT.
A Summer in Leslie Goldthwaite's Life. By Mrs. WHITNEY.
Faith Gartney's Girlhood. By Mrs. WHITNEY.
Real Folks. By Mrs. WHITNEY.
Dred. By Mrs. STOWE.
My Wife and I. By Mrs. STOWE.
An Only Sister. By Madame DE WITT.
Spinning Wheel Stories. By Miss ALCOTT.
My Summer in a Garden. By C. DUDLEY WARNER.

Low's Pocket Encyclopædia: a Compendium of General Know-ledge for Ready Reference. Upwards of 25,000 References, with Plates. New ed., imp. 32mo, cloth, marbled edges, 3s. 6d.; roan, 4s. 6d.

Low's Handbook to London Charities. Yearly, cloth, 1s. 6d.; paper, 1s.

Lusignan (Princess A. de) Twelve years' Reign of Abdul Hamid II. Crown 8vo, 7s. 6d.

M*cCULLOCH (H.) Men and Measures of Half a century.* Sketches and Comments. 8vo, 18s.

Macdonald (D.) Oceania. Linguistic and Anthropological. Illust., and Tables. Crown 8vo, 6s.

Mac Donald (George). See LOW'S STANDARD NOVELS.

Macgregor (John) "Rob Roy" on the Baltic. 3rd Edition, small post 8vo, 2s. 6d.; cloth, gilt edges, 3s. 6d.

—— *A Thousand Miles in the "Rob Roy" Canoe.* 11th Edition, small post 8vo, 2s. 6d.; cloth, gilt edges, 3s. 6d.

—— *Voyage Alone in the Yawl "Rob Roy."* New Edition, with additions, small post 8vo, 3s. 6d. and 2s. 6d.

Mackenzie (Sir Morell) Fatal Illness of Frederick the Noble. Crown 8vo, limp cloth, 2s. 6d.

Mackenzie (Rev. John) Austral Africa: Losing it or Ruling it? Illustrations and Maps. 2 vols., 8vo, 32s.

Maclean (H. E.) Maid of the Golden Age. Illust., cr. 8vo, 6s.

McLellan's Own Story: The War for the Union. Illust. 18s.

Maginn (W.) Miscellanies. Prose and Verse. With Memoir. 2 vols., crown 8vo, 24s.

Main (Mrs.; Mrs. Fred Burnaby) High Life and Towers of Silence. Illustrated, square 8vo, 10s. 6d.

Malan (C. F. de M.) Eric and Connie's Cruise in the South Pacific. Crown 8vo, 5s.

Manning (E. F.) Delightful Thames. Illustrated. 4to, fancy boards, 5s.

Markham (Clements R.) The Fighting Veres, Sir F. and Sir H. 8vo, 18s.

———— *War between Peru and Chili,* 1879-1881. Third Ed. Crown 8vo, with Maps, 10s. 6d.

———— See also "Foreign Countries," MAURY, and VERES.

Marston (W.) Eminent Recent Actors, Reminiscences Critical, &c. 2 vols. Crown 8vo, 21s.; new edit., 1 vol., 6s.

Martin (J. W.) Float Fishing and Spinning in the Nottingham Style. New Edition. Crown 8vo, 2s. 6d.

Matthews (J. W., M.D.) Incwadi Yami: Twenty years in South Africa. With many Engravings, royal 8vo, 14s.

Maury (Commander) Physical Geography of the Sea, and its Meteorology. New Edition, with Charts and Diagrams, cr. 8vo, 6s.

———— *Life.* By his Daughter. Edited by Mr. CLEMENTS R. MARKHAM. With portrait of Maury. 8vo, 12s. 6d.

Melio (G. L.) Manual of Swedish Drill for Teachers and Students. Cr. 8vo, 1s. 6d.

Men of Mark: Portraits of the most Eminent Men of the Day. Complete in 7 Vols., 4to, handsomely bound, gilt edges, 25s. each.

Mendelssohn Family (The), 1729—1847. From Letters and Journals. Translated. New Edition, 2 vols., 8vo, 30s.

Mendelssohn. See also "Great Musicians."

Merrifield's Nautical Astronomy. Crown 8vo, 7s. 6d.

Mills (J.) Alternative Elementary Chemistry. Ill., cr.8vo, 1s.6d.

Mitford (Mary Russell) Our Village. With 12 full-page and 157 smaller Cuts. Cr. 4to, cloth, gilt edges, 21s.; cheaper binding, 10s. 6d.

Mody (Mrs.) Outlines of German Literature. 18mo, 1s.

Moffatt (W.) Land and Work; Depression, Agricultural and Commercial. Crown 8vo, 5s.

Mohammed Benani: A Story of To-day. 8vo, 10s. 6d.

Mollett (J. W.) Illustrated Dictionary of Words used in Art and Archæology. Illustrated, small 4to, 15s.

Moore (J. M.) New Zealand for Emigant, Invalid and Tourist. Cr. 8vo.

Morley (Henry) English Literature in the Reign of Victoria. 2000th volume of the Tauchnitz Collection of Authors. 18mo, 2s. 6d.

Mormonism. See STENHOUSE.

Morse (E. S.) Japanese Homes and their Surroundings. With more than 300 Illustrations. Re-issue, 10s. 6d.

Morten (Honnor) Sketches of Hospital Life. Cr. 8vo, sewed, 1s.

Morwood. Our Gipsies in City, Tent, and Van. 8vo, 18s.

Moss (F. J.) Through Atolls and Islands of the great South Sea. Illust., crown 8vo, 8s. 6d.

Moxon (Walter) Pilocereus Senilis. Fcap. 8vo, gilt top, 3*s.* 6*d.*
Muller (E.) Noble Words and Noble Deeds. Illustrated, gilt edges, 3*s.* 6*d.*; plainer binding, 2*s.* 6*d.*
Musgrave (Mrs.) Miriam. Crown 8vo, 6*s.*
Music. See "Great Musicians."

*N*ETHERCOTE *(C. B.) Pytchley Hunt.* New Ed., cr. 8vo, 8*s.* 6*d.*
New Zealand. See BRADSHAW and WHITE (J.).
New Zealand Rulers and Statesmen. See GISBORNE.
Nicholls (J. H. Kerry) The King Country: Explorations in New Zealand. Many Illustrations and Map. New Edition, 8vo, 21*s.*
Nordhoff (C.) California, for Health, Pleasure, and Residence. New Edition, 8vo, with Maps and Illustrations, 12*s.* 6*d.*
Norman (C. B.) Corsairs of France. With Portraits. 8vo, 18*s.*
North (W. ; M.A.) Roman Fever: an Inquiry during three years' residence. Illust., 8vo, 25*s.*
Northbrook Gallery. Edited by LORD RONALD GOWER. 36 Permanent Photographs. Imperial 4to, 63*s.*; large paper, 105*s.*
Nott (Major) Wild Animals Photographed and Described. 35*s.*
Nursery Playmates (Prince of). 217 Coloured Pictures for Children by eminent Artists. Folio, in col. bds., 6*s.*; new ed., 2*s.* 6*d.*
Nursing Record. Yearly, 8*s.*; half-yearly, 4*s.* 6*d.*; quarterly, 2*s.* 6*d*; weekly, 2*d.*

O'BRIEN *(R. B.) Fifty Years of Concessions to Ireland.* With a Portrait of T. Drummond. Vol. I., 16*s.*, II., 16*s.*
Orient Line Guide. New edition re-written; by W. J. LOFTIE. Maps and Plans, 2*s.* 6*d.*
Orvis (C. F.) Fishing with the Fly. Illustrated. 8vo, 12*s.* 6*d.*
Osborne (Duffield) Spell of Ashtaroth. Crown 8vo, 5*s.*
Our Little Ones in Heaven. Edited by the Rev. H. ROBBINS. With Frontispiece after Sir JOSHUA REYNOLDS. New Edition, 5*s.*

*P*ALGRAVE *(R. F. D.) Oliver Cromwell and his Protec*torate. Crown 8vo.
Pallser (M. s.) A History of Lace. New Edition, with additional cuts and text. 8vo, 21*s.*
——— *The China Collector's Pocket Companion.* With upwards of 1000 Illustrations of Marks and Monograms. Small 8vo, 5*s.*
*Panton (J. E.) Homes of Taste. Hints on Furniture and Deco*ration. Crown 8vo, 2*s.* 6*d.*
*Parsons (James ; A.M.) Exposition of the Principles of Partner*ship. 8vo, 31*s.* 6*d.*

Pennell (H. Cholmondeley) Sporting Fish of Great Britain
    15s. ; large paper, 30s.
—— *Modern Improvements in Fishing-tackle.* Crown 8vo, 2s.
Perelaer (M. T. H.) Ran Away from the Dutch ; Borneo, &c.
    Illustrated, square 8vo, 7s. 6d; new ed., 2s. 6d.
Perry (J. J. M.) Edlingham Burglary, or Circumstantial Evi-
    dence. Crown 8vo, 3s. 6d.
Phelps (Elizabeth Stuart) Struggle for Immortality. Cr. 8vo, 5s.
Phillips' Dictionary of Biographical Reference. New edition,
    royal 8vo, 25s.
Philpot (H. J.) Diabetes Mellitus. Crown 8vo, 5s.
—— *Diet System.* Tables. I. Diabetes ; II. Gout ;
    III. Dyspepsia ; IV. Corpulence. In cases, 1s. each.
Plunkett (Major G. T.) Primer of Orthographic Projection.
    Elementary Solid Geometry. With Problems and Exercises. 2s. 6d.
Poe (E. A.) The Raven. Illustr. by DORÉ. Imperial folio, 63s.
Poems of the Inner Life. Chiefly Modern. Small 8vo, 5s.
Poetry of the Anti-Jacobin. New ed., by CHARLES EDMONDS.
    Cr. 8vo, 7s. 6d.; large paper, 21s.
Porcher (A.) Juvenile French Plays. With Notes and a
    Vocabulary. 18mo, 1s.
Porter (Admiral David D.) Naval History of Civil War.
    Portraits, Plans, &c. 4to, 25s.
Portraits of Celebrated Race-horses of the Past and Present
    Centuries, with Pedigrees and Performances. 4 vols., 4to, 126s.
Powles (L. D.) Land of the Pink Pearl : Life in the Bahamas.
    8vo, 10s. 6d.
Poynter (Edward J., R.A.). See " Illustrated Text-books."
Prince Maskiloff: a Romance of Modern Oxford. By ROY
    TELLET. Crown 8vo, 10s. 6d.
Prince of Nursery Playmates. Col. plates, new ed., 2s. 6d.
Pritt (T. E.) North Country Flies. Illustrated from the
    Author's Drawings. 10s. 6d.
Publishers' Circular (The), and General Record of British and
    Foreign Literature. Published on the 1st and 15th of every Month, 3d.
Pyle (Howard) Otto of the Silver Hand. Illustrated by the
    Author. 8vo, 8s. 6d.

QUEEN'S Prime Ministers. A series. Edited by S. J. REID.
    Cr. 8vo, 2s. 6d. per vol.

RAMBAUD. History of Russia. New Edition, Illustrated.
    3 vols., 8vo, 21s.

Reber. History of Mediæval Art. Translated by CLARKE.
422 Illustrations and Glossary. 8vo, .
Redford (G.) Ancient Sculpture. New Ed. Crown 8vo, 10s. 6d.
Redgrave (G. R.) Century of Painters of the English School
Crown 8vo, 10s. 6d.
Reed (Sir E. J., M.P.) and Simpson. Modern Ships of War.
Illust., royal 8vo, 10s. 6d.
Reed (Talbot B.) Sir Ludar: a Tale of the Days of good Queen
Bess. Crown 8vo, 6s.
Remarkable Bindings in the British Museum. India paper,
94s. 6d.; sewed 73s. 6d. and 63s.
Reminiscences of a Boyhood in the early part of the Century: a
Story. Crown 8vo, 6s.
Ricci (J. H. de) Fisheries Dispute, and the Annexation of
Canada. Crown 8vo, 6s.
Richards (W.) Aluminium: its History, Occurrence, &c.
Illustrated, crown 8vo, 12s. 6d.
Richter (Dr. Jean Paul) Italian Art in the National Gallery.
4to. Illustrated. Cloth gilt, £2 2s.; half-morocco, uncut, £2 12s. 6d.
———— See also LEONARDO DA VINCI.
Riddell (Mrs. J. H.) See Low's STANDARD NOVELS.
Roberts (W.) Earlier History of English Bookselling. Crown
8vo, 7s. 6d.
Robertson (T. W.) Principal Dramatic Works, with Portraits
in photogravure. 2 vols., 21s.
Robin Hood; Merry Adventures of. Written and illustrated
by HOWARD PYLE. Imperial 8vo, 15s.
Robinson (Phil.) In my Indian Garden. New Edition, 16mo,
limp cloth, 2s.
———— *Noah's Ark. Unnatural History.* Sm. post 8vo, 12s. 6d.
———— *Sinners and Saints: a Tour across the United States of*
America, and Round them. Crown 8vo, 10s. 6d.
———— *Under the Punkah.* New Ed., cr. 8vo, limp cloth, 2s.
Rockstro (W. S.) History of Music. New Edition. 8vo, 14s.
Roe (E. P.) Nature's Serial Story. Illust. New ed. 3s. 6d.
Roland, The Story of. Crown 8vo, illustrated, 6s.
Rose (F.) Complete Practical Machinist. New Ed., 12mo, 12s. 6d.
———— *Key to Engines and Engine-running.* Crown 8vo, 8s. 6d.
———— *Mechanical Drawing.* Illustrated, small 4to, 16s.
———— *Modern Steam Engines.* Illustrated. 31s. 6d.
———— *Steam Boilers. Boiler Construction and Examination.*
Illust., 8vo, 12s. 6d.

Rose Library. Each volume, 1s. Many are illustrated—
- Little Women. By LOUISA M. ALCOTT.
- Little Women Wedded. Forming a Sequel to "Little Women."
- Little Women and Little Women Wedded. 1 vol., cloth gilt, 3s. 6d.
- Little Men. By L. M. ALCOTT. Double vol., 2s.; cloth gilt, 3s. 6d.
- An Old-Fashioned Girl. By LOUISA M. ALCOTT. 2s.; cloth, 3s. 6d.
- Work. A Story of Experience. By L. M. ALCOTT. 3s. 6d.; 2 vols., 1s. each.
- Stowe (Mrs. H. B.) The Pearl of Orr's Island.
- —— The Minister's Wooing.
- —— We and our Neighbours. 2s.; cloth gilt, 6s.
- —— My Wife and I. 2s.
- Hans Brinker; or, the Silver Skates. By Mrs. DODGE. Also 2s.6d.
- My Study Windows. By J. R. LOWELL.
- The Guardian Angel. By OLIVER WENDELL HOLMES. Cloth, 2s.
- My Summer in a Garden. By C. D. WARNER.
- Dred. By Mrs. BEECHER STOWE. 2s.; cloth gilt, 3s. 6d.
- City Ballads. New Ed. 16mo. By WILL CARLETON.
- Farm Ballads. By WILL CARLETON. ⎫
- Farm Festivals. By WILL CARLETON. ⎬ 1 vol., cl., gilt ed., 3s. 6d.
- Farm Legends. By WILL CARLETON. ⎭
- The Rose in Bloom. By L. M. ALCOTT. 2s.; cloth gilt, 3s. 6d.
- Eight Cousins. By L. M. ALCOTT. 2s.; cloth gilt, 3s. 6d.
- Under the Lilacs. By L. M. ALCOTT. 2s.; also 3s. 6d.
- Undiscovered Country. By W. D. HOWELLS.
- Clients of Dr. Bernagius. By L. BIART. 2 parts.
- Silver Pitchers. By LOUISA M. ALCOTT. Cloth, 3s. 6d.
- Jimmy's Cruise in the "Pinafore," and other Tales. By LOUISA M. ALCOTT. 2s.; cloth gilt, 3s. 6d.
- Jack and Jill. By LOUISA M. ALCOTT. 2s.; Illustrated, 5s.
- Hitherto. By the Author of the "Gayworthys." 2 vols., 1s. each; 1 vol., cloth gilt, 3s. 6d.
- A Gentleman of Leisure. A Novel. By EDGAR FAWCETT. 1s.

See also LOW's STANDARD SERIES.

Ross (Mars) and Stonehewer Cooper. Highlands of Cantabria; or, Three Days from England. Illustrations and Map, 8vo, 21s.

Rothschilds, the Financial Rulers of Nations. By JOHN REEVES. Crown 8vo, 7s. 6d.

Rousselet (Louis) Son of the Constable of France. Small post 8vo, numerous Illustrations, gilt edges, 3s. 6d.; plainer, 2s. 6d.

—— *King of the Tigers: a Story of Central India.* Illustrated. Small post 8vo, gilt, 3s. 6d.; plainer, 2s. 6d.

—— *Drummer Boy.* Illustrated. Small post 8vo, gilt edges, 3s. 6d.; plainer, 2s. 6d.

Russell (Dora) Strange Message. 3 vols., crown 8vo, 31s. 6d.

Russell (W. Clark) Betwixt the Forelands. Illust., crown 8vo, 10s. 6d.

Russell (W. Clark) English Channel Ports and the Estate of the East and West India Dock Company. Crown 8vo, 1s.

—— *Sailor's Language.* Illustrated. Crown 8vo, 3s. 6d.

—— *Wreck of the Grosvenor.* 4to, sewed, 6d.

—— See also "Low's Standard Novels," "Sea Stories."

S*AINTS and their Symbols: A Companion in the Churches* and Picture Galleries of Europe. Illustrated. Royal 16mo, 3s. 6d.

Samuels (Capt. J. S.) From Forecastle to Cabin: Autobiography. Illustrated. Crown 8vo, 8s. 6d.; also with fewer Illustrations, cloth, 2s.; paper, 1s.

Saunders (A.) Our Domestic Birds: Poultry in England and New Zealand. Crown 8vo, 6s.

—— *Our Horses: the Best Muscles controlled by the Best* Brains. 6s.

Scherr (Prof. J.) History of English Literature. Cr. 8vo, 8s. 6d.

Schuyler (Eugène) American Diplomacy and the Furtherance of Commerce. 12s. 6d.

—— *The Life of Peter the Great.* 2 vols., 8vo, 32s.

Schweinfurth (Georg) Heart of Africa. 2 vols., crown 8vo, 15s.

Scott (Leader) Renaissance of Art in Italy. 4to, 31s. 6d.

—— *Sculpture, Renaissance and Modern.* 5s.

Sea Stories. By W. CLARK RUSSELL. New ed. Cr. 8vo, leather back, top edge gilt, per vol., 3s. 6d.

Frozen Pirate.	Sea Queen.
Jack's Courtship.	Strange Voyage.
John Holdsworth.	The Lady Maud.
Little Loo.	Watch Below.
Ocean Free Lance.	Wreck of the *Grosvenor*.
Sailor's Sweetheart.	

Semmes (Adm. Raphael) Service Afloat: The "Sumter" and the "Alabama." Illustrated. Royal 8vo, 16s.

Senior (W.) Near and Far: an Angler's Sketches of Home Sport and Colonial Life. Crown 8vo, 6s.; new edit., 2s.

—— *Waterside Sketches.* Imp. 32mo, 1s. 6d.; boards, 1s.

Shakespeare. Edited by R. GRANT WHITE. 3 vols., crown 8vo, gilt top, 36s.; *édition de luxe*, 6 vols., 8vo, cloth extra, 63s.

Shakespeare's Heroines: Studies by Living English Painters. 105s.; artists' proofs, 630s.

—— *Macbeth.* With Etchings on Copper, by J. MOYR SMITH. 105s. and 52s. 6d.

—— *Songs and Sonnets.* Illust. by Sir JOHN GILBERT, R.A. 4to, boards, 5s.

—— See also CUNDALL, DETHRONING, DONNELLY, MACKAY, and WHITE (R. GRANT).

Sharpe (R. Bowdler) Birds in Nature. 39 coloured plates and text. 4to, 63s.

Sheridan. Rivals. Reproductions of Water-colour, &c. 52s. 6d.; artists proofs, 105s. nett.

Shields (C. W.) Philosophia ultima; from Harmony of Science and Religion. 2 vols. 8vo, 24s.

Shields (G. O.) Cruisings in the Cascades; Hunting, Photography, Fishing. 8vo, 10s. 6d.

Sidney (Sir Philip) Arcadia. New Edition, 3s. 6d.

Siegfried, The Story of. Illustrated, crown 8vo, cloth, 6s.

Simon. China: its Social Life. Crown 8vo, 6s.

Simson (A.) Wilds of Ecuador and Exploration of the Putumayor River. Crown 8vo, 8s. 6d.

Sinclair (Mrs.) Indigenous Flowers of the Hawaiian Islands. 44 Plates in Colour. Imp. folio, extra binding, gilt edges, 31s. 6d.

Sloane (T. O.) Home Experiments in Science for Old and Young. Crown 8vo, 6s.

Smith (G.) Assyrian Explorations. Illust. New Ed., 8vo, 18s.

——— *The Chaldean Account of Genesis.* With many Illustrations. 16s. New Ed. By PROFESSOR SAYCE. 8vo, 18s.

Smith (G. Barnett) William I. and the German Empire. New Ed., 8vo, 3s. 6d.

Smith (Sydney) Life and Times. By STUART J. REID. Illustrated. 8vo, 21s.

Spiers' French Dictionary. 29th Edition, remodelled. 2 vols., 8vo, 18s.; half bound, 21s.

Spry (W. J. J., R.N., F.R.G.S.) Cruise of H.M.S. "Challenger." With Illustrations. 8vo, 18s. Cheap Edit., crown 8vo, 7s. 6d.

Stanley (H. M.) Congo, and Founding its Free State. Illustrated, 2 vols., 8vo, 42s.; re-issue, 2 vols. 8vo, 21s

——— *How I Found Livingstone.* 8vo, 10s. 6d.; cr. 8vo, 7s. 6d.

——— *Through the Dark Continent.* Crown 8vo, 12s. 6d.

Start (J. W. K.) Junior Mensuration Exercises. 8d.

Stenhouse (Mrs.) Tyranny of Mormonism. An Englishwoman in Utah. New ed., cr. 8vo, cloth elegant, 3s. 6d.

Sterry (J. Ashby) Cucumber Chronicles. 5s.

Stevens (E. W.) Fly-Fishing in Maine Lakes. 8s. 6d.

Stevens (T.) Around the World on a Bicycle. Vol. II. 8vo. 16s.

Stockton (Frank R.) Rudder Grange. 3s. 6d.

——— *Bee-Man of Orn, and other Fanciful Tales.* Cr. 8vo, 5s.

——— *Personally conducted.* Crown 8vo, 7s. 6d.

——— *The Casting Away of Mrs. Lecks and Mrs. Aleshine.* 1s.

——— *The Dusantes.* Sequel to the above. Sewed, 1s.; this and the preceding book in one volume, cloth, 2s. 6d.

Stockton (Frank R.) The Hundredth Man. Small post 8vo, 6s.
—— *The Late Mrs. Null.* Small post 8vo, 6s.
—— *The Story of Viteau.* Illust. Cr. 8vo, 5s.
—— See also LOW'S STANDARD NOVELS.
Stowe (Mrs. Beecher) Dred. Cloth, gilt edges, 3s. 6d.; cloth, 2s.
—— *Flowers and Fruit from her Writings.* Sm. post 8vo, 3s. 6d.
—— *Life, in her own Words . . . with Letters and Original Compositions.* 10s. 6d.
—— *Little Foxes.* Cheap Ed., 1s.; Library Edition, 4s. 6d.
—— *My Wife and I.* Cloth, 2s.
—— *Old Town Folk.* 6s.
—— *We and our Neighbours.* 2s.
—— *Poganuc People.* 6s.
—— See also ROSE LIBRARY.
Strachan (J.) Explorations and Adventures in New Guinea. Illust., crown 8vo, 12s.
Stranahan (C. H.) History of French Painting, the Academy, Salons, Schools, &c. 21s.
Stutfield (Hugh E. M.) El Maghreb: 1200 *Miles' Ride through Marocco.* 8s. 6d.
Sullivan (A. M.) Nutshell History of Ireland. Paper boards, 6d.
Sylvanus Redivivus, Rev. J. Mitford, with a Memoir of E. Jesse. Crown 8vo, 10s. 6d.

TAINE (H. A.) "Origines." Translated by JOHN DURAND.
    I. **The Ancient Regime.** Demy 8vo, cloth, 16s.
    II. **The French Revolution.** Vol. 1. do.
    III. Do. do. Vol. 2. do.
    IV. Do. do. Vol. 3. do.
Tauchnitz's English Editions of German Authors. Each volume, cloth flexible, 2s.; or sewed, 1s. 6d. (Catalogues post free.)
Tauchnitz (B.) German Dictionary. 2s.; paper, 1s. 6d.; roan, 2s. 6d.
—— *French Dictionary.* 2s.; paper, 1s. 6d.; roan, 2s. 6d.
—— *Italian Dictionary.* 2s.; paper, 1s. 6d.; roan, 2s. 6d.
—— *Latin Dictionary.* 2s.; paper, 1s. 6d.; roan, 2s. 6d.
—— *Spanish and English.* 2s.; paper, 1s. 6d.; roan, 2s. 6d.
—— *Spanish and French.* 2s.; paper, 1s. 6d.; roan, 2s. 6d.
Taylor (R. L.) Chemical Analysis Tables. 1s.
—— *Chemistry for Beginners.* Small 8vo, 1s. 6d.
Techno-Chemical Receipt Book. With additions by BRANNT and WAHL. 10s. 6d.

Technological Dictionary. See TOLHAUSEN.
Thausing (Prof.) Malt and the Fabrication of Beer. 8vo, 45*s.*
Theakston (M.) British Angling Flies. Illustrated. Cr. 8vo, 5*s.*
Thomson (Jos.) Central African Lakes. New edition, 2 vols. in one, crown 8vo, 7*s.* 6*d.*
—— *Through Masai Land.* Illust. 21*s.*; new edition, 7*s.* 6*d.*
—— *and Miss Harris-Smith. Ulu: an African Romance.* crown 8vo, 6*s.*
Thomson (W.) Algebra for Colleges and Schools. With Answers, 5*s.*; without, 4*s.* 6*d.*; Answers separate, 1*s.* 6*d.*
Thornton (L. D.) Story of a Poodle. By Himself and his Mistress. Illust., crown 4to, 2*s.* 6*d.*
Thorrodsen, Lad and Lass. Translated from the Icelandic by A. M. REEVES. Crown 8vo.
Tissandier (G.) Eiffel Tower. Illust., and letter of M. Eiffel in facsimile. Fcap. 8vo, 1*s.*
Tolhausen. Technological German, English, and French Dictionary. Vols. I., II., with Supplement, 12*s.* 6*d.* each; III., 9*s.*; Supplement, cr. 8vo, 3*s.* 6*d.*
Topmkins (E. S. de G.) Through David's Realm. Illust. by the Author. 8vo, 10*s.* 6*d.*
Tucker (W. J.) Life and Society in Eastern Europe. 15*s.*
Tuckerman (B.) Life of General Lafayette. 2 vols., cr. 8vo, 12*s.*
Tupper (Martin Farquhar) My Life as an Author. 14*s.*; new edition, 7*s.* 6*d.*
Tytler (Sarah) Duchess Frances: a Novel. 2 vols., 21*s.*

*U*PTON (*H.*) *Manual of Practical Dairy Farming.* Cr. 8vo, 2*s.*

*V*AN DAM. *Land of Rubens; a companion for visitors to* Belgium. Crown 8vo, 3*s.* 6*d.*
Vane (Young Sir Harry). By Prof. JAMES K. HOSMER. 8vo, 18*s.*
Veres. Biography of Sir Francis Vere and Lord Vere, leading Generals in the Netherlands. By CLEMENTS R. MARKHAM. 8vo, 18*s.*
Verne (Jules) Celebrated Travels and Travellers. 3 vols. 8vo, 7*s.* 6*d.* each; extra gilt, 9*s.*
Victoria (Queen) Life of. By GRACE GREENWOOD. Illust. 6*s.*
Vincent (Mrs. Howard) Forty Thousand Miles over Land and Water. With Illustrations. New Edit., 3*s.* 6*d.*
Viollet-le-Duc (E.) Lectures on Architecture. Translated by BENJAMIN BUCKNALL, Architect. 2 vols., super-royal 8vo, £3 3*s.*

BOOKS BY JULES VERNE.

WORKS. (LARGE CROWN 8vo.)	Containing 350 to 600 pp. and from 50 to 100 full-page illustrations.		Containing the whole of the text with some illustrations.	
	In very handsome cloth binding, gilt edges.	In plainer binding, plain edges.	In cloth binding, gilt edges, smaller type.	Coloured boards, or cloth.
	s. d.	s. d.	s. d.	
20,000 Leagues under the Sea. Parts I. and II.	10 6	5 0	3 6	2 vols., 1s. each
Hector Servadac	10 6	5 0	3 6	2 vols., 1s. each
The Fur Country	10 6	5 0	3 6	2 vols., 1s. each
The Earth to the Moon and a Trip round it	10 6	5 0	2 vols., 2s. ea.	2 vols., 1s. each
Michael Strogoff	10 6	5 0	3 6	2 vols., 1s. each
Dick Sands, the Boy Captain	10 6	5 0	3 6	2 vols., 1s. each
Five Weeks in a Balloon	7 6	3 6	2 0	1s. 0d.
Adventures of Three Englishmen and Three Russians	7 6	3 6	2 0	1 0
Round the World in Eighty Days	7 6	3 6	2 0	1 0
A Floating City	7 6	3 6	2 0	1 0
The Blockade Runners			2 0	1 0
Dr. Ox's Experiment	—	—	2 0	1 0
A Winter amid the Ice	—	—	2 0	1 0
Survivors of the "Chancellor"	7 6	3 6	3 6	2 vols., 1s. each
Martin Paz			2 0	1s. 0d.
The Mysterious Island, 3 vols.:—	22 6	10 6	6 0	3 0
I. Dropped from the Clouds	7 6	3 6	2 0	1 0
II. Abandoned	7 6	3 6	2 0	1 0
III. Secret of the Island	7 6	3 6	2 0	1 0
The Child of the Cavern	7 6	3 6	2 0	1 0
The Begum's Fortune	7 6	3 6	2 0	1 0
The Tribulations of a Chinaman	7 6	3 6	2 0	1 0
The Steam House, 2 vols.:—				
I. Demon of Cawnpore	7 6	3 6	2 0	1 0
II. Tigers and Traitors	7 6	3 6	2 0	1 0
The Giant Raft, 2 vols.:—				
I. 800 Leagues on the Amazon	7 6	3 6	2 0	1 0
II. The Cryptogram	7 6	3 6	2 0	1 0
The Green Ray	6 0	5 0	—	1 0
Godfrey Morgan	7 6	3 6	2 0	1 0
Kéraban the Inflexible:—				
I. Captain of the "Guidara"	7 6	3 6	2 0	1 0
II. Scarpante the Spy	7 6	3 6	2 0	1 0
The Archipelago on Fire	7 6	3 6	2 0	1 0
The Vanished Diamond	7 6	3 6	2 0	1 0
Mathias Sandorf	10 6	5 0	3 6	2 vols., 1s. each
The Lottery Ticket	7 6	3 6		
The Clipper of the Clouds	7 6	3 6		
North against South	7 6			
Adrift in the Pacific	7 6			
Flight to France	7 6			

CELEBRATED TRAVELS AND TRAVELLERS. 3 vols. 8vo, 600 pp., 100 full-page illustrations, 12s. 6d. gilt edges, 14s. each :—(1) THE EXPLORATION OF THE WORLD. (2) THE GREAT NAVIGATORS OF THE EIGHTEENTH CENTURY. (3) THE GREAT EXPLORERS OF THE NINETEENTH CENTURY.

WALFORD (Mrs. L. B.) *Her Great Idea, and other Stories.*
  Cr. 8vo, 10s. 6d.; also new ed., 6s.
Wallace (L.) *Ben Hur: A Tale of the Christ.* New Edition,
  crown 8vo, 6s.; cheaper edition, 2s.
Wallack (L.) *Memories of* 50 *Years; with many Portraits, and*
  Facsimiles. Small 4to, 63s. nett; ordinary edition 7s. 6d.
Waller (Rev. C.H.) *Adoption and the Covenant.* On Confirmation. 2s. 6d.
—— *Silver Sockets; and other Shadows of Redemption.*
  Sermons at Christ Church, Hampstead. Small post 8vo, 6s.
—— *The Names on the Gates of Pearl, and other Studies.*
  New Edition. Crown 8vo, cloth extra, 3s. 6d.
—— *Words in the Greek Testament.* Part I. Grammar.
  Small post 8vo, cloth, 2s. 6d. Part II. Vocabulary, 2s. 6d.
Walsh (A.S.) *Mary, Queen of the House of David.* 8vo, 3s. 6d.
Walton (Iz.) *Wallet Book,* CIƆIƆLXXXV. Crown 8vo, half
  vellum, 21s.; large paper, 42s.
—— *Compleat Angler.* Lea and Dove Edition. Ed. by R. B.
  MARSTON. With full-page Photogravures on India paper, and the
  Woodcuts on India paper from blocks. 4to, half-morocco, 105s.;
  large paper, royal 4to, full dark green morocco, gilt top, 210s.
Walton (T. H.) *Coal Mining.* With Illustrations. 4to, 25s.
War Scare in Europe. Crown 8vo, 2s. 6d.
Warner (C. D.) *My Summer in a Garden.* Boards, 1s.;
  leatherette, 1s. 6d.; cloth, 2s.
—— *Their Pilgrimage.* Illustrated by C. S. REINHART.
  8vo, 7s. 6d.
Warren (W. F.) *Paradise Found; the North Pole the Cradle*
  of the Human Race. Illustrated. Crown 8vo, 12s. 6d.
Washington Irving's Little Britain. Square crown 8vo, 6s.
Watson (P. B.) *Swedish Revolution under Gustavus Vasa.* 8vo.
Wells (H. P.) *American Salmon Fisherman.* 6s.
—— *Fly Rods and Fly Tackle.* Illustrated. 10s. 6d.
Wells (J. W.) *Three Thousand Miles through Brazil.* Illustrated from Original Sketches. 2 vols. 8vo, 32s.
Wenzel (O.) *Directory of Chemical Products of the German*
  Empire. 8vo, 25s.
Westgarth (W.) *Half-century of Australasian Progress. Personal*
  retrospect. 8vo, 12s.
Wheatley (H. B.) *Remarkable Bindings in the British Museum.*
  Reproductions in Colour, 94s. 6d., 73s. 6d., and 63s.
White (J.) *Ancient History of the Maori; Mythology, &c.*
  Vols. I.-IV. 8vo, 10s. 6d. each.
White (R. Grant) *England Without and Within.* Crown 8vo,
  10s. 6d.
—— *Every-day English.* 10s. 6d.

L.

White (R. Grant) Fate of Mansfield Humphreys, &c. Cr. 8vo, 6s.
—— *Studies in Shakespeare.* 10s. 6d.
—— *Words and their Uses.* New Edit., crown 8vo, 5s.
Whitney (Mrs.) The Other Girls. A Sequel to "We Girls." New ed. 12mo, 2s.
—— *We Girls.* New Edition. 2s.
Whittier (J. G.) The King's Missive, and later Poems. 18mo, choice parchment cover, 3s. 6d.
—— *St. Gregory's Guest, &c.* Recent Poems. 5s.
William I. and the German Empire. By G. BARNETT SMITH. New Edition, 3s. 6d.
Willis-Bund (J.) Salmon Problems. 3s. 6d.; boards, 2s. 6d.
Wills (Dr. C. J.) Persia as it is. Crown 8vo, 8s. 6d.
Wills, A Few Hints on Proving, without Professional Assistance. By a PROBATE COURT OFFICIAL. 8th Edition, revised, with Forms of Wills, Residuary Accounts, &c. Fcap. 8vo, cloth limp, 1s.
Wilmot (A.) Poetry of South Africa Collected. 8vo, 6s.
Wilmot-Buxton (Ethel M.) Wee Folk, Good Folk: a Fantasy. Illust., fcap. 4to, 5s.
Winder (Frederick Horatio) Lost in Africa: a Yarn of Adventure. Illust., cr. 8vo, 6s.
Winsor (Justin) Narrative and Critical History of America. 8 vols., 30s. each; large paper, per vol., 63s.
Woolsey. Introduction to International Law. 5th Ed., 18s.
Woolson (Constance F.) See "Low's Standard Novels."
Wright (H.) Friendship of God. Portrait, &c. Crown 8vo, 6s.
Wright (T.) Town of Cowper, Olney, &c. 6s.
Wrigley (M.) Algiers Illustrated. 100 Views in Photogravure. Royal 4to, 45s.
Written to Order; the Journeyings of an Irresponsible Egotist. By the Author of "A Day of my Life at Eton." Crown 8vo, 6s.

YRIARTE (Charles) Florence: its History. Translated by C. B. PITMAN. Illustrated with 500 Engravings. Large imperial 4to, extra binding, gilt edges, 63s.; or 12 Parts, 5s. each.

ZILLMAN (J. H. L.) Past and Present Australian Life. With Stories. Crown 8vo, 2s.

London:
SAMPSON LOW, MARSTON, SEARLE, & RIVINGTON, LD.,
St. Dunstan's House,
FETTER LANE, FLEET STREET, E.C.

www.ingramcontent.com/pod-product-compliance
Lightning Source LLC
Chambersburg PA
CBHW031932230426
43672CB00010B/1893